Copyright 2000 by Jules Smith

A Wrecking Ball Press Publication

Editorial Offices
9 Westgate
North Cave
East Yorkshire
HU15 2NG
U.K.

All rights reserved. No part of this book may be reproduced in any form, except by a reviewer who wishes to quote brief passages in a review or article.

Bukowski poems and correspondence copyright Black Sparrow Press, 24 Tenth Street, Santa Rosa, CA 95401, U.S.A.

Drawings copyright 2000 by David Hernandez

Editor-in-chief: Shane Rhodes
Production editor: Ryan Newdick
Cover design: Owen Benwell

Queries regarding rights and permissions should be addressed to:

Wrecking Ball Press,
9 Westgate, North Cave,
East Yorkshire,
HU15 2NG
U.K.

Printed in Great Britain

"Art, Survival and So Forth":
The Poetry of Charles Bukowski

Jules Smith

ACKNOWLEDGEMENTS

This book is partly based on my Ph.D thesis *The Poetry of Charles Bukowski* (University of Hull, 1990). I would firstly like to thank my former tutors at Hull during the 1980s. Professor Geoffrey Moore (1920-1999) was a pioneer of American Studies in Britain. He inspired me with anecdotes about all the poets he had met, from e.e. cummings to Robert Lowell - and Bukowski himself. He anthologised Bukowski in the *Penguin Book of American Verse* (1979, rev. 1983), placed his poetry on the undergraduate literature course, and was the first academic to accept a research student on his works. From Dr. John Osborne I learned a great deal about poetry and criticism while we played numerous games of chess, and by being involved with his important literary magazine *Bête Noire* from 1984-94, and its accompanying series of international readings. He remains an outstanding teacher and a good man to debate literature with.

Library staff, from the Brynmor Jones Library to the Little Magazines archive at University College, London, have been unfailingly helpful. I particularly wish to thank Irene Still Meyer, Special Collections Librarian at California State University, Long Beach, for her assistance during my trip there. My friends in Long Beach, especially Fred Voss and Joan Jobe Smith, were essential to the eventual writing of this book. They sent a great deal of valuable materials relating to Bukowski and West Coast poetry over the years, shared their enthusiasm for C.B., and generously hosted me during a memorable visit to Southern California at the end of 1996. I owe special debts of gratitude also to my sister Diana, her husband Ian, and to my brother Richard, for their support at a vital time. Many thanks to Ryan Newdick for the loan of a computer and for his expertise. John Martin, editor-publisher of Black Sparrow Press, has kindly given permission to quote from the published poetry and correspondence of Charles Bukowski.

CONTENTS

Preface by Gerald Locklin 11

Introduction 13

Chapter 1
    Whitman's Wild Child 17

Chapter 2
    Bukowski as Underground Hero 1944-1970 41

Chapter 3
    The No-Holds Bard 1970-1994 73

Chapter 4
    Reactions to Modernism and The Beats 95

Chapter 5
    Three Essential Collections 121

Chapter 6
    At the Movies and the Racetrack 149

Chapter 7
    Bukowski and West Coast Poetry 177

Chapter 8
    Das Ist Alles: Charles Bukowski Reconsidered 207

Notes 227

Bibliography 237

Artwork by David Hernandez

PREFACE

This culmination of twenty years of loving labor on the work of Charles Bukowski by Jules Smith represents a critical breakthrough, a shift in perspective, and an elevation of Bukowski Studies to a new plane of serious technical analysis and informed historical positioning. Although the book takes into consideration the best of the American and Continental commentary that currently exists, it also offers an intriguing and uniquely British point of view. Buk's work is seen as heavily indebted to the Hollywood movies of the 1930s and '40s and to the young author's outsider status as having been declared psychologically unfit for service in the Second World War.

Smith investigates in detail the formal influences of Whitman's broadening of subject matter, iterative parallelisms, and revival of narrative, Robinson Jeffers' Inhumanism, and the long, strophic lines of both predecessors. As a poet based for thirty-six years in Southern California, I am especially grateful for the insightful attention paid to the complex relationship of subsequent generations of L.A./Long Beach writers to the Bukowskian model. I share, furthermore, his conviction that Bukowski's work is of at least the stature of Ginsberg's, Kerouac's, and Henry Miller's - I would, in fact, place him a notch above all three. I also find of great significance the "anxiety of influence," to invoke Harold Bloom's terminology, of Bukowski's Oedipal relationship to his towering, glowering forefather, Ernest Hemingway.

All who value the achievements of Charles Bukowski will rejoice that he is at last enjoying the high level of scholarly attention and prestige signalled by the publication of this landmark study.

Gerald Locklin, Ph.D.
Professor of English
California State University, Long Beach
Author of *Charles Bukowski: A Sure Bet* (Water Row Press, 1995)

INTRODUCTION

Charles Bukowski is the great romantic mongrel of contemporary American verse, the cold dog in its courtyard; the former postal carrier who became the best-selling poet in the world. A figure for whom the term 'legendary' is for once justified, numerous anecdotal memoirs by his erstwhile lovers, literary associates and correspondents are now appearing. Perhaps to his own surprise, he lasted well into his eighth decade, and was totally fulfilled as a writer. During his heyday in the 1970s he was a most notorious reader-performer, a compelling Rabelaisian presence on stage and in riotously funny live recordings. By turns witty, profane, and serious, he succeeded in his self-imposed task of 'humanising' poetry, arguably bringing it closer to ordinary American speech than any poet ever has, and giving his art an unprecedented ease and naturalness. Formally, he helped to reinstate the narrative element to poetry, meanwhile through his readings deliberately breaking down the usual rhetorical barriers between poet and audience. Six years after his death, interest in Bukowski is phenomenal. There are world-wide sales, fanzines and websites; movie rights to all his novels have been sold. His artefacts and rare items are eagerly sought in Internet auctions on eBay, with early chapbooks and original drawings commanding thousands of dollars. 'Hank' to his friends, 'Buk' to the fans, he is the cult figure who found a genuinely popular audience. Co-opted, at least posthumously, as one of the Beat Generation, he is currently at least as influential with the young as any of his major contemporaries or rivals.

Like many another American cultural icon, Bukowski was born overseas, in Andernach, Germany, and brought to the States as a small child. Perhaps fittingly he was the offspring of conflict. In a general sense, through the occupation of Germany by Allied troops after the First World War; and as the son of a wretchedly unhappy marriage. Nevertheless, the brutality of his German-American father - of the same name - eventually gave him a rich seam of material, as well as the resentful harshness of his world-view. Bukowski's youth was disrupted by the Great Depression and he avoided military service during World War II. After a period of restless travelling during the 1940s, he returned to Los Angeles and took menial jobs or no job before finding long-term employment within the Post Office. Two major biographies, *Hank* (1991) by Neeli Cherkovski, and *Locked In the Arms of a Crazy Life* (1998) by Howard Sounes, have traced this personal background in some detail. He found his subject matter waiting for him on the hot streets of Los Angeles, in its tough bars and roominghouses, the underside of the Californian Dream.

With his trademark holy trinity of beer, classical music and the racetrack, he took on a persona as the uninhibited 'Dirty Old Man' of American letters in the mid-1960s, typing a scabrously funny weekly column for underground newspapers. His career gained lift-off when he became a full-time author in 1970, and his lengthy apprenticeship with little magazines and small presses began to pay off. He was one of the most powerfully charismatic voices in American poetry from then onwards, vigorously anti-academic and - therefore - a great favourite with students. Despite commercial success, his work managed to retain an air of Outsiderdom, a mystique of No Compromise. A back-handed compliment has been paid to his continuing popularity in a recent report in the *Times Literary Supplement*. A correspondent in New York had visited his local Barnes and Noble bookstore, searching for Jack Kerouac titles. "On enquiring he was invited to proceed to the back of the shop, where, high on a lofty shelf, were Kerouac's novels, together with those of William Burroughs and Charles Bukowski. 'We keep them up there', the assistant explained, 'because they're the shoplifters' favourites'"(17 March 2000).

The essence of Bukowski's appeal can be encapsulated in the words simplicity, vividness, personality. Essentials, surely, for anyone who wishes to get a message across. Writing in a 1974 issue of the San Francisco magazine *Second Coming*, Bukowski claimed that his contribution had been "to loosen and simplify poetry, to make it more humane. I made it easy for them to follow. I taught them that you can write a poem the same way you can write a letter, that a poem can even be entertaining, and that there need not be anything necessarily holy about it".[1] This seductive line of reasoning raises immediate questions. Should poetry be loosened and simplified? Probably, if it wants to reach a wide audience. Can this still be 'great' poetry? In the hands of a stylist like Bukowski, the answer is emphatically yes - at least sometimes. (We can safely disregard the Beat slogan "you're a genius all the time").

Bukowski's works are uneven, and are regarded as being provocatively insulting to women. They are undeniably repetitious, with the same material frequently being cheerfully repackaged as poem, story, novel extract or anecdote. His thousands of published poems certainly contain much dross. But such is his amazing prolificness that there is also a cornucopia: of wonderfully alive, entertaining and profound works, with an abundance of narrative, imagery, emotion, comedy. And they have above all - to cheekily borrow a phrase from the patrician critic Helen Vendler - "the excess of distinctive manner...common to all remarkable poetry".[2] Or as John Bennett, editor of *Vagabond*, succinctly put it: "When Bukowski was 'on', he hit ground zero of the human condition and was second to none".[3] Regarded by mainstream critics for most of his writing life as a crude and marginal figure, he is posthumously moving towards acceptance as a contemporary classic American author.

The most basic observation to make about his career, in retrospect, is that Bukowski was actually far more of an all-round artist and man of letters than is generally appreciated. He wrote poems, stories and novels, an unperformed play, and gave numerous self-mythologising interviews. He wrote the screenplay for a fairly commercially successful movie, *Barfly* (1989) - the only other significant poet to have written a movie being James Dickey, from his novel *Deliverance*. Bukowski also produced a long-running newspaper column, reviews, essays, and thousands of letters to hundreds of correspondents. He did expressionist-type paintings, and drawings in a Thurberesque mode, continuing creation right through his years of serious illness in later life. All this brought him an enthusiastic cult following, for decades within avant-garde coteries and the little magazine scene, later from more established cultural figures. Among his friends or fans have been singer-songwriters such as Tom Waits, Bono of U2, and Sinead O'Connor. Film directors Jean-Luc Godard, Barbet Schroeder, Paul Verhoeven, Taylor Hackford, and David Lynch; screen actors Sean Penn, Dennis Hopper, James Woods, Elliot Gould, Harry Dean Stanton, and Helen Mirren. Madonna visited Bukowski when she was married to Sean Penn, and later wanted him to pose for her book *Sex* - a request refused.[4] Fellow writers on both sides of the Atlantic have been among his greatest advocates, including Roddy Doyle (who wrote an introduction to the current British edition of *Ham on Rye*), Raymond Carver, James Kelman, Irvine Welsh, Patrick Marber, Gerald Locklin and Fred Voss.

Bukowski is best understood as a stylist who emphatically declared new possibilities for poetry in simple language and recording quotidian experience. The importance of 'style', whether in art or life, was what he constantly stressed. Style "is the answer to everything/...style is the difference,/ a way of doing,/ a way of being done" ('Style').[5] Contrary to his rhetoric, Bukowski's poetry did not spring fully formed from bar talk, but evolved over the years, from early literariness towards a hard-edged 'unpoetic' manner. Yet even in his late, heavily flattened-out mode he habitually slips in a mellifluous phrase or exotic simile to augment the demotic.

This study takes Bukowski's poetry seriously, though not solemnly, tracing a truly remarkable career's distinctiveness, achievement and influence. Though clearly written from a British perspective, this book sets out his essential West Coast context, arguing that Bukowski is far more of an insider to U.S. cultural mythology and traditions than he appears. This may seem presumptuous for a British critic, but 'American' is a world culture and Bukowski a world author now. It has turned out to be something of a revisionist view, with a number of received 'truths' about Charles Bukowski needing to be qualified. My critical opinions are based on more than a decade's research, and over 15 years' involvement with magazines, poets and poetry in Britain and the States. On offer is a mix of literary history, critical commentary and views from a wide variety of sources. There is relatively little overlap between this study and the most recent critical book, by Gay Brewer in the Twayne's U.S. Authors series (1997).

Outlining Bukowski's formative influences, literary contacts, and development in the first half of the book, I then look at specific poems, collections, and issues in his poetry. The importance of early Hollywood movies as an identifiable source of his characters is, I believe, just one of the original features of my argument. Bukowski's place within and influence upon West Coast poetry is shown, connecting him up to the current generation of poets in Southern California. A concluding chapter summarises his peculiar achievement as a poet, and looks at critical and biographical reaction following his death in March 1994 - almost exactly 50 years after his first appearance in print. There follows a full bibliography of secondary critical sources. This will hopefully be of use and interest to fans, general readers, and future scholars of the burgeoning Bukowski industry, with new items of reminiscence and criticism appearing all the time.

Chapter 1

Whitman's Wild Child

"It appears that certain people think that poetry should be a certain way. For these, there will be nothing but troubled years. More and more people will come along to break their concepts. It's hard, I know, like having somebody fuck your wife while you are at work, but life, as they say, goes on".
Preface to *Poems Written Before Jumping Out of an 8 Story Window* (1968)[1]

Open almost any page of any one of his poetry volumes: it has a hard-bitten authority of style which says 'Charles Bukowski', even within a few lines. His typical narrator is closely identified with the author himself, reporting to us, the readers, on the world through half-closed, suspicious eyes. It is a distinctive posture, with a tone and subject matter that may suggest other masculine figures and authors but is ultimately *sui generis*. How did Bukowski do it? How did he get this unmistakable style and content? The short answer is: by a process of evolution after decades of struggle to become a writer and achieve acceptance, on his own terms. The long answer is: the subject of the first three chapters of this book. As a tyro he was brash, literary, resentful of authority, anxious, aggressive, 'self-taught', and full of his vocation as a writer. He took some early artistic decisions which conditioned the rest of his career. Despite being regarded as a completely untheorised writer, Bukowski nevertheless constructed his art by some basic critical principles. Chief amongst these was that writing had to come out of harsh, physical life experiences, that it could not be merely word games. This was a theme he returned to again and again, in poems, prose, interviews and letters. He told his Black Sparrow editor John Martin, for instance, that "the writing must come out of the living, the reaction to living" (31 March 1972). It seems an obvious point, yet for Bukowski this was crucial, colouring his whole approach to the business of writing, as well as to past and present-day literature. His letters of the early 1960s are surprisingly literary; but when he had settled in to his maturity, he refused to discuss writing and aesthetics except in life-related terms.

His second essential was encapsulated in a 1969 letter to Neeli Cherkovski, a young associate and his future biographer. Bukowski told him that "a good style comes primarily from a lack of pretentiousness, and what is pretentious changes from year to year and from day to day and from minute to minute. We must be evermore careful".[2] If this sounds close to Hemingway's usages, it is. Part of what Bukowski took from Hemingway was abhorrence of empty rhetoric, abstractions, intellectual concepts, and polysyllabic vocabulary. Avoidance of "pretentiousness" meant that the raw material of Bukowski's art had to be structurally 'simple' language. Accordingly, the vast majority of words in any Bukowski poem are of one or two syllables, and seldom require a dictionary, except perhaps a dictionary of American slang. Bukowski eventually 'broke the rules' in a thoroughly romantic way, but only to live and write by self-imposed rules, strictures, and prejudices.

The confidence inherent in the above two statements only emerged after a long apprenticeship, an anxious struggle to become a writer, in the face of continual rejection, he continually emphasised, from more tradition-minded editors. Bukowski once claimed to have covered an entire wall with rejection slips. Apocryphal or not, the story is symbolically right. Conflict seems to have been necessary in both his relationships and in his works. He gathered the strength and endurance to succeed from his own feelings of antagonism to authority, estrangement from the poetry 'establishment', however conceived.

Allied to experience and lack of pretentiousness, Bukowski constantly stressed the importance of 'truth' in art: the latter a loaded and relative term, of course. Part of what he meant was to do with style, simplicity as against over-elaboration; and partly he meant not avoiding ugly realities of the self or the world. It makes his works both appealing and at times uncomfortable. (He carried this into real life, not minding being photographed unshaven, or in his underpants!). Another strand of the unvarnished 'truth' for Bukowski was self-revelation, preparedness to reveal 'unacceptable' desires in himself, and much else besides. As a poet emphatically in the Whitman tradition, he echoes the disreputable Walt's plea, in the introduction to *Leaves of Grass* (1855) for "the great poets...to be known...by the justification of perfect personal candour". He very seldom spares anyone, including himself, in presenting unflattering portraits of men and women in bars, on the street, and at the racetrack. His contemporary, the New York poet and anthologist Edward Field, characterised this as 'The Bukowski Option':

... his beauty was
    that he insisted on thrusting
his entire ugly face in our faces...
    Even as he snarled at the world.[3]

Notwithstanding his eventual commercial success, Bukowski retains the aura of being a 'cult' figure. But could the author who in 1989 gave an interview to the supermarket tabloid *People* still be a cult? Yes - poetry is very much a niche market in sales terms. Bukowski's works continue to have the air of being somehow 'unacceptable' - much to its commercial advantage. Many people otherwise uninterested in contemporary poetry or novels buy Bukowski books.

The English poetry 'establishment' is still rather sniffy; his work has still never been printed, reviewed or discussed in *Poetry Review*, the official organ of the Poetry Society in London. Yet in other respects, the Brits can actually claim credit for latching onto Bukowski fairly early on, taking him seriously, and having assisted his career. The first-ever critical article on his work appeared in a Newcastle little magazine, *Satis*, in 1962; at the end of that decade, inclusion in the London-based Penguin Modern Poets series gave his verse international exposure. Carl Weissner, later Bukowski's influential German translator and agent, in fact first spotted his work during the mid-1960s in *Iconolatre*, a West Hartlepool little mag. Professor Geoffrey Moore of the American Studies Department at Hull University placed his poetry on an undergraduate literature course during the mid-1970s, and a few years later accepted the first graduate student. By far the most revealing interview that Bukowski ever gave was printed in *London Magazine*, which around the same time also brought out a selection of his short stories, *Life and Death in the Charity Ward* (1974), to widespread acclaim.

Excellent current coverage of the Bukowski phenomenon is found within Kevin Ring's Coventry-based magazine *Beat Scene*. The best of Bukowski's biographers so far, Howard Sounes, is British; as is the present author. The arts pages of British national newspapers regularly feature Bukowski, and he has been reviewed in the *Times Literary Supplement*, often favourably, since the late 1970s. There were obituary tributes on

BBC Radio 4, mentioning him as an early exponent of so-called 'dirty realism'; and several years later a documentary on BBC TV, 'The Ordinary Madness of Charles Bukowski'. For all his 'underground' credentials, Bukowski has not exactly been excluded from coverage by the mainstream media, even in a generally conservative literary culture like Britain's.

But Bukowski has thus far rarely commanded the attention of influential literary critics in the States. One can't imagine a Hugh Kenner, Guy Davenport, or Harold Bloom deigning to write about Bukowski; the latter's favourite being the abstract, games-playing poetry of John Ashbery. Helen Vendler's taste in her *Faber Book of Contemporary American Poetry* (1986) extended to Allen Ginsberg, Gary Snyder and Frank O'Hara, among her selected academic poets, careerists, and duds like Howard Nemerov. There was no place for Bukowski. My own post-reading conversation in 1992 with the agenda-setting New Formalist poet and critic Dana Gioia indicated his surprisingly high regard for Bukowski, but he has remained silent in print. Bukowski's work seldom featured in major mainstream anthologies, though he appeared in many others. He continues to be excluded from the latest editions of *The Norton Anthology*, the most widely-used college-level teaching textbook, and was absent from *The Harvard Guide to Contemporary American Writing* (1979) at a time when much of his best work was being written. He rated only a brief mention within *Los Angeles in Fiction* (1984), despite his stature as easily the leading figure in Angeleno writing over the past thirty years. One conspicuous exception was Geoffrey Moore's *Penguin Book of American Verse* which included four classic Bukowski poems, including 'Don't come round but if you do...' and 'Something for the touts'.

Even in Germany, the land of his birth, where Bukowski's reputation and name-recognition among the general reading public has been highest, opinions on the value of his work have been sharply divided. He enjoyed bestseller status there from the early 1970s onwards, famous enough to feature in advertisements; and he was once hailed in *Die Welt* as "the greatest American writer since Hemingway". But, according to Carl Weissner, his detractors have ranged from "a former speechwriter of Willy Brandt who called Bukowski the most overrated writer of the century to the right-wing Munich paper that tried to put him down as 'a marginal figure of the U.S. porn scene'".[4] More recently, The Buk Center, associated with Falko Hennig, of the Bukowski Society, has been established in Berlin.

His admirers and detractors are agreed on one thing, at least: Bukowski's poetry, at its best and worst, is distinctive. It makes its impact, in part, by a sheer difference from smoother, more intellectual writing. His slangy departures from politeness, his 'roughness' of diction, and anti-depressant humour, go along with satirical invocations of composers, painters, writers and other culture heroes. Bukowski must be one of the funniest poets of the 20th century. His voice - in maturity at least - is not that of anguished alienation, but of disreputable sanity. His is a poetry that, because of its directness and simplicity, seems able to talk directly to readers, speaking to their situation.

We can again draw upon Whitman's introduction to *Leaves of Grass* to understand the Bukowski agenda: "The messages of great poets to each man and woman are, Come to us on equal terms, Only then can you understand us, We are no better than you, What we enclose you enclose, What we enjoy you may enjoy".[5] Bukowski includes rather than excludes readers, even those without higher education: not for him the 'obscurity' of modern poetry. He can be read during tough times and personal crises. He usually has a poem on the subject, and a comment to put one's own problems in perspective. He continues to appeal to young people, as a social rebel, albeit mostly on the 'wearing-the- t-shirt' level. During the 1970s era of student protest, a college in West Germany was reportedly taken over by its students and re-named 'Bukowski University' for a few days. Many of his readings were on the U.S. college circuit, and few campus bookshops in Europe now fail to stock his books.

Notwithstanding this, Bukowski's badmouthing of academics and the 'academic approach' to literature was consistent. In a 1957 'Call for Our Own Critics', clearly endorsing the Beats' attack on academia, he identified himself with "loiterers in pool halls and back alleys", wary of the university critics who have "lost in pulling the blinds around their little ivy world" but "gained in direction and prestige". Nearly thirty years later, he was still persuaded that "the academics are...playing secret and staid games, snob and inbred games which are finally anti-life and anti-truth".[6] However, his most sophisticated critics, from J.W. Corrington to Gerald Locklin, Russell Harrison to Gay Brewer, have each been University teachers of long standing.

One of the elements in Bukowski's achievement that these academic critics have pointed to is his restoration of narrative structures, that is, storytelling, to verse. This was partly instinctive, linked to the fact that Bukowski started out as a short story writer, and partly a conscious decision to do with the kind of poetry he wished to write. By the time that Bukowski got into his stride as a poet, narrative had been a poor relation to the lyric impulse for most of the century. It was squeezed by Modernism's concentration on reform of the lyric, notwithstanding Frost, Jeffers, Auden's ballads, or the light verse of Ogden Nash and Don Marquis. In the post-war scene, the Beats and the Confessionals had little reason to tell stories in verse, concentrating on the self under pyschological pressure.

Bukowski made it his business to be different. Storytelling is one of the most obvious facets of his work, even if it is composed of everyday details, and sets it apart from the works of his contemporaries: lyric experimentalists (Creeley), language dandies (Ashbery), or operatic embracers (Ginsberg). Certainly by the late 1960s-early 1970s onwards, narrative predominates. In *Crucifix in a Deathhand* (1965), there are still romantic lyrics; by *War All the Time* (1984) there are virtually none, and the works are full of dialogue and the kind of readerly instructions (I said, she said) commonly found in prose. Bukowski switched easily between verse and prose, in his maturity saw little formal difference between the two, and helped break down absolute distinctions between them.

Bukowski's is a poetry of ordinary words, mundane details and the frustrations of life. There are few moments of epiphany. To young would-be writers he seems to be saying: express yourself, don't worry about intellectualising, or the Great Tradition (itself now an outdated notion), just go ahead and do it. Be true to your own personal idiom but remain this side of accessibility - sound advice for any writer. Bukowski himself revelled in ambivalent or unflattering epithets, being variously called "America's sewer Shakespeare" (Morris Edelson) and "an ursine slob with a heart of tin" (Ken Tucker).[7] Like any 'strong' writer, Bukowski attracted his friends and enemies in academia and in literary journalism. The poetry world is nothing if not subjective, prone to infighting and long-running feuds. He has been portrayed as a *naif* writing off the top of a muddled head, his writing put down as simplistically autobiographical and lacking identifiable literary techniques. The nadir of this kind of reaction was reached by Guy Davenport, who reportedly called Bukowski a barbarian, and by the late Martin Seymour-Smith, who patronised Bukowski's work, observing its "relative mildness", that it "might have been jotted down by any half-cut middlebrow. But his titles are fun". This should now be seen in its true context, as a personal spite. Seymour-Smith was a close friend of Robert Creeley - and Robert Graves - during the 1950s on Mallorca, Spain. Creeley and Bukowski had a lifelong mutual antipathy, neither understanding the other's conception of poetry. Neeli Cherkovski told Lawrence Ferlinghetti an amusing story about their 'rivalry', which extended even to alcohol-inspired bad behaviour: "Bukowski said he had been to a party and the host showed him a window that Robert Creeley had busted when he had gotten drunk. According to Bukowski, they asked Creeley to autograph the wall next to the window and made a big deal about how great it was. 'When I shattered their goddamn window', Bukowski said, 'they called the cops'".[8]

The Bukowski Personality Cult has been the bane of much critical reaction, both for and against. The whiff of autobiographical immediacy that his work gives off has been stupefying to his most vehement admirers and detractors, leading them to confuse the persona created by Bukowski in his writing with their supposed knowledge about the author's life. Undeniably personal works have been reduced by overly autobiographical readings. His deliberated informality has likewise been smeared as sloppiness or incompetence, rather than conscious decision-making: few poets can hang as loose as Bukowski does, and yet retain a sense of 'poemness'. Instead of departing for the Lake Isle of Innisfree, as Yeats does, or rhapsodizing about the best minds of his generation, as Ginsberg does, we find Bukowski simply telling us something: "yeah sure, I'll be in unless I'm out/ don't knock if the lights are out/ or you hear voices or then..." ('Don't come round but if you do...'). His trademark poem is emphatic, heavily cadenced lines vary in length from one or two words or to the edge of the page. It is conversational, 'rough and ready', full of feeling; elegiac or humorous. But - and this is the main contention of this book - Bukowski's apparent artlessness disguises his artifice. The tools in his craftsman's bag are employed to create an impression of conversational spontaneity, and he shows great resource in working this through on the linguistic level. By the last decades of his life and writing, Bukowski had succeeded in eradicating from his poetry everything that smacked of the artificial.

His poems have an air of improvisation, a feeling that their destinations are not fixed in advance, but arrived at after a journey in language which might have gone elsewhere. Bukowski's, in more senses than one, is a free verse. He was of the generation that assumed that all the rhymes had been exhausted. The strait-jacket of regular metrics would have been intolerably conformist to him, inimical to someone who wanted to capture living life. The writer of any formal verse - sonnets, say, or blank verse - knows the poem's destination in advance, because he or she is obliged to fulfil metrical norms. There have been plenty of American poets skilled in formal metres, and latterly a whole New Formalist movement, but the nationalist mode remains, as Carlos Williams notoriously put it, a free verse for a free country. ("Do I contradict myself? Very well I contradict myself". Bukowski did actually publish at least one rhyming poem in *Flame* magazine, in 1961, and a few other early poems approximate to syllabic verse. These were experiments, not repeated in his maturity).

Bukowski made it his business to be 'free'. He was against self-conscious writing, against tradition-bound too-careful 'craft'. He wrote in the vernacular, the American language; again, this was a choice indicating the kind of writing he wanted to do. It fitted in with his working class subject matter, his territory of bars, roominghouses and racetracks. So, part of the answer to the question - how does he do it? - is by making his work seem as unliterary as possible. By avoiding conventions such as rhyme schemes, and by deploying lines of irregular length attuned to the contours of his own voice. By the predominant use of first-person narrators, with a street-wise language unencumbered by complex words or intellectual concepts; and by a no-bullshit stance, his speakers busy 'telling it like it is'. His poems uninhibitedly incorporate repetitions, jokes and asides to the reader; digressions, ungrammatical constructions, split-infinitives and sentences with no verbs. They often contain 'bad language'. His use of slang and swear words (fuck, whore, jerk-off, blow-job, etc) alone would make him unusual, even today, as the vast number of poets do not challenge or break decorum. He also includes innuendoes and other linguistic ambiguities that enable him to splice together sex and violence, nastiness and humour. By leaving in features common to speech but usually repressed within books, Bukowski signalled that he wanted to align his poetry with spoken rather than written conventions. To identify all these component parts, one must look at what formed him, unravel his influences. Bukowski's vigorous, mongrel style - one decidedly of mixed parentage - did not arrive at once, fully-formed, but evolved from a variety of sources in literature, the movies of the 1930s-40s, and popular culture in general.

The French novelist Céline, and the Los Angeles novelist and screenwriter John Fante, who began being published during the 1930s, are often cited as influences, not least by Bukowski himself. Céline's energetic use of slangy street language was certainly absorbed, though he can have read him only in translation. The novel which Bukowski constantly refers to is *Journey to the End of the Night* (1932), whose misanthropic vehemence definitely seeps onto the Bukowski page. Literally so in the novel *Post Office* (1970), whose first sentence ("It began as a mistake") clearly echoes the opening of *Journey*: "It all began just like that".

Fante's autobiographical fictions, particularly his early novels and stories, have a lyrical, starkly emotional feel for the developing, low-rent Los Angeles of the 1930s. 'Arturo Bandini', the streetwise narrator of Bukowski's favourite novel *Ask the Dust* (1939, 1980) was the first writer-hero that he identified with. Fante himself, ostensibly starving in order to write short stories - recognized by one of the great magazine editors of the day, H.L. Mencken, of *The American Mercury* - gave him a role model. Even Fante's subsequent life as a saccharine scriptwriter, a self-confessed 'Hollywood whore', connected Bukowski to his movie-watching youth. Reminiscing in the introduction to the Black Sparrow edition of *Ask the Dust*, which he was instrumental in having re-published, Bukowski warmly commended "a man who was not afraid of emotion. The humour and the pain were intermixed with a superb simplicity".[9] The novel's portrayal of human frailties, self deception about romantic love, and the grinding nature of urban poverty in the midst of consumer plenty, no doubt made a big impression. Nor was Bukowski alone in his appreciation:

Robert Towne, writer of the movie *Chinatown*, declared it the best novel ever written about Los Angeles. And yet Fante was not a strong enough author to be Bukowski's sole artistic father. Both Fante and Céline certainly contribute to Bukowski's works, but they mainly influence his prose, not his poetry.

Bukowski began absorbing literature while living through the dark shadow of the 1930s Depression, and the build-up to the Second World War. Indeed, the hard-bitten character of his work is largely inexplicable unless the historical experiences that he and his generation lived through - he was slightly older than most of the Beats - are taken account of. He achieved distinctiveness during the 1960s partially by reflecting earlier values and writing, by contrasting strongly with the young hippies surrounding him at underground papers and at readings. The Wall Street Crash, engendering a decade of economic and political turmoil, took place when Bukowski was aged 9. Unemployment climbed in the U.S. from 2 to 15 million within the period 1929-33, at the peak affecting one-third of the workforce including Bukowski's father. Its effects in California were marked, by shanty-towns, or 'Hoovervilles', full of desperate migrants in the agricultural heartlands of the Golden State. The novelist Upton Sinclair ran unsuccessfully for office, despite his slogan 'End Poverty in California': no less than 1 in 7 Californians were on relief at the worst. And, as the historian Piers Brendon has pointed out, the Depression by the Winter of 1932-3 had reached through to affect Hollywood: "Even the affluent ran short of cash. Groucho Marx, with 50 dollars, was a plutocrat. Fay Wray, heroine of the newly-opened *King Kong*, found herself with only $2.80, and...civilization under assault from the monster Depression seemed as vulnerable as the Empire State Building in the grip of the giant ape". Though Bukowski is in no sense a documentary writer, or even a 'realist', a lot of his poetry - and the novel *Ham on Rye* (1982) - makes reference to the events and personnel of the 1930s. Sometimes this is explicit:

I remember much:
men in unemployment lines forever
good men
frightened and laughing and real
nothing wrong with them
hardly as much wrong as with those who were
sullenly and righteously
working.
('Drunk again and wondering, wondering...')[10]

Much more typical of Bukowski's rendering of the 1930s is a 1981 poem, 'The lady in red', which contains all kinds of social detailing as well as hindsight. People pulling up greens in vacant lots to cook, raising chickens in their backyards, smoking Wings (10c a pack). The exploits of bank-robbing gangsters are recalled, especially John Dillinger - gunned down coming out of a gangster movie - and others:

Pretty Boy Floyd, Baby Face Nelson, Machine Gun Kelly, Ma
Barker, Alvin Karpis, we loved them all...

The narrator shows his New Deal sympathies by his final phrase: "it was a glorious/ non-bullshit time, especially after we got rid of Herbert Hoover". The social experience is glamorised, tinged with nostalgia: romance beats reportage. Thus though there are apparent antecedents for Bukowski's working class subject matter in the so-called Proletarian writers of the 1930s, there are artistic and political differences. These are now-neglected novelists such as Horace McCoy, Tom Kromer and Jack Conroy; poets Sol Funaroff, Joseph Kalar, Herman Spector and Kenneth Fearing. Their bitter, disillusioned tone and concern for the downtrodden industrial worker or the unemployed is suggested in early Bukowski works such as 'Poem for personnel managers' or 'Winter comes to a lot of places in August'. But these were politically engaged writers, often active within the Communist Party. Bukowski flies from political commitment as so much delusion; he announces himself as 'apolitical' (usually a cover for conservatism), underlying extreme individualism. And there is no evidence that Bukowski ever read any of these authors. Jack Conroy, who was active again in the 1960s as an editor, did read and comment favourably on his work. Bukowski's vastly greater output, sceptical distance from party politics, and frankly much greater creative intelligence, meant that his work developed far beyond any possible 'proletarian' origins.

If one had to point to the essential figures standing behind Bukowski, they would be Walt Whitman and Ernest Hemingway. As a generalisation, his work combines an 'open to experience' stance with the stripped-down language of the prose technician. Robinson Jeffers' works also crucially suggested to Bukowski the restoration of narrative to verse. More widely, Bukowski's reading of the American Moderns such as W.C. Williams, E.E. Cummings, even Ezra Pound, crucially qualified his essential romanticism. Bukowski himself, though nodding to Fante, Céline and Hemingway, spent much of his time denying his debts or bad-mouthing writers and artists he had palpably learned from. Bukowski certainly suffered from what Harold Bloom famously termed 'the anxiety of influence'; especially early on. Partly this was to make his work appear more original than it is. It was a psychologically understandable reaction: as his biographers have confirmed and his work makes clear, Bukowski suffered extreme anxiety as a child and adolescent, caused by his father's excessive severity. In his struggle to become a writer, this scorn for authority, the father-figure, and consequent desire for independence, extended into the realm of art. (These factors may also account for Bukowski's consistent anti-bourgeois rhetoric, setting himself against his parents' material ambitions).

This is not to deny that Bukowski ended up as a very different kind of writer from either Whitman or Hemingway: he clearly did. Neither has the humour that gloriously informs Bukowski's perspectives. Bukowski does not share Walt's 'kosmic' ambitions, his positive faith in American democracy, and of course implicit homosexuality. Hemingway was a famously careful, painstaking writer, constantly going over what he had written the previous day. Bukowski habitually uses terms like 'gamble' and 'risk' when explaining his intentions. Hemingway's authenticity of words and feelings seeps through to Bukowski. But anarchic humour makes his writings more divided, ambiguous, and harder to pin down ideologically than others (say, Norman Mailer) who recycle Hemingway's male mythology.

Whitman's modern admirers, from Henry Miller to Harold Norse and Neeli Cherkovski, have appreciated Bukowski. As did, more uneasily, a more conservative literary figure, the recently-deceased Karl Shapiro, one-time editor of *Poetry* and a Pulitzer Prize winner. Interviewed in 1978, the veteran bibliophile, from the generation of Lowell, Berryman, Bishop and Schwartz, ruefully observed: "Now Bukowski, I think, is an authentic poet. He was over at our house and threatened to tear it apart. A wonderful artist had loaned us a couple of his paintings, beautiful abstractions. Bukowski sat down on the sofa, and somebody said to him, 'What do you think of that painting? He said, 'Vulgar bourgeois shit'".[11] Cherkovski made a more convincing link, including a chapter on his old friend Bukowski in his highly informative book of anecdotal essays *Whitman's Wild Children* (1988, 1999).

Whitman's fatherhood of 20th Century American poetry, at least on its so-called 'redskin' side, has become a cliché. It is worth recalling that the first edition of *Leaves of Grass* (1855) was known only to a tiny number of enthusiasts, becoming recognised as an epoch-making book by academia many decades later. Whitman himself was a self-mythologiser, greatly exaggerating the impact of his work on audiences and on his times. Within his poems, the first person narrator is sometimes himself and sometimes a dramatisation of his fantasy self (cf. 'Henry Chinaski', the fictional stand-in for Bukowski). Bukowski's larger than life writing persona was also somewhat at odds with his private self. Fuelled by drink, he was rowdy and banteringly provocative at readings. In private, he was by most accounts courteous and soft-spoken (when sober), kind to animals, a devoted if distant late father. Certainly up to 1970, Bukowski lived in the Whitman mode as a poverty-stricken bohemian poet; even in his comfortable San Pedro home from 1979 onwards he worked in a battered, smoke-filled room to recreate his early writing conditions.

Newspaper journalists and critics showed much of the same dismissive, even disgusted, attitude to Bukowski as they had a century earlier to Whitman. Both never won general acceptance in America during their lifetimes, but did attract specific adulation from coteries, with passionate admirers of both sexes. Many of their earliest and most fervent supporters were Europeans rather than Americans. Whitman himself was by no means the unsophisticated working man of his persona; he was a devotee of symphony music and opera, especially Beethoven and Wagner. (Does this sound familiar?) There are sadder personal parallels. Whitman, the great poet of vitality, spent his last 19 years as a semi-paralysed invalid. Bukowski, far from going out face-down drunk on his typewriter as he intended, died lingeringly in hospital after years of serious illness; frail, sober, and away from his writing.

Whitman's posthumous influence started working upon those American literary nationalists, and modernists, intent upon re-declaring independence from English Literature. His appeal was as a rebel against puritanism and convention, as the chief radical in American poetry - intriguing Ezra Pound (who concluded 'A Pact' with Whitman, and called him the first man to write in the American idiom) and his friend W.C. Williams. T.S. Eliot and his New Critical followers were largely dismissive of Whitman's 'incompetence' as a poet, which made him unsuited to close readings. Whitman was unfashionable when the highly intellectual, closely-argued poetry and criticism of an Eliot, Auden or even an Yvor Winters ruled fashion. It took a more liberal, younger generation New Critic, Randall Jarrell, to bring him somewhat back into academic critical favour, in *Kenyon Review* essays such as 'Walt Whitman: He Had His Nerve' (1952). And it took an Allen Ginsberg to restore him as a vital resource for contemporary American poets. Even as late as 1963, Robert Creeley said in an interview with the English poet Charles Tomlinson, that Whitman had been "suppressed" by the influence of the New Criticism, but was nevertheless far more "available" to contemporary poets than, say, T.S. Eliot.[12]

Whitman's long lines, measured by the number of major stresses in each line, were indispensable for Robinson Jeffers, and later for Allen Ginsberg's great long poems 'Howl' and 'Kaddish'. For Bukowski also, albeit not in the same operatic way. He habitually used the Whitmanic verse paragraph and the parallelism as structuring elements in his early work, bringing order and cadence to lines of irregular length. In his later poetry, these long lines are simply squeezed down the page rather than across it. Bukowski told Neeli Cherkovski about the revelatory impact of first reading 'Song of Myself' in the L.A. Public Library. A number of poems make brief references to Whitman, though there is no explicit homage in verse form. Whitman should be regarded as the nationalist foundation of Bukowski's work, but only that. There are many layers on top, and ultimate differences.

The most important element that Whitman bequeathed to Bukowski was an air of familiarity, an intimate relationship with his readers. Not addressing them as a comrade, but as a bar-buddy listening to a story. Equally vital was that for Whitman, poetry's essence was located in life itself: "the poetic quality is not marshalled in rhyme or uniformity or abstract addresses to things nor in melancholy complaints or good precepts, but is the life of these and much else and is in the soul". Bukowski didn't find "the soul" a useful concept: there are certainly more references to the asshole than the soul in his works! But he too maintains that poetry is not in rhyme, uniformity, or abstractions, still less in "good precepts". Bukowski too constructs an heroic myth of himself within the work; his persona is also as "one of the roughs.../ Disorderly, fleshy and sensual".[13] Both write 'list' poems of Americana, catalogues of human life in all its vulgarity and disorder. Like Whitman, Bukowski's is the eye of experience which has seen, accepted and memorialised it all:

ask the man sleeping in an alley under
a sheet of paper
ask the conquerors of nations and planets
ask the man who has just cut off his finger
ask a bookmark in the Bible
ask the water dripping from a faucet while
the phone rings
ask perjury
ask the deep blue paint
ask the parachute jumper
ask the man with the bellyache
ask the divine eye so sleek and swimming
('They, all of them know')[14]

"The divine eye" is a typical Whitmanism. His demand that poets should walk the Open Road of life, embracing the world in all its endlessly fascinating, sordid reality, impressed itself on Henry Charles Bukowski, Jr, a young man searching for a father figure. Whitman's 'Song of Myself', his line "I am the man, I suffered, I was there", became a rallying cry. Eventually Bukowski himself realised Whitman's demand for "great audiences" for poetry. That is, by deliberately seeking a wide, and popular audience rather than an elite one. In 'A Rambling Essay On Poetics and the Bleeding Life Written While Drinking a Six-Pack (Tall)', a prose piece originally written in the mid-1960s, Bukowski mythologised his past, invoked Whitman, and incidentally summarised a good deal of his own future subject matter.

> Call me a hardhead if you wish. uncultured, drunken, whatever. The world has shaped me and I have shaped what I can. I have carried the bleeding 1/2 steer on my shoulder that was alive a minute ago and swung him on the dull hook on the truck-roof through gristle; I've entered the women's can with a mop while you've slept; I've rolled and been rolled; I've prayed to a toteboard; I've been black-jacked in a pisser for making a play for a gangster's moll; I was married to a woman with a million dollars and left her; I have crawled drunken in alleys from coast to coast; I've pumped gas, worked in a dog biscuit factory, sold Xmas trees, even been a foreman; I've been a truck driver, I've guarded door,
>
> looking for boots, in a Texas whorehouse; I lived a year on a yacht by learning how to start the auxiliary engine and by making love to the women of a rich madman with one arm who thought he was a genius at playing the organ and I had to write the words for his damned operas, and I was drunk most of the time and it worked until he died, but why go on with the rest? the subject is poetry.
> The subject is dull.
> Poetry must become, must right itself. Whitman had it backwards. I'd say that to have great audiences we must first have great poetry. I've never said this before but I am now high enough as I write this to perhaps say that Ginsberg has been the most awakening force in American poetry since Walt W.[15]

Bukowski here is not just indulging in self-aggrandizement. He is pleading for poets to go all out, to go for broke, burst out of shackles of convention and good taste, and take risks. He praises Ginsberg, qualifying it with the "perhaps", but behind the phrase "poetry must become, must right itself" is the burgeoning ego of someone who passionately wants to correct the perceived dullness of poetry: Bukowski himself. The "most awakening force" also surely refers to himself and his own ambitions. Bukowski's writing, which for the previous five and more years had been stalled, was given the kiss of life around 1955-57, when the Beats, a self-proclaimed Whitmanic brotherhood, were making their moves into public awareness.

Whitman's influence also falls upon Bukowski's social perspectives, which gravitate towards those on the economic margins. *Pace* the critic

Russell Harrison, Bukowski's poetry in general does not in my view offer a politicised critique of American society, nor "depict as class experience what might otherwise be viewed as confessional material".[16] Certainly he is not political in the sense of calling for a change in the economic system: one early title makes a joke of politicking, 'I wanted to overthrow the government but all I brought down was somebody's wife'. There is ample evidence that Bukowski debunks political radicals as self-serving or deluded, and is only concerned with individuals, not the working class as a whole. His narrators do not believe in collective solutions to individual problems: those daylabourer or working characters are more likely to drown their sorrows in drink than join a trade union.

Bukowski does use a great deal of anti-bourgeois rhetoric, from the avant-gardist's antagonistic viewpoint rather than the leftist ideology. He celebrates ethical, psychological and economic estrangement from the goals of mainstream society. His typically alienated early narrator despises routinised work, fulminating against an America whose materialism leads to work without life - choosing instead life without work. The title of 'Machineguns towers and timeclocks', for instance, makes an implied connection between Concentration camp and workplace. He is "not wanting"

a front lawn
sing-togethers
new shoes, Christmas presents
life insurance, *Newsweek*
162 baseball games
a vacation in Bermuda.
not wanting not wanting,
and I judge the purple flowers
better off than I [17]

These final two lines recall Christ's admonition to regard the lilies of the valley, who neither toil nor give thought for the morrow - a rare Biblical flourish again nodding towards Whitman. Bukowski habitually writes in sympathy with the socially excluded - all those unwilling or unable to conform to society's values and standards. Deliberately choosing to write about the bottom of the social hierarchy, Bukowski's sympathies are with those excluded from the pursuit of money, status and consumerism. His works, until his last few books, feature economic failures: skid row bums, barflies and brassy barstool hustlers; convicts, daylabourers, dishwashers, losing boxers and racetrack punters, struggling writers and criminals. "I went by what I felt and my feelings went to the crippled, the tortured, the damned and the lost, not out of sympathy but out of brotherhood because

I was one of them, lost, confused, indecent, petty, fearful and cowardly...knowing it didn't help, it didn't cure it, it only solidified it" (*Shakespeare Never Did This*, 21).[18]

Commentators who have remarked on this aspect of his work often claim that Bukowski records "the voices of the streets, the factories, the racetracks....the pathos of poverty, blue collar jobs, hangovers and jailyards".[19] Bukowski is more self-centered as an artist than this: he goes to the racetrack, as he went to skid row, as an observer, to see humanity *in extremis*. He actually alternates sympathy for toiling, exploited humankind with disgust at their bovine behaviour; empathy as well as misanthropy. He does not truly adopt "the vantage point of the underclass"; rather, his typical narrator is a writer who knows the streets and is not just slumming. He investigates the Lower Depths but is not of them. His culture-knowledge, keeps him apart, free to take sidelong looks at high art and low life. He is as familiar with Van Gogh and Beethoven as with racetrack whores and fights in alleys. Culture is tossed in among the beercans. A quintessential early title is 'On going back to the streets after visiting an art show'. Bukowski Man knows that he needs the consolations of art.

But he is equally scornful of connoisseurs, 'poetry lovers', and precious attitudes to culture. A "boy" is overheard talking about recitals, virtuosi, conductors, and "the lesser known novels of Dostoyevsky":

he gabbles about the Arts until
I hate the Arts,
and there is nothing cleaner
than getting back to a bar or
back to the track and watching them run.
('The talkers')[20]

Bukowski liked to antagonise pure aesthetes, and to comically deflate the illusions of those who naively imagine poets to be elevated or exquisite beings. The post-coital laughter of the racetrack pick-up in 'A 340 dollar horse and a hundred dollar whore' disperses the narrator's reluctant admission ("you, you...a poet? / I guess you're right I said, I guess you're right"). A harsh rebuke is sent to a literary lady: "Brooke? no. I am a monkey with an olive lost in the/ circus sand of your laughter..." ('Note to a lady who expected Rupert Brooke').[21] For such attitudinizing, Bukowski was accordingly parodied, lampooned, and sent up by his fellow little maggers often enough. Felix Pollak's 'Letter to Chuck Buk' in *The Smith* in 1966 was but one example; other parodies have been written by Ron Offen, P.O. Arone, and Joan Jobe Smith. Ron Androla and Paul Weinman (*We Puked Together In a Rusty Tub*) even made up a whole chapbook in the mid-1980s.

What is often overlooked is how romantic and literary Bukowski was in his poems of the late 1950s, works which yet contain the seeds of his later manner. A prime example is 'On seeing an old civil war painting with my love'. Its two sections encompass calmly elegiac description of the unnamed painting ("the conceited drummer boy/ dumber than the tombs/ lies in a net of red") and the human interest, a couple going out into the rain. The first section is self-consciously poetic, the second 'realistic' with a line of idiomatic speech, referring back to the painting, ending with marvellously descriptive similes which enables us to see - as well as the canvas, the poem's humanity, and its narrator's love for this woman:

And on the battlefield the rocks are wet and cool,
the fine grains of rock glint moon-fire,
and she curses under a small green hat
like a crown
and walks like a gawky marionette
into the strings of rain.[22]

Bukowski was here stumbling towards a type of poetry which would allude to rather than describe artworks, and include narrative and dialogue elements. But he had to fight his corner, writing several artistic credos early on, as in, 'In Defence of a Certain Type of Poetry, a Certain Type of Life...'. Bukowski's self-defence sometimes touched on formal issues, such as the breaking down of the absolute distinction between poetry and prose. The debate was drawn out of his early correspondence with J.W. Corrington, then teaching at the University of Louisiana, one of Bukowski's best critical champions. The letters to Corrington are highly literary, discussing aesthetics as well as the likes of Hemingway, Yeats, Carlos Williams, Camus, even Pascal, but are almost too anxious to justify his own purposes as a writer. And he was quick to rebut any perceived slight. In a letter dated 14 February 1961, for instance, Bukowski was responding to an 'Essay on the Recent History of Immortality' by Robert Vaughan, in J.B. May's *Trace* (January-March 1961). Bukowski asked "What the hell's wrong with a 6 or 7 or 37 line long prose statement that is broken into the readable advantage and clearness of the poem-form?" Bukowski's observations concluded in typically combative vein. "Writing poems is not difficult: living them is....simply sit down and write the god damned thing throwing on the colour and sound, shaking us alive with the force....let's make poetry the way we make love...and some day, Robert, I'll think of you, pretty and difficult, measuring vowels and adverbs, making rules instead of poetry".

Bukowski's oppositional aims were also stated in Jon Edgar Webb's significantly-titled magazine *The Outsider*. The third issue in 1963 proclaimed him 'Outsider of the Year'. (He was the only such recipient, and it was the only poetry prize that he ever won). The issue brought together the first batch of critical responses to his work, an important *festschrift* for a writer virtually unknown outside little magazines. Their editors were asked to write about Bukowski's special qualities. Comments by Felix Stephanile (editor of *The Sparrow*) brought out an interesting riposte, and the two pieces were printed alongside each other. Stephanile had appeared to brand Bukowski as a primitive: "Let the man alone; let him cavort in left-field, where he belongs, way out, alone, performing with both hands, and at the top of his voice, waving his poems like a flag. He only wants the thing that is himself in his poems; we need such men to remind us how poetry got started. I have compared the man to a brick-layer, a pugilist, and a baseball player".[23] Bukowski's reply stated that he was "against concepts & preconcepts of what poetry should be". His short, bewhiskered avant-garde credo is worth quoting almost in its entirety.

> The politicians and newspapers talk a lot about freedom but the moment you begin to apply any, either in Life or in the Art-Form, you are in [for] a cell, ridicule or misunderstanding. I sometimes think when I put that sheet of white paper in the machine: you will soon be dead, we will all soon be dead...while you're living it might be best to live from the source stuck inside of you....If you come to the poem, you are not going to worry too much about [writing like] Keats, Swinburne, Shelley; or acting like Frost. You are not going to worry about spondees, counts, or if the endings rhyme. You want to get it down, hard or crude or otherwise - any way you can truly send it through.... The mass, both actual mass and the artistic mass (in the sense of large practising numbers only) are always far behind, practising safety not only in the material and economic life but in the life of the so-called soul....If you write a poem that escapes the mass-hypnosis of the 19th Century slick-soft poesy they think you write badly because you do not sound right. They want to hear what they have always heard. But they forget that it takes 5 or 6 good men every century to push the thing ahead out of the staleness and death. I'm not saying that I am one of these men but I sure as hell am saying I am not one of the others. Which leaves me hanging - OUTSIDE.[24]

Moving from an oppositional stance, from stating what he was against, what he did not want, the other essential was insistence on freedom. Freedom from a 'rules' mentality in art, freedom to write about anything and as much as he wanted. (He would have to wait for a publisher to arise who would satisfy this last demand - and give him a large income, the final requirement of personal freedom). Freedom is of course an American shibboleth, what the nation was founded upon, and broke away from Britain to enjoy. Rebellious freedom from authority is 'American', from the Boston Tea Party to *Butch Cassidy and the Sundance Kid*. Rebellious freedom for the individual is even more American, and moves towards Hollywood - which is where Bukowski's work, his novels at least have ended up. Any critique of the status quo that Bukowski does advance invariably comes from his own 'majority of one'.

He thereby joins a lengthy list of American writers who conceived themselves as rugged individualists, anti-aesthete aesthetes, and Advertisers for the Self: Thoreau, Melville, Twain, Whitman, Jack London, Jeffers, Hemingway, Miller, Mailer, most of the Beats, Ken Kesey and many others. Bukowski emerged in a culture that stresses individual freedoms and distrusts collectivity. America, so its cherished national creed holds "self-evident", is the Land of the Free, where anyone may find life, liberty, and pursue happiness. This ideal is partly a wish-fulfillment stemming from the idea of America itself, which gave religious freedom to the early Puritan settlers, and freedom from European class and economic barriers to later arrivals. Election-seeking politicians have only to couple the words 'America' with 'Freedom' to provoke an invariably enthusiastic crowd response.

American individualism has self-reliance on one side of its coin, and dissidence on the reverse. Cultural mythology has nurtured the outlaw spirit, as Leslie Fiedler maintained, from "the frontiersman, the pioneer, at last the cowboy...[to] the beatnik, the hippie, one more wild man seeking the last West".[25] Fiedler's book title, *The Return of the Vanishing American* alludes to an early Hollywood treatment of the victims of Frontier freedoms, the Native American. Nevertheless, in U.S. mythology, only the individual can live up to the ideals on which America was reared; the collective is potentially corrupt and corrupting. Even Whitman, usually stereotyped as the poet of American Optimism, complained in his 1871 essay 'Democratic Vistas' that

> The depravity of the business classes of our country is not less than has been supposed, but infinitely greater. The official services of America, national, state, and municipal, in all their branches and departments, except the judiciary, are saturated in corruption, bribery, falsehood, mal-administration; and the judiciary is tainted. The great cities reek with respectable as much as non-respectable robbery and scoundrelism....I say that our New World democracy...is, so far, an almost complete failure.[26]

Not only is there a "perpetual failure to live up to the nation's preconceived foundation myths" (John Osborne), but America's historical record shows something not far from a dystopia. Witchcraft trials, extermination of native peoples, slavery, the Civil War, endemic financial scandals from Presidents Grant to Clinton, McCarthyism, the Vietnam War, the assassinations of progressive political figures during the 1960s, and the pervasive influence of the 'Military-Industrial Complex' on U.S. domestic and foreign policy since 1945. America's history is - almost as bad as Europe's.[27]

Bukowski's work is written within this widespread sense of disillusionment with the idea of America, the falling short of America's ideals in the face of reality. He shares in the influential strain in U.S. cultural mythology which dissents from straight society's values and institutions. This has been endlessly recycled by Hollywood and in Classic American Literature. The hero of such imaginings lives on the moral Frontier, wary of encroachment - by Big Government or the neighbours - lighting out for the territory ahead of civilization and domesticity, in constant emulation of the pioneer, the outlaw. Leslie Fiedler long ago noted Huck Finn's symbolic status as "a marginal American type, who only wants to stay alive; but who does not find this very easy to do".[28] And Hemingway stated that that 'all' subsequent American literature came out of *Huckleberry Finn*. Disaffiliation and individualism are the essential characteristics of fictional descendants, who find that their insistence upon independence leads to conflict with conformists, mass culture, and with the law.

This is the typical situation of Bukowski's characters, including fictional stand-ins for himself, who resist society's attempts to make them conform. (This is distinct from the real-life Charles Bukowski, who throughout the 1960s worked for the U.S. Postal Service, paid child support, ran a car, paid his taxes, and conspicuously failed to plot Capitalism's downfall). For all the wealth of contemporary detail and streetwise perspectives within his works, Bukowski is no social realist. While he did write poems, especially later in his career, about financial success, restaurants, parenthood, property ownership, memories of work and school, and even about vacations and watching television, they do not characterise his writing. His pages are crowded, not with 'realistic' characters, but with archetypes and stereotypes taken from American popular culture, films and literature. Rarely does one find the middle-class American, who typically works for a large corporation, worries about the mortgage and dental bills, and lives in the suburbs, confining the Great Outdoors to weekends or holiday homes. Instead, he renders the contemporary in mythic terms, complete with recognisable fictional types - the sentimental tough guy, the vamp, the tart with a heart, the schlemiel comically mugged by fate, the rebel with no cause except drink.

All these elements make Bukowski, ultimately, very much an insider to American cultural traditions, and not the outsider that surface indications - and his anti-Establishment rhetoric - might lead one to suppose. Even when he enters his own texts as 'Bukowski ' or 'Henry Chinaski', he is restating the awareness "of being so much a 'self' - constantly explaining oneself and telling one's own story" which is, as Alfred Kazin claimed, "as traditional in the greatest American writing as it is in a barroom".[29]

Bukowski is unusual in that he very rarely quotes from other writers, a practice which would undermine his 'anti-literary' bent; but he is a champion name-dropper. His poems have an enormous number of irreverent references to culture heroes: poets, men of letters, film stars, painters, and composers.

we talked about Klee,
the death of cummings,
Art, survival and so forth.
('Experience')

But rather than acknowledging that literature comes from other art and writing, Bukowski insists that it was rooted in things and in the relish of life itself. This lies behind his bravura definition of poetry, given to Allen de Loach, editor of *Intrepid*: "I think of it...as a loaf of bread, a long fat hot loaf, sliced in half down the middle, spread with pickles, onions, meats, garlic, chilies, old fingernails...add ice beer and a shot of scotch, ram it down under electric light, forget the mountains of faces and eyes and wrinkles and bombs and rent and graves, get it in, warm, smelling, filling, light a cigar, blow the whole room paint the whole room blue with smoke, play the radio, think of the bones of Chopin's left foot - that, to me, is poetry" (February 1967).[30]

He never lost an essentially romantic conception of the artist-hero transforming ordinary realities with genius. He proclaimed, sometimes preached, the American gospel of independence, dissidence, and individualism. Over the course of several decades, he found the artistic means to present this 'spontaneity' and 'rawness', his direct speaking. Freedom is what Bukowski's work is all about, and part of its unmistakable 'Americanness'; he embodied this in his language, subject matter, and tactics as a writer.

But it was achieved by a constant process of evolution. Literariness can be seen, for instance, in the very large number of similes scattered throughout his early work. He cut down on such features through time, but by no means eliminated them from his repertoire. Bukowski, beyond two years at L.A. City College where he studied journalism, was largely self-taught. This had consequences for the variability of his art, which can seem at times like a Casanova making a pass at every woman he meets in order to seduce every so often. If his works don't have the formal satisfactions of the well-made poem, when they do succeed, they have an inimitable force which makes most other poets seem dull and artificial by comparison.

If one wants to know what kind of a writer Bukowski was, look at the rich variety of magazines, papers and publishers which handled his work. And at his arresting, melodramatic titles, which almost burst with an amazing energy, a controlled anarchy. They suggest alienation, exclusion and embattlement, an attempt at capturing messy life itself. They also have airs of pain and suffering, perhaps even masochistic enjoyment. He appreciated that the ugliness of life was expressive, offered more fertile territory for him as an artist. This tied in with his own youthful feelings of being badly treated, by his parents and by the world in general. During the 1960s it was *Flower, Fist and Bestial Wail*; *Cold Dogs in the Courtyard*; *At Terror Street and Agony Way*. During the 1970s: *Love is a Dog from Hell*; *Play the Piano Drunk Like a Percussion Instrument Until the Fingers Begin to Bleed a Bit*. Even in the 1980s it remains *War All the Time*.

Numerous early poem titles are 'spontaneous' and, as even Martin Seymour-Smith conceded, "fun": 'So much for the knifers, so much for the bellowing dawns' (*Nomad*, 1960); 'You can't get something without the bellyache of a bullet and I guess the mushroom now" (*Simbolica*, 1961), 'A disorganised poem on a disorganised day with women running in and out and the price of beer up two cents a can' (*The Anagogic and Paideumic Review*,1961), and 'Rimbaud be damned: I have withstood 99,000 seasons in hell' (*Earth*, 1965). Bukowski moved on from excitable garrulity to his later stoic terseness. He was far from being a man without art, ignorant of aesthetics. His letters alone refute any such notion. But giving that impression was important to his artistic purpose, and to his eventual success.

Photograph of Charles Bukowski, New Orleans, 1962/3
by Jon or Gypsy Lou Webb

Chapter 2

Bukowski As Underground Hero 1944-1970

"All a writer can ask for is a bare survival...so that he can go on writing until he dies" - C. B., *Notes of a Dirty Old Man*.

Bukowski was the small press and little magazine poet *par excellence*. He was proud to have become big through 'the littles', remained loyal to them, and even up to the last weeks of his life was sending out poems, and corresponding with editors. His work was only ever published by a major mainstream press once in his lifetime - the *Bukowski Reader* issued by Harper Collins in 1993. The natural territory of Bukowski's writing was that of the little mag, and he straddled the developing continuum between magazines, small presses and underground newspapers. From this energetic environment came his earliest editors, fans, critics, lampooners, correspondents and even lovers. Far from being an isolato, an urban Robinson Jeffers, Bukowski's involvements - usually via correspondence but sometimes by personal contact - were wide-ranging, especially during the 1960s and 1970s.

Bukowski's reputation as a literary outsider is and was somewhat exaggerated, usually by himself. His lifetime total of appearances in magazines, faithfully catalogued by Al Fogel, was well over 1100. He was, in the fullness of time, published by almost every poetry publication of importance in the U.S., as well as by many of little or no importance.[1] By legendary avant-garde magazines of the 1940s-1960s; later by establishment entities such as *Poetry* (Chicago), *Antaeus*, and *American Poetry Review*; and between, within organs of the counterculture too numerous to list. Even the usual lament of West Coast writers, neglect by the New York/ East Coast literary marketplace, didn't apply to Bukowski. From Whit Burnett's *Story* in the mid-1940s onwards, numerous magazines on the East Coast embraced his work; Ed Sanders' *Fuck You, Unmuzzled Ox* and especially William Packard's *New York Quarterly*. Only those associated with particular coteries such as Robert Bly's, or the New York School and the Black Mountaineers, and certain academic quarterlies, remained closed to him. This is not to downplay Bukowski's struggle; but his rapid increase in name-recognition throughout the 1970s meant that he ended up with an exponential increase in general approval, and an incredible amount of such acceptance. This of course translated into his income from writing; until the mid-1960s at least it was virtually nothing, but by his last years he was receiving $7000 in royalties per month from Black Sparrow alone.

If Donald M. Allen's canonical anthology *The New American Poetry 1945-1960* had been published a few years later, Bukowski would probably have been included. 1960 was simply too early, for his work had hardly begun to develop its true character. But Bukowski knew, or his work was known to, virtually everyone of importance in the small press scene in America during these years; he was widely reviewed, talked about, ridiculed, imitated and criticised. He had participated in certain free speech and censorship *cause célèbres* of the 1960s small press scene, giving his support to editors facing obscenity charges - at least once because of his own activity. Through literary involvements he gained a wife (Barbara Frye, editor of *Harlequin*), and numerous relationships: Frances Smith and Linda King were both enthusiastic small press poets. His major personal friendships were linked with his writing, notably Jon and Gypsy Lou Webb, the "miracles in flesh" who were his breakthrough publishers. Later in the decade, around 1964, at the home of bohemian poet John Thomas, he had the pivotal meeting with John Martin, who founded Black Sparrow Press specifically to cater for Bukowski's publishing needs, making their fortunes in the process.

The 1960s were key to his development, as it was for alternative publishing media in general. The mimeograph magazine revolution speeded up, got cheaper, and democratised the production process, displacing the old-fashioned fine printing tradition exemplified by the Webbs' Loujon Press. Bukowski himself began the decade by having his first, much delayed, chapbook published, and ended it nationally-known and about to become a full-time author. To do so, he had to become a 'precedent' writer, an authoritative figure able to inspire disciples. His first such were Douglas Blazek's so-called 'Meat Poets', most of them midwesterners who moved to the West Coast. For this, Bukowski's anti-academic approach was essential. It brought him the regard, the adulation (and in some cases the later disillusionment), of a young generation of energetic activists, notably John Bryan, editor of *Renaissance*, *Notes from Underground* and then *Open City*; Blazek, one of the leaders of the 'mimeo revolution'; and the legendary d.a. levy. Also of great significance within Bukowski's career was a then-young German student, Carl Weissner, well connected within the U.S. literary avant-garde, who became his life-long friend, translator and agent.

Other associated names within the 1960s scene were Kirby Congdon, Hugh Fox, John Bennett, Steve Richmond, Neeli Cherkovski, and William Wantling. These became Bukowski's "hot little prophets", freely promoting his name, and propagating his mystique of No Compromise; his aura of rebellion against authority, his image as an embattled outsider. Through their advocacy, his work began its rise to prominence and notoriety. The publishing contacts that the 'mimeo revolution' and underground press brought him transformed his standing. This in turn created the conditions in which independent publishers could spring up and deliver his work to wider, eventually international, audiences. After a lengthy apprenticeship he emerged blinking from the literary 'underground' into the sunshine of widespread name-recognition. After years of wanting and waiting, he was finally able to leave the L.A. Post Office at the age of 50.

Though tangential to his poetry, the 'Notes of a Dirty Old Man' column that Bukowski wrote for his local underground papers, *Open City* and *L.A. Free Press*, and the stories that began appearing in papers all over the country, greatly boosted his public image. Many of those who attended his live readings from 1970 onwards, and bought his books, first came across the name in underground papers. In a newspaper advertisement for *Crucifix in a Deathhand* (1965), Henry Miller praised Bukowski as "the poet-satyr of today's Underground"; the veteran literary leftist Walter Lowenfels called him "the Houdini of the Literary Underground". Even as late as 1980, the British journalist David Montrose still felt able to refer to him as "the quintessential Underground Man of American Letters".[2] This recurrent term 'underground' has several elements. In general, it means the non-mainstream, non-commercial arm of new literature. It has an inherently political, anti-establishment dimension. Further, it specifically refers to that late phase of the avant-garde active during the 1960s American scene: the younger successors of the Beats and Black Mountaineers. Lastly, it refers to the phenomenon of underground newspapers, which emerged in the mid-1960s on the West Coast with *The Berkeley Barb* and *Los Angeles Free Press*, and rapidly spread all over the continent and to Europe. All of these strands are heavily represented in Bukowski's career: this is why he was an 'underground hero'.

But - to begin at the beginning. He spent two years at Los Angeles City College just before the war, majoring in journalism. (One of his contemporaries was the science fiction writer Ray Bradbury, though they appear not to have met). Bukowski's first experience of literature was of course as a reader. Declared psychologically unfit by the Draft Board, he saw war service instead in libraries, chiefly at the Los Angeles Public Library but also elsewhere. This is what his own accounts focus upon, his pleasure at discovering novelists such as Dostoyevsky, Sherwood Anderson and Hemingway, and his instinctive reaction to the magazines he encountered then. In 'A Rambling Essay on Poetics and the Bleeding Life...', originally written for Blazek's magazine *Olé* (#2, 1965), he retrospectively shaped his ambivalent feelings when voraciously reading through the philosophy and religion section, to Current Affairs and *The New York Times*; finding only "the old joke of a knowledge that didn't really exist, dressed up in a pretty and painted terminology". He then says he moved on to the literary-academic quarterlies, naming *The Sewanee Review* and *The Kenyon Review*: "the magazines really said nothing real, nothing about the streets outside, the park benches, the faces, the almost uselessness of living".[3] Bukowski singles out, in fact, the two leading critical journals of that era. *Sewanee* in Tennessee was edited in the mid-1940s by Allen Tate, who had been previously associated with John Crowe Ransom in the so-called Southern 'Fugitives' group of writers and critics. *Kenyon* had only recently been founded in Gambier, Ohio, and was edited by Ransom from 1939 to 1958.

It is instructive to take a look at what Bukowski was actually reading. A poem published in 1984, 'Kenyon Review, after the sandstorm', specifically refers to a revelatory reading experience in El Paso, Texas, during 1940. It contrasts the narrator's memory of his own impoverished situation with that of the comfortable 'professors' writing about literature, with their leisurely and safe lives. As it happens, each of the four issues that year was of great interest. In the first two issues he would have read a poem by W.H. Auden memorialising the recently-deceased Sigmund Freud, and other poetry by Wallace Stevens, Robert Penn Warren, Randall Jarrell, and Weldon Kees. There were articles by R.P. Blackmur on Henry Adams, by Milton Hindus on Emily Dickinson, John Crowe Ransom on 'The Pragmatics of Art', Wyndham Lewis on Picasso, an attacking piece by Julian Symons titled 'Obscurity and Dylan Thomas', and high-powered reviews by Lionel Trilling, John Gould Fletcher, and Mark Schorer.

In the Summer 1940 issue he would have seen poems by Marianne Moore and Frederic Prokosch. He might have relished this particular sentence in 'On the Semantics of Poetry' by Philip Wheelwright: "Poetry is never entirely sober; its acquaintance with the language of sobriety is casual and varying". There were also articles on Brecht, Balzac, and even on the widely-banned Henry Miller: "Mr Miller takes his place in the widespread revolt against intellect. 'There's no improving the mind', he insists, 'look to your heart and gizzard'. And he might well have added another organ". The chief feature of the Autumn number was a symposium, 'Literature and the Professors', contributed to by Cleanth Brooks and Arthur Mizener. This issue included a brilliantly enthusing review by John Berryman of a new book by Dylan Thomas, rebutting Symons' earlier critiques of the Welsh poet. William Empson wrote on 'Basic English and Wordsworth', Philip Blair Rice on George Santayana, and Klaus Mann on 'Karl May, Hitler's Literary Mentor'. The point of listing these contents is that, whatever Bukowski's mid-1960s and mid-1980s characterisations of this reading experience, for or against, *Kenyon* and the other magazines constituted a wonderful education, a widely-based introduction to all the arts at a very high level. He was then free to make of it what he wanted. If Bukowski was rebelling against all this, he was at least taking on the very best writers and critics of his time.

Bukowski's education by reading continued throughout the war years and beyond. Another issue, *Kenyon* (1944, volume 6) is worth looking at. He would have opened it to find a long poem, 'Seasons of the Soul' by Allen Tate, complete with obligatory Eliot-like epigraph in Italian. He would have read in it rhythmical but somewhat meaningless lines such as "It had its timeless day/ Before it kept the season/ of time's engaging jaws". Ah, the lifeless late Modernist-Southern poesy of an Allen Tate had to die before the populist art of a Bukowski could be born! Elsewhere in this issue, Bukowski read work by new young poets Randall Jarrell, Muriel Rukeyser, Jean Garrigue; articles on Jean Cocteau and André Gide; reviews by Arthur Mizener, Delmore Schwartz and Horace Gregory. He could have read a lengthy essay by Ransom himself, 'Art Needs a Little Separating', written in the most professorial manner: "We commonly say that a work of art is a discourse, or piece of ordered language; that it makes statements and conducts an argument; or, if it is not literature, that at any rate it is a composition having logical relations among its parts".[4] Perhaps most galling for the young man's eyes was its announcement of a short story contest, with prizes of $500 and $250. Bukowski's first stories were now busy being written and rejected by the likes of *The New Yorker* and *Atlantic Monthly*.

What he learned from the magazine and the libraries' shelves, what he wanted and what he didn't want, was vital to his later writing. He learned in particular about the kind of language he was to use. "I was aware of the glass-prison terminology: that fancy, long, and twisted words were evasions, crutches, weaknesses. And so I used to think of it as 'bullshit padding': talking about useless things in useless terminology".[5] Bukowski is here echoing Hemingway's prejudices, and endorsing, a decade late, the

Beats' attack on academia's safe and stale orthodoxies. He goes on later in the *Olé* piece to portray himself in a role familiar to avant-garde myth, that of the youthful martyr to Literature - like his heroes John Fante in L.A. and Hemingway in Paris before him, starving and drinking and trying to write One True Sentence.

Bukowski himself constantly refers to his 'late start' in the writing game, usually stating that he began poetry at the age of 35: see his introduction to the early selected poems *Burning in Water, Drowning in Flame* (1974). This isn't accurate. Most of his first appearances in print were indeed short stories, but he had poems published in several issues of a highly reputable magazine, *Matrix*, when he was in his mid-to-late 20s. Bukowski in fact died exactly 50 years after his first prose acceptance, 'Aftermath of a Lengthy Rejection Slip', appeared in the March 1944 issue of Whit Burnett's *Story* magazine. *Story* began in Vienna during the mid-1930s before transferring to New York, and was later called "the most distinguished short story magazine in the world" (Edward J. O'Brien).[6] In the war years, for instance, among the new young writers it published were J.D. Salinger, Norman Mailer, Truman Capote and Joseph Heller. Inclusion in such a magazine heralded the start of a serious writing career, and his first payment. Burnett also contributed indirectly to Bukowski's career by encouraging Jon Edgar Webb, then incarcerated in a Midwestern prison, and publishing him in *Story* (February 1936). Webb's model of a magazine editor, of catholic taste without regard to literary cliques, was partly Burnett's, and he followed this in *The Outsider*.

Another story was taken by Caresse Crosby's *Portfolio*, placing Bukowski in the same issue as the international avant-garde: Sartre, Lorca, Camus, Henry Miller and Picasso. It was a beautiful if somewhat haphazardly-produced magazine, as her friend Daisy Aldan, editor of *Folder*, remembered: "she had published it during the war when paper was scarce and had used any paper she could find, all sizes and colours. The pages were unbound". Bukowski's first separately printed work was a story, published in 1946, 'Twenty tanks from Kasseldown'. This, Al Fogel's *Bukowski Price Guide* informs us, was included in a collection of broadsides by the Black Sun Press, and titled *Portfolio III*.[7] Caresse, widow of poet Harry Crosby, was a left-over of the glamorous artistic bohemia of 1920s Paris. She had relaunched her Black Sun Press in Washington during the war, with Henry Miller as associate editor in charge of prose, publishing works by a range of emergent figures such as Charles Olson. Bukowski's early writing, far from being totally rejected, was thus known to, encouraged, and accepted by well-connected international figures in the arts.

Bukowski's poems appeared during 1946 in *Matrix* (Vol. 9, no.2), established since 1938 and edited by Joseph Moray and S.Z. Mackey. It was located in New York, later in California; they published Bukowski poems and stories in five issues between 1946 and 1951. (One of their regular contributors, J.B. May, went on to regularly support Bukowski's work in *Trace*, which he started after the closure of *Matrix* in 1952). Looking at two of these apprentice poems, their manner is strangely indirect and muted, but their themes - a young writer's despair, and an existential perception of the alien nature of things - have something in common with later work. In 'Object lesson', *Matrix* (Winter 1946) an unnamed voice tells us about depression, bitterness, the temptations of suicide.

He who pauses is
one damn fool.

I remember a discourse
with a leper
who suggested using
hooks and pulleys....

Tell him to seek the stars
and he will kill himself with climbing.

Tell him about Chatterton. Villon....

He will do it himself.[8]

This name-dropping identification with persecuted artists - the 18th Century suicide Thomas Chatterton, imprisoned Francois Villon - is characteristic. So is the simplicity of the language, though it veers between the sub-Hemingway "one damn fool" and a word such as "discourse". The piece is vague, unfocussed, monolithic. Whatever later Bukowski poems may lack, they do not lack emphasis. 'The look', published in *Matrix* during 1951, is short, enigmatic, slightly comical. If it has a discernible meaning, it may be the perception of the gap between human consciousness and the alien world of objects. It reads, in its entirety:

I once bought a toy rabbit at a department store
and now he sits and ponders me with pink sheer eyes.
He wants golfballs and glass walls.
I want quiet thunder.

Our disappointment sits between us.[9]

Bukowski, having made a highly promising start and being featured by three leading magazines, suddenly stopped. 'The Look' was followed by a publication break of about five years. Not, that is, the "ten year drunk" repeatedly referred to by him. The drought was ended by the fundamental event in The Bukowski Legend. This was a near-fatal spell in hospital around 1955, the consequence of years of heavy drinking, which galvanised a release into genuine creativity. In artistic terms, Bukowski's bleeding stomach ulcer performed the same function as the shrapnel wounds suffered by Hemingway on the Italian-Austrian front while serving as a Red Cross ambulance driver during the First World War. The changed perspectives caused by a close encounter with death characterise Hemingway's subsequent creations Nick Adams and Jake Barnes. Bukowski's typical early narrator, though far less heroic, is also highly aware of the fragility of human existence. His own energetic response to near-fatality, however much embellished and fictionalised (cf. one of his great short stories, 'Life and death in the charity ward'), is undeniable in the sheer amount of work that he began producing.

And, like Hemingway, he was concerned with the authenticity of words and feelings. His working experiences reinforced this; it was hard for him to come out of the factories and write a poem that he "didn't quite mean". His initial struggle was simply to gain acceptance from more literary-minded editors. He wrote to Jon Edgar Webb about his release from hospital, "A couple of days later I had the first drink, the one they said would kill me. A week or so later I got a typewriter, and after a 10 year blank (sic)....I found my fingers making the poem. Or rather, the bar talk. The non-lyrical, non-singing thing. The rejects came quickly enough".[10] Even such an offhand account shows the essence of the image and the work that Bukowski had begun creating. That is, disrespect for established authority and official opinion (the doctors) and, rhetorically, of death itself. Drink is to be essential for his art and life - an escape, but also a way of dramatising existence, connecting with people, giving him the courage to take risks. His efforts are described as coming from overheard speech, bar talk. Then they are 'quickly' rejected by more tradition-bound editors. Bukowski's poems, and the authorial self created in them, therefore carry an indelible mark of rejection and resentment against authority. (It was something he never really lost). Nonetheless, this rejection can be "good for the soul", he told the Canadian poet Al Purdy, "if you are not a quitter".[11] Bukowski's speakers wear their rejection with pride. To echo Jean Genet, they reject those who have rejected them.

One of the earliest significant magazines to latch on to Bukowski's resumed creativity was *Quixote*, which published him in several issues in the period 1956-58, then later during the 1960s under the editorship of Morris Edelson. One of Bukowski's poems was accepted in 1956 by Judson

Crews' *The Naked Ear*, a one-man magazine located in the ranches of Taos, New Mexico (near where members of the D.H. Lawrence gang were still alive). 'Layover' is an elegiac remembrance of a lost lover, its speaker scorning the work ethic, "headlines/ and Cadillacs", observing an alley where poor men "poke" domestic rubbish for bottles to sell. He remembers being in a cheap hotel, making love "by a photograph of Paris/ and an open pack of Chesterfields". Reiterations, characteristic in this period of his work, impart rhythm to uneven line-lengths. Of all the words used in the poem, only its title, and two others are of more than one or two syllables. It thereby establishes the predominant trait of all Bukowski's subsequent verse: the use of structurally simple language. The second paragraph's attempt to arrest the fatal flow of time is concluded with a simile.

That moment - to this -
may be years in the way they measure,
but it's only one sentence back in my mind -
there are so many days
when living stops and pulls up and sits
and waits like a train on the rails.[12]

Those magazines hospitable to Bukowski in the first few years of his new career were mainly Californian, favouring Beat-inspired free verse and open forms. Jory Sherman remembered that, in spite of many later admonitions against rhyming poetry, Bukowski did publish a rhymer, probably 'I think of the olden armies' in an August 1959 issue of the Texas magazine *Flame*. Clearly still casting around for styles, he also published a few poems that approximate to syllabic forms, notably 'I taste the ashes of your death' in Andrew Linick's San Francisco-based *Nomad* (Winter, 1959). A magazine unusual for its humour was E.V. Griffith's *Hearse*, whose deadpan subtitle was "A Vehicle Used to Convey the Dead". An irreverent quarterly, its successor was *Gallows*. Griffith was a discerning if slow-motion operator, his Hearse Press publishing Bukowski's first chapbook; and much later on, his publication *Poetry Now* included him in numerous issues.

Gene Frumkin's *Coastlines* and. J.B.May's *Trace* were then situated in Hollywood. George Hitchcock's *San Francisco Review* was active just up the coast. Wallace Berman's L.A. based *Semina* highlighted Bukowski's work among the Beats, as did *Beatitude* (in 1960) and Barney Rossett's *Evergreen*. A native of Texas, Barbara Frye, published *Harlequin* in Los Angeles; one issue in 1957 devoted twenty-six pages to Bukowski poems and stories. A copy, if any can be found, now carries a valuation of $1750. He liked the magazine so much that he married the editor! During the first decade of his resumed career, several magazines came out with special issues, and his work percolated through to a wide geographical spread. These included Carl Larsen's *Rongwrong* (New York), Margaret Randall's bilingual Spanish/ English magazine *El Corno Emplumado/ The Plumed Horn* (Mexico City), Felix Stephanile's *The Sparrow*, Harry Smith's *The Smith* (both New York), Marvin Malone's *Wormwood Review*, which moved from Connecticut to California with its editor, and *Midwest* edited by R. R. Cuscaden in Chicago. *Epos*, described by the hip Hugh Fox as "a rather square and traditional magazine", was edited by Evelyn Thorne and Will Tullos from Florida; they dedicated a special issue to Bukowski in 1962. *Targets* made a booklet in 1961 for Bukowski's own use; there were only 6 copies of *Signature* #2 (currently carrying an amazing value of $4500).[13]

Bukowski accumulated the inevitable rejection slips: he once claimed to have papered a room with them. He scorned these judgements in the introduction to one of his first collections: "I found out that the editors wanted everything in a cage....Boil it down, they said. You're all over the placenta (sic). But I found that all they wanted was dullness and the poetic pose". He further lambasted their tastes in a letter to Webb, his confessor in literature, dated 2 September 1962: "Went someplace last night against my wishes and listened to being told I do not write lyric poetry, and that my pessimism was exaggerated etc. Hell, I know I don't write lyric poetry....I am sick of the mess, and g.d. sick of being told 'how' I should write with my 'talent' and what POETRY IZ (sic). I don't care what POETRY IZ. I write from my own marble and f. everybody".[14] 'I Am Visited By an Editor and a Poet', published in 1962, notes the difference between the visitors, named as J.B. May and Leslie Woolf Hedley, who are "very immaculate" - and its roughhouse narrator ("You're Charles Bukowski, aren't you?"). He is more used to the cops calling, and has just got back from the racetrack.

and I looked at the five magazines with my name on the cover
and wondered what it meant,
wondered if we are writing poetry or all huddling in
one big tent
         clasping assholes.[15]

All of Bukowski's first chapbooks were brought out by little magazines, published in editions of no more than two hundred copies. Most were probably given away to subscribers or to friends, sales being minimal. *Flower, Fist and Bestial* Wail was published by E.V. Griffith's Hearse Press, based in the quaintly-named town of Eureka, California, in November 1960. Bukowski's correspondence with him shows that he actually paid half of the printing costs, and was prepared to consider doing so again: "if this works out o.k., sometime in the future we can go in on another half and half deal" (2 June 1960). It also shows that publication had been delayed for two years, from 1958, and that Bukowski suffered considerable exasperation and anxiety over this.

But he enjoyed a burst of publishing in 1962 and 1963. *Poems and Drawings* from Epos Press; *Longshot Pomes for Broke Players* from Carl Larsen's 7 Poets Press in New York; and *Run With the Hunted* was edited by R.R. Cuscaden as one of *Midwest's* poetry chapbooks. Bukowski was grateful for their interest, time and care, but he was impatient. He could be scathing about the back-scratching and infighting within the small press world, and its highly variable standards. In an article written for Len Fulton's *Small Press Review*, Bukowski complained that the littles had degenerated into "a vast grinding lonely hearts club of no talents", and that there were only a few where the editing was "professional rather than personal".[16]

Jon Edgar Webb, and his wife 'Gypsy Lou', satisfied both demands. They became his personal friends and professional champions, sustaining his morale and sense of purpose as a writer in the aftermath of the death of Jane Cooney Baker. The Webbs' magazine *The Outsider* highlighted Bukowski's work and placed it among an eclectic mix of writers, various generations of the international avant-garde, while their Loujon Press published his two beautifully-produced 'breakthrough' volumes. Webb and Bukowski had first established contact in August 1960, through Jory Sherman, a young writer living in Los Angeles who was *The Outsider's* talent scout on the West Coast. Webb was a survivor of 1920s bohemia and 1930s radicalism, had worked as a journalist and teacher, and written a prison novel - *Four Steps to the Wall* (1948). Webb had known Hemingway, Sherwood Anderson, Jack Conroy and Henry Miller. An informative 1979 article by Jim Burns, in the British critical magazine *Poetry Information*, tells about the Webbs' hand-to-mouth existence over many years. Theirs was the old-fashioned skill of fine printing, laboriously setting type and hand printing on a Chandler & Price 8" x 12" Press. They even won a national printing award for a mid-1960s volume by Henry Miller. But their dedication was pursued at a considerable - if sometimes exaggerated - personal cost.[17]

Wormwood Review devoted an entire issue in tribute to Jon Edgar Webb in 1972. In it, Bukowski praised Webb (who had died in June 1971), comparing him as an editor to Whit Burnett, and to H.L Mencken. He wrote that "in the brief span of its existence, THE OUTSIDER made more of a landing upon our literature than any other magazine....it was literature jumping and screaming, it was a record of voices and... a record of the time".[18] Befitting its usual base in New Orleans, the magazine's subtitle was 'Today's Poetry and Prose, Yesterday's Jazz'. Its international cast and excellent production values ensured that the magazine found its way into University libraries, bookstores all over the U.S., and the eager hands of collectors. But, as so often, the economics were wrong: even a virtual sell-out of its 3,000 copies print run made little or no profit for future projects. Three numbers appeared between 1961 and 1963. Their final flourish, a double issue to which Bukowski also contributed, featured works by and tributes to the painter and poet Kenneth Patchen, and was delayed until 1969 when they were living in Tucson, Arizona.

The first *Outsider* was dated Fall 1961, and exhibited Webb's taste, blending new and established writers. Among those featured were Kay Boyle, Colin Wilson, Russell Edson, Jonathan Williams, Langston Hughes, and the (relatively) young turks Ginsberg, Corso, Olson, Creeley, Kerouac, Snyder, Gael Turnbull, and Gilbert Sorrentino. The largest individual contribution, 'A Charles Bukowski Album', had eleven poems. The second issue had many of the same names, plus William Burroughs, Howard Nemerov, Jonathan Williams, and the Scottish poet Edwin Morgan. Only two poems by Bukowski were printed. It was the third *Outsider* which showcased Bukowski, carrying three new poems, 'The house', 'Event', and 'Dinner, rain and transport'. Webb liked printing letters, featuring the Henry Miller-Lawrence Durrell correspondence of the 1930s-40s. The third issue printed some of rather more recent vintage: agonised letters sent by Bukowski to the Webbs in the aftermath of the death of Jane, in January 1962. It included several photographs, probably the first of Bukowski to appear in print, in which he looks not unlike a young Humphrey Bogart.

The 'Editors Congratulate Bukowski' section found Gene Frumkin of *Coastlines* stating that had "made the sense of spontaneity his trademark....he is the only poet I can think of who can be utterly raw, and, at the same time, genuinely poetic". Joseph Friedman, editor of *Venture*, remarked upon Bukowski's 'offensive laughter', and his "attack, an impertinent zany attack on death, for like the farthest out of the Outsiders he is keenly sensitive to the innermost innards of being alive". The two critical essays in this issue remain among the best short assessments of Bukowski 's verse, at least in its earliest phase. 'Charles Bukowski: Poet in a Ruined Landscape' by R.R.Cuscaden (reprinted from the Newcastle magazine *Satis* of the previous year) drew attention to a "Jeffers-like pessimism", an obsession with art and music, and the "sense of a desolate, abandoned world". Cuscaden concluded that "Bukowski is a poet of the permanent opposition. He opposes 'the ruin' on a basis of personal anarchy which must attempt the impossible and create its own order". J.W. Corrington's essay examined 'The tragedy of the leaves', 'The priest and the matador' and 'Old man, dead in a room', linking the poems with the Existentialism of Sartre and Camus, and with T.S. Eliot's alienated characters.[19]

Bukowski's prize for being 'Outsider of the Year' was to have his first full-length collection printed by the Webb's Loujon Press. This was a volume of new and selected poems, *It Catches My Heart in Its Hands*, a title slightly adapted from a line in Robinson Jeffers' poem 'Hellenistics'. This hand-printed and hand-bound volume, #1 in the so-called Gypsy Lou Series, was a work of art in itself and appeared in an edition of 777 copies between June and September. The copy that I have seen, a mostly orange and green cover with an image of a skeleton in sand, was printed on several shades of paper and signed on 2 June 1963. Hugh Fox recalled seeing the special copy made for Bukowski himself, "with its textured grass-paper cover, so beautiful that you almost hated to touch it". The author was, for once, highly appreciative: "Never such a book! Where? Where? In all the libraries in all the cities I have never seen such a book put together...[with] inventive creativeness and love" (23 November 1963).

One of the features of the volume was a remarkably prescient introduction by J.W. Corrington, whose large claims for Bukowski's importance were eventually borne out, if not always by the poems he discussed. It began in magisterial fashion: "critics at the end of our century may well claim that Charles Bukowski's work was the watershed that divided 20th Century American poetry between the Pound-Eliot-Auden period and the new time in which the human voice speaking came into its own". Corrington called Bukowski's poetry "the spoken voice nailed to paper", and went on to praise its "nearly perfect balance between the ideal of spontaneous composition and the obvious requirements of the written word", a style that "transcends and merges the outer edges of prose and poetry". He compared and associated Bukowski with some of the giants of modern literature - Lorca, Faulkner, and Hemingway - concluding with a rhetorical flourish, hailing "works which will bear whatever is worth the cartage from our time into another".[20]

The creativity that the Webbs had engendered went into a further lovingly produced volume, necessarily financed by Lyle Stuart Inc. of New York, in an edition of 3100 copies, *Crucifix in a Deathhand* (1965). Webb himself remarked on Bukowski's astounding productivity, stating on the volume's wrap-around that the book was "a painstakingly pruned selection from the 326 poems Bukowski submitted for this title between October 1963 and March 1965". Many were written on a visit to New Orleans, during a hot lyrical month, August 1964. Bukowski told the Canadian poet Al Purdy at the time that:

> The Webbs are miracles in flesh. They work in this dive full of roaches and rats and paper and press and no room - they have hung the wall with a bed and climb up there on a ladder and they starve and print pages of poetry and a magazine...and no thought of anything but the work. And me - I roar into town drunk as 90 sailors and piss over everybody.[21]

The book itself, which included striking artwork by Noel Rockmore, was "a multi-layered assemblage of coloured weave Spectra paper in shades of white, winestone, saffron, bayberry, peacock, ivory, bittersweet, gobelin & tabasco, intermixed with rice paper and madras tissue, between several overlapping covers of cork and other exotic paper". The printing was done from June to September 1964 "in a slave quarters workshop back of a sagging ex-mansion" in the French Quarter of New Orleans. One of the book's many favourable reviews appeared in a local newspaper, *The Vieux Carré Courier*, on 28 May 1965. Its reviewer noted the 9 months' gestation, seven shades of paper being fed into an antique press, the result being "a labor of heat, ink, glue and love". He records revealing comments by Webb on his editing: "Sometimes I'd take out a four-letter word - I'm really a moralist if the word doesn't help the poem - and then I'd write Bukowski asking permission. We'd correspond for several weeks about the word, and he'd get very worried, wondering if another word could go in its place".[22] So much for the idea of Bukowski as a slapdash, devil-may-care word-slinger.

Despite his gratitude, Bukowski made virtually no money from sales of the Loujon Press books, waiving royalties because of the Webbs' precarious finances, a situation that the correspondence shows that Bukowski was often suspicious about. But the Webbs continued to be his friends and correspondents, to whom he reported significant advances in his career. He wrote to them about the first radio broadcast of his work: "a tape of a poetry reading of mine I made on my machine and which was broadcast over KPFK [station in Los Angeles] in August 1962. Of course, they deleted a lot of vulgarity" (1 July 1963). He also told them about his first offer of a paid reading: "Some outfit in Frisco wants me to give a reading in Feb[ruary], offer of 2/3rds of house but I can't see myself on the boards in front of the yak hyenas, lonely hearts and homos. Not yet". (19 October 1963).

One of Bukowski's other significant correspondents at this time was the Ontario poet Al Purdy. Born in 1918, like Bukowski he had had an early succession of menial jobs, travelled extensively, and published precociously. His first collection appeared in 1944; he had six books out by the start of their correspondence, and was far more established. As both hell-raiser and philosopher-poet, he became recognized as one of Canada's leading talents, alongside Irving Layton. In the introduction to Purdy's *Selected Poems* (1972), the critic George Woodcock characterised both himself and Purdy as "autodidacts, omnivorous readers, furious generalists, restless travellers, maverick radicals, gluttons for variety of experience....Rare types a decade ago when every other poet in the groves...seemed to sport at least an M.A.".[23] As a poet observing nature, Purdy owes something to D.H. Lawrence, his natural world usually the Canadian Arctic of ice and frozen tundra. His lyrics are counterpointed by comically vulgar episodes, such as the difficulties of excreting when huskies are around. They shared an admiration for the poetry of Robinson Jeffers. In his brief preface to *The Bukowski/Purdy Letters 1964-1974* (1983), Bukowski observed that "getting a letter from Purdy always got my day up off the floor....[it was] like hearing from another world...his poems read bright in my darkness". On other occasions, he was less than complimentary.[24] Some Purdy poems have affinities with Bukowski's, but are more avuncular in their celebration of wine, women and song:

I am drinking
I am drinking beer with yellow flowers
in underground sunlight
and you can see that I am a sensitive man
('At the Quinte Hotel')[25]

Their correspondence was one of mutual admiration. Bukowski warmly commended Purdy's *Poems for All the Annettes* (1962) and *The Cariboo Horses* (1965). Their letters mostly belong to the period 1964-66, and began after Purdy's enthusiastic review of *It Catches...*, in *Evidence* # 8, a Canadian magazine edited by Alan Bevan which also regularly published C.B. Incidentally, Bukowski committed the little mag 'sin' of simultaneous publication a number of times; for example 'Men's crapper' appeared in *Evidence* #7 (1967) as well as in *Evergreen* that same year. For his part, Bukowski turned Purdy on to *The Outsider* and to young Doug Blazek's *Olé*. By 1968, Bukowski's star had risen and Purdy wrote asking for an endorsement to help sell his latest collection in the U.S.

Henry Miller wrote to him during August 1965, praising but counselling him against drinking, "a sure way" to kill the source of inspiration - advice which Bukowski naturally ignored. And his correspondence had expanded. As he told Purdy, this was a mixed blessing: "young poets...talk on and enclose poems - most of them rather thin as if drizzled through a fog with a hackneyed sense of the melodramatic". Joe Wolberg commented that by 1965, Bukowski's "underground reputation was remarkable, considering how few people actually knew him personally. That situation changed as more young poets, fans and sycophants began to seek out the now-notorious 'dirty old man' in his East Hollywood tenement".[26] Wolberg is anticipating the soubriquet earned by the writings within *Open City*, which did not begin until May 1967, when the self-styled "old man" was a mere 46. (The column's title can perhaps be seen as Bukowski's irony at the expense of the Californian youth-hippy culture surrounding him at the paper).

Bukowski's next significant publishing contact after Webb was Douglas Blazek, who was then married to the poet Alta [Gerrey]. She went on to become a leading light in West Coast feminist writing and publishing, founding the Shameless Hussy Press in 1969. Blazek was originally just one of a number of young writers from the Midwest who corresponded with Bukowski, and each other. Blazek, Charles Potts, and William Wantling all came from Illinois, though Potts and Blazek moved to San Francisco during the latter 1960s. They in turn had links with more politicised activists in Cleveland, Ohio; d.a. levy, t.l. kryss, kent taylor, d.r. wagner, who all affected lowercase names à la e.e.cummings. The proliferation of mimeo mags all over the States during the mid-1960s owed much to Blazek and levy's energetic activities. Mimeographs had been pioneered in the 1950s by *Matrix* and *Trace*. Their machines used typewriter cut stencils, allowing magazines and chapbooks to be produced quickly and cheaply, though not with high quality production values. Networks of communication and exchange were set up, freeing new writing from the grip of university presses and established publishers. Mimeo mags were thus ideally suited to the anti-academic and the avant-garde. A recent anthology, *The Outlaw Bible of American Poetry* (1999) has recognised their historical importance in the development of alternative publication media. In Felix Pollak's view at the time, they represented "a kind of populist thrust that held that any man could be a publisher and, perhaps, a poet too".[27]

Blazek first surfaces in Bukowski's life during late 1964, when he wrote asking for poems for his new magazine. C.B. told Al Purdy about this "kid with his mimeo machine in the kitchin (sic) in Illinois, who seemed full of beans so I sent him some verse which he took. I do wish he'd learn to operate the machine better". The subtitle of *Olé* was "the original consciousness-raising magazine", though this implied psychological extremity, altered states of mind induced by drugs, and relative sexual explicitness rather than politics. Some of the featured talents, notably Gil Orlovitz, William Wantling, Ray Newton, and d.a. levy, died prematurely either from drug overdoses or suicide. Blazek's editorials expressed alienation from the mainstream, as well as his hopes as an entrepreneur. He frequently referred to Bukowski's opinions. "Poetry is dying on the vine like a whore on the end stool on a Monday night.... He knows that good writing is merely good opinion. Style wise the same thing goes....All we intend to do is join the already present revolution. By mass force, good poetry, and a belief in our cause we hope to make poetry respected in this country and make it into a financially independent art form with a new audience who will purchase our work....We shun the word 'literary'...poetry must disturb and upset".[28]

The magazine was unpaginated, sold for 75 cents, and used garish shades of blue or purple paper; typography was sometimes as shaky as its grammar and spelling. Blazek, a believer in the "we prefer crude vigour to polished banality" motto of proletarian magazines of the 1930s, termed his principles 'Meat Poetry'. He urged poets to "find out where the bones break, get down...to where the hair is, where the blood spurts like ejaculating whales and lay it on the line whatever you feel you see". He summarised this as: I WANT POETRY THAT IS LIFE NOT POETRY. Blazek also wanted to further extend the subject matter of poetry - a neo-Beat demand. "Every inch of the planet earth, every curse word, every thimble, every spot of dirt, every slam, bang, jing, every chug in the harbor is poetry" (*Olé* #1).

Bukowski was a constant feature in *Olé*; in fact he was listed as a patron (i.e. financial contributor). In *Olé* # 3 (November 1965) there were several adverts for his publications. Blazek's Mimeo Press edition of *Confessions of a Man Insane Enough to Live with Beasts* was available for $1, or $2 for one of 25 copies with "specially autographed drawings by Buk". Readers were also informed of the "long awaited" chapbook *Cold Dogs in the Courtyard*, produced in an edition of 500 copies by the *Literary Times* (where his first interview appeared) and Cyfoeth, in Chicago. Its contents were poems that had been rejected from earlier publications, notably by Jon Edgar Webb and E.V. Griffith. Bukowski protested that "very lately, I can tell a good woman when I see one, a good fire, a good whiskey, a good car, a good painting...why couldn't I tell a good poem?" The thirteen poems had appeared in magazines such as *Epos*, *Impetus*, *Sciamachy*, and *Wormwood Review*. There are two unusual poems in the chapbook, neither of which have been reprinted since.'It's nothing to laugh about' is a Jeffers-like observation of mankind and nature interacting. A small toad is minutely described, "a greener living green than any green leaf...the leg-ends seeming to grip for notches in the air..../ his green skin happy against the blue-chill water". 'Existence' is possibly his only poem that directly describes Bukowski's working routine at the Los Angeles Post Office Terminal Annexe:

I huddle in front of this cheesebox of numbers
poking in small cards
addressed to non-existent
lives...
this is my job, my rent, my whore, my shoes...
on the street is so hard, at least
give me the walls I have paid a life for.[29]

Also advertised was a book of drawings to be produced by Border Press "at the end of 1965", which never appeared. The same page informed readers that "Charles Bukowski is raping the Mad Virgin Press with his forthcoming book of new poems" - *Poems Written Before Leaping (sic) Out of an Eight Story Window* - which was not published until 1968. This issue of *Olé* signalled the shape of things to come. The bookseller Jim Roman, of Fort Lauderdale, Florida, was "drafting a bibliography on Bukowski"; and the Alumni Memorial Library in Orchard Lake, Michigan, was "collecting anything published" by him.

In *Olé* # 4 (May 1966), Blazek hyperbolically reviewed *Cold Dogs in the Courtyard*: "Bukowski a poet? he's 100% poet who writes the way he lives....Bukowski is the unameable, the undefinable, the illimitable - a man filtering in & out of Everything in existence....Bukowski talks face-to-face with his typewriter...his scream of consciousness poems are relatively simple but this simplicity is underwritten by a most confounding understanding...Bukowski is immersed in life & reading any of his books is like swallowing an ocean". Bukowski's endorsement of Steve Richmond's Earth Books and Gallery in Santa Monica was recorded: "I was down there last night....[it has] better paintings than the L.A. Art Museum, even in the washroom". This issue also advertised a forthcoming Loujon Press project, which, probably for lack of money, was another that never appeared: "BUKOWSKI TALKING a drunken lifespew by the Dean of Hardmouthed Poets gleaned from about 50 hrs of talking into a borrowed tape recorder". Bukowski's propensity for talking in an unstructured way was shortly to be captured on tape by John Thomas. (And later by another friend, the French film director Barbet Schroeder, the many hours of 'The Bukowski Tapes' recorded at the time of *Barfly*).

Bukowski's poems in *Olé* have been mostly reprinted by Black Sparrow in variant versions. Words such as 'bung-hole' and 'cock' are curiously cut out (a literal emasculation), presumably self-censored by Bukowski when he sent material off to John Martin. If so, he also removed rhythm and pungency from, for instance, an entertaining satirical blast at his fellow little maggers in 'O we are the outcasts, O we burn in wondrous flame' (*Olé* # 4). Here is the original opening:

ah, christ, what a bung-hole crew:
more
poetry, always more
P O E T R Y.

if it doesn't come, squeeze it out with a
laxative. get your name in LIGHTS,
get it up there in
81/2 x 11 mimeo.

keep it coming like a miracle
cock.[30]

Bukowski wrote reviews for the magazine, using it to sound off about the dullness and timidity of poetry. He lambasted Louis Zukofsky's (to him) arid experimentalism, stating "the fraud is over". Of Kathleen Fraser's *Change of Address and Other Poems* he observed "No wonder the world has gone to hell - stick a knife in the average poet and he (she) will only hiccup". (There were no hard feelings. During the 1970s, as director of the Poetry Center at San Francisco State University, she put on a reading by Bukowski, with William Stafford). Ill-informed as criticism, these pieces are only valuable as reflections on his own practices, and contain his usual mix of melodrama, exaggeration, and horse sense. C.B. characterises writing as physical, a last ditch stand doomed to defeat. "Itz (sic) sweet stale shit, this poeming....none of us knows what it is....its like awakening in the morning with a boil on your back and it won't go away....But there sure as hell aren't any fuhrers of enlightenment, baby, and sometimes it makes for long evenings, sharp razors, accident while cleaning shotguns....good writing, without fucking relent, is nothing but g.d. trying to bust through a wall of steel and we are just not going to make it".

The "accident while cleaning shotguns" is a reference to Hemingway's suicide, which was initially represented to the world as such. The phrase "fuhrers of enlightenment" is taken from a line by Harold Norse, subject of an *Olé* special issue in 1965. He had close links with the Beats as well as with Bukowski, though they later fell out. Though Bukowski was a stay-at-home, he had several expatriate correspondents who kept him in touch, among whom was Norse. He had lived for three years, circa 1960-63, in Paris, at 9 rue-git-le-coeur, "a fleabitten roominghouse" whose stairs were sweetened "by the green fragrance of cannabis being smoked in practically every room". Harold Chapman's *The Beat Hotel* (1984) details many of the bohemian and experimental happenings there. William Burroughs recalled that he, Norse, and Brion Gysin "held constant meetings and conferences", "with exchange of ideas and comparisons of cut-up writing, painting, and tape-recorder experiments".[31] Norse's poetry was rated highly, especially in the 1960s, and he was instrumental in Bukowski appearing in Penguin Modern Poets 13, later publishing him in his own magazine *Bastard Angel*.

Another of the indigent artists who lived in the Paris hotel was the painter and poet Kay Johnson, a.k.a. 'kaja'. She was from New Orleans, moved to Greece and France, and her work appeared in both *The Outsider* and *Olé*. She was one of the woman artists that Bukowski corresponded with - no doubt for a mix of artistic and personal reasons, though they never met - and he reviewed at least one of her collections, probably *Human Songs* (City Lights, 1964). One of her rather mournful poems was included in Walter Lowenfels' anthology *Poets of Today* (1964):

...Sorrow

tempers the heart to a compass point.
When all is lost, then I begin.
When hope is gone, the marrow of my bones
   Begins to sing.
I ride wild the winds of torment,
Soar, like a laughing bird
   Through the harm meant.

Strike me freedom on the anvil of your hate!
Unleash necessity to love, to smile,
To wait the common cage of brotherhood
To snare me, like a vice.

I'm not your kind, cannot be wooed,
   By else but blood.
And I must fall, like homing birds
   Into the sun.
('A defiant song')[32]

   Bukowski also appeared in Lowenfels' anthology, and several of his poems, such as 'Letter from too far', refer to her ultimately sad story. She killed herself in Paris around 1971, apparently over an unhappy love affair.
   Olé was fairly widely-distributed for a little mag, even selling in Britain, being sold in alternative bookshops in London and elsewhere. It had British contacts, carrying poems, articles, and letters by Glyn Pursglove in Oxford, Dave Cunliffe (editor of *Poetmeat*, based in Blackburn, Lancashire) and Barry Miles, the London-based editor of *International Times* (later biographer of Ginsberg and Kerouac). One great thing that Blazek did for Bukowski was to encourage him back to writing prose. The Mimeo Press brought out the first fruits of this stimulus, *Confessions of a Man Insane Enough To Live With Beasts* (1965) and *All the Assholes in the World and Mine* in 1966. Blazek also edited *A Bukowski Sampler* for Morris Edelson's Quixote Press in 1969, collecting together poems from out-of-print early books, a significant 'Rambling Essay...', letters, and admiring comments by Wantling, Lowenfels, and Blazek himself. Characteristically, Bukowski was not wholly grateful. In correspondence with Carl Weissner, Bukowski described the *Sampler* as "all mixed up", comments on his work as "burblings", though "they meant well".[33]
   But Bukowski was supportive of Blazek when faced with obscenity charges and police harassment. Steve Richmond was another who at this time fell foul of the law, at his Earth Books and Gallery in Santa Monica.

The F.B.I visited Blazek and told him that they were "formally investigating" his magazines. Blazek wrote to Brown Miller on 28 December 1966: "seems as tho someone has reported me for publishing pornography....the agent asked for Buk's address and a list of my subscribers. i refused to give either. he said he would be back. i am waiting".[34] Blazek was never charged. But there were court cases involving d.a. levy, and the book-seller Jim Lowell. Levy was the editor-publisher of *The Marrawannah Quarterly*, arrested after a reading at 'The Gate', a Cleveland coffee shop. The police charge stated that the reading had included references to "death, suicide, use of marijuana and LSD, unnatural sex, immoral acts, and had described the city administration in foul terms". Eric Mottram's account of the proceedings quotes a letter written to a Cleveland newspaper at the time, which, with unintentional irony, justified the prosecution: "Levy is alleged to have read poetry to juveniles. That being the case, the police have a right to arrest him".[35] Bukowski and levy had been acquainted through Blazek, and levy's 7 Flowers Press brought out a hand-printed edition of a single poem, 'The Genius of the Crowd', a doom-laden Jeffers-like dirge, in an edition of only 103 copies. All but 40 were destroyed by the police. (It is now one of the most sought-after collecting rarities). C.B. in turn contributed to an anthology of poems and tributes to levy, titled *ukanhavyrfuckincitibak*, printed by Ghost Press.

Bukowski also wrote in *A Tribute to Jim Lowell* (1967), supporting The Asphodel bookshop in Cleveland, Ohio, which had been raided by the police. His short essay raised general issues of relations between the writer and the public. In true avant-gardist fashion it claims an embattled, independent status for the artist in the face of hostility from both the state and the public, the forces of social conformity, prejudice and ignorance:

> Good Art, Creation, is generally 2 decades to 2 centuries ahead of its time in relationship to the establishment ...good Art is not only not understood but also feared because to make the future better it must state that the present is bad, very bad, and this is hardly an endearment to those in control.... 'Obscenity' is the word they use to excuse their own rot in order to raid the works and outposts of creative men....The creative artist has always been continually harassed by officialdom and the public itself - Van Gogh was hooted by children who threw stones against his window....I do not ask mercy for the artist, I do not ask public funds, I do not even ask understanding; I only ask that they leave us alone in the joy and horror and mystery of our work.[36]

A 1966 letter from Jim Lowell to Marvin Malone explains more about the circumstances of the police raid, and its connection to levy's activities. "My raid developed from a marijuana investigation by the local narcotic gestapo. It seems a high school boy, coming off a not too successful LSD trip went home and his father found in his possession either a copy of the *Marijuana Quarterly* or the M. Newsletter...and of course my address was listed. Anyway the father made a complaint to the police, then on two successive days plain clothesmen purchased at the shop copies of the MQ and several other Levy publications. A secret indictment was drawn up charging me with "sale & possession"....They confiscated 9 cartons of books and periodicals and searched the place for narcotics. Of course, they didn't find any....[And] to top it off an excessive punitive bond was set ($10,000) but through the efforts of the local ACLU [American Civil Liberties Union] it was reduced to $1000".[37]

Malone himself commented on the other literary figures involved: "while this is pending, d.a. levy is dodging a warrant for arrest. Moreover the Peace Eye Bookstore [of Ed Sanders] in N.Y. is closed under similar circumstances. Moreover Steve Richmond's Earth Books has been raided because his *Earth Rose* periodical said "Fuck Hate" on the cover - trial pending. City Lights Book Store in similar circumstances. D.R. Wagner's mail under surveillance. Blazek's *Olé*, and [even] *Wormwood* reported to the FBI - no action. Something's in the air - a touch of mass paranoia...".[38] The fate of The Asphodel bookstore was alluded to in a cryptic flyer sent out by levy and kryss which stated that the bookstore "is being torn down as part of which (sic) is called an 'urban renewal' project and is being replaced by a modern CULT-yrall center which will be known as 'parking lot'".[39] Lowell continued trading at Burton, Ohio, and The Asphodel celebrated its twenty-fifth anniversary in 1988. But levy's fate was more sombre; he began direct action against the authorities. One of *Open Skull's* correspondents claimed to have just heard on the radio that Kent Taylor and levy had been cited by the Food and Drug Commission "as local leaders of the neo-American church advocating political assassinations by drugs" and "dumping hallucinogens in public water supplies'". Eric Mottram claimed that levy - found shot dead on 24 November 1968 - "had come to believe that the country was 'programmed to fall apart', and that state of the nation reaches into his poems, many of which contemplate the possibility of suicide as the accurate response to the 1960s".[40]

A modest but far more significant enterprise, a true 'little magazine' which championed Bukowski throughout almost its entire existence, was the aforementioned Marvin Malone's *Wormwood Review*. This came under his editorship in 1961 and ended only with Malone's decease in 1996. Malone himself, a professor of Pharmacology at the University of the Pacific, moved to California in 1969, and was a collector of rare books and literary magazines. (As was, significantly, John Martin: Bukowski owed a great deal to bibliophiles). Brief statistics in 1986 show that Malone had published Bukowski poems in 68 out of the first 102 issues, beginning in issue 7, including special sections and chapbooks. Bukowski - latterly listed as a patron of the magazine under the pseudonym 'Two-Ton Tony Galento' - had a great deal of respect for Malone, who (like Jon Webb) had no hesitation in turning down second-rate work even by writers he admired. The magazine's manifesto was summarised as "non-beat, non-academic, non-sewing circle and non-profit", and was later self-assessed by Malone as "a small winner in a crowded field often marred by unreadable mags and literary politics". An interview with Mark Weber included in the posthumous last issue of *Wormwood* indicated that he had first come across Bukowski's work very early on, in the pages of *Hearse*, "and was attracted to his unique energy. With the publication of *Flower, Fist and Bestial Wail*, I became a fan and collector".[41] *Wormwood* regularly brought out special Bukowski issues over the decades. Notable among these, all collectors' items now, is #24 (1966), titled 'Night's work (including buffalo bill)', with several humorous illustrations by Bukowski, one showing a man scrubbing an 'A-bomb' in a tub. (The effect, combining poems and drawings, works so well that one wonders why Bukowski's main publishers did not use them together). This issue also included 'a beginner's bibliography of Bukowski', the first such listing to appear, albeit with only 14 items. The magazine kept him in touch with an evolving roster of featured writers, from Ann Menebroker and Lyn Lifshin to Gerald Locklin, Fred Voss *et al.*

During the late 1960s, Bukowski's poems continued to appear in quixotically-named littles redolent of the burgeoning counterculture - *Acid* (from Germany), *Meatball*, *Copkiller*, *Sixpack*. But he was always in more lasting enterprises: John Bennett's *Vagabond*, Len Fulton's *Dust*, Allen de Loach's *Intrepid*, Jerome Rothenberg's *Some/Thing*. *Intransit*, edited by Andy Warhol and Gerard Malanga, included three poems in a remarkable 1968 issue that placed Bukowski's work alongside photos of Factory models and an eclectic range of avant-gardists. *Quixote*, a magazine that had printed Bukowski since the mid-1950s, became more politicised under Morris Edelson's editorship, and found space for levy, Blazek, Wantling, and Charles Potts. It carried interviews with figures in the New Left, discussed its political splits and confrontations, and arranged benefit performances by Allen Ginsberg, Ed Sanders' group The Fugs, and radical theatre groups Brand X, The Human Race, and The San Francisco Mime Troupe. Edelson defined its aim as "working to create a climate for art as well as art itself - by which we mean revolutionary art".[42] That Bukowski's work was highly acceptable to small press editors of radical, liberal and anarchist persuasions is clear. His poems were anthologised in old leftist Walter Lowenfels' *Poets of Today* (1964) and *This is Vietnam* (1967). Dan Georgakas included Bukowski in his *Anthology of Revolutionary Poetry* (1968).

By 1968, Hugh Fox claimed, "the underground editor... himself isolated from the dubious 'mainstream' of American life and letters, found in Bukowski a spokesman for his own nihilism". Fox went on to state that Bukowski, "anti-war, anti-bomb, anti-blind patriotism, anti-practically everything" had become "a spokesman for the growing rebelliousness of the Sixties".[43] This was an oversimplification, given that Bukowski even in the heady atmosphere of those times maintained a sceptical distance from the ideals of the Counterculture. He fully participated in the iconoclastic spirit of the age, but not its political campaigns. Editors in the underground press may have seized upon his works as the acme of rebellion against authority, but Bukowski's scepticism can be seen within poems and stories of the period, e.g. 'The Underground' in *The Days Run Away...*, or 'The Birth, Life and Death of an Underground Newspaper' in *Erections...* It can also be seen in his personal dealings with the underground press.

The first such papers emerged on the West Coast; the *L A. Free Press* which began in 1964, followed by *The Berkeley Barb*, *The San Francisco Chronicle* and many similar operations all over the States. These libertarian publications came to focus opposition to Government policies on drugs, race issues and Vietnam. They spread information throughout their readership of students, disaffected liberals, the exponents of radical chic. They were supposedly run on strictly egalitarian lines, with every worker receiving the same salary whatever their part in the production process. But, just like their capitalist cousins, they had to attract circulation, attract advertisers, and pay the costs of printing, staffing and distribution. (A contradiction not lost on Bukowski).

Bukowski was first featured when *The East Village Other* in 1966 ran an extract from *All the Assholes...*, published by Blazek's Mimeo Press. Al Fogel points out that the 'Notes of a Dirty Old Man' column was anticipated years earlier by Bukowski's "rambling dialogue" which appeared in a 1960 issue of *Simbolica* magazine.[44] *Open City*, a weekly paper set up by John Bryan, was an alternative to the established *L.A. Free Press* which he had managed previously. Another of Bryan's former publications, *Renaissance*, was perhaps alluded to in the paper's subtitle, 'Weekly Review of the Los Angeles Renaissance'. Issue 83 (20 December 1968) conveys its style and concerns, headlines CAMPUS REVOLT HITS L.A. HIGH SCHOOLS and YAPPING SAM'S RED BAITING STRIKES OUT AGAIN. The editorial approved a situation where "the halls and quadrangles of academe now echo with the sounds of sit-ins, building occupations, strikes, sanctuaries and disruptions of many kinds".[45] The paper was interested in 'Black Power', carrying an interview with Eldridge Cleaver when he was on the run. It covered the New Left and student unrest, particularly resistance to the Vietnam Draft. Alongside exposés of local civic and police corruption appeared information about drugs, and adverts for sexual partners and services.

Editor Bryan persuaded a slightly baffled Bukowski to write a weekly column, opening on 5 May 1967 with a review of A.E. Hotchner's book of memoirs *Papa Hemingway*, under the heading AN OLD DRUNK WHO RAN OUT OF LUCK. The writing quickly turned into a high-proof cocktail of fiction mixed with opinion. It can be compared to Brian O'Nolan/ Flann O'Brien's fantasy writings, as 'Myles na Gopaleen', in *The Irish Times* during the 1940s-50s, though Bukowski's is infinitely less intellectual and more sexually explicit. The great attraction for readers was that from week to week "the gloriously impertinent Bukowski" appeared, summoning up a cast of whores, comically inept muggers, murderers and gangsters, racetrack punters, struggling writers, bums, idiots and geniuses. The subjects of his poetry, in fact, though far more outspoken. Writing for the paper had obvious attractions for Bukowski, a sizeable audience and rapid access to it. A hip generation of readers got to know him. After the closure of *Open City* in 1969, Bukowski continued the iconoclastic column in *Nola Express*, edited by Bob Head and Darlene Fife fortnightly from New Orleans. They dubbed him 'King of the Hard-Mouthed Poets". A memorable advert in the paper, appearing when C.B. had just left the Post Office, showed a naked man sat on the toilet, with the caption: "Bukowski? Sure as Shit - I read him in the *Nola Express*".[46] It was one of several Bukowski-associated titles to be prosecuted for obscenity. Bukowski moved to the *L.A. Free Press*, edited by Art Kunkin, until around 1974, also publishing poems and extracts from forthcoming novels *Factotum* and *Women* there. Quite as much as R.Crumb, Bukowski was associated with underground papers, sex mags, and other disreputable outlets: his "dirty and immortal stories" regularly appeared in *The Berkeley Barb*, *Adam*, *Pix*, *Knight* and *Evergreen Review*.

Bukowski was still writing for virtually no money. He told Charles Potts on 26 April 1968 that *Open City* was going to miss a column now and then, and that he had just sold "2 Notes columns to the National Underground Review [in New York] for 25 bucks a piece...I need money. Bryan slips me a tenner now and then but I sell out to the highest bidder".[47] Bukowski was in fact partly responsible for the paper's demise, through his editorship in 1968 of a literary supplement judged obscene. The paper was fined $2000, a decision reversed on appeal, but too late. Events were staged to raise money for the *Open City* legal fund, notably a benefit reading at the Ash Grove Theater in Los Angeles. A retrospective account of the evening by Tony Quagliano called it "the truest embodiment of a sense of community that the 'underground' literary scene in Los Angeles was ever able to muster". It was billed as a gathering of L.A. poets and a Free Speech protest. Jack Micheline, whose story 'Skinny Dynamite' had caused the obscenity charge; John Thomas, Harold Norse, William

Margolis, and Jack Hirschman - all of whom were born elsewhere in the States - turned up. The true Angeleno Bukowski did not; he was presumably working the evening shift at the Post Office.[48]

Meanwhile, critical attention was starting to gather. There had been many reviews of Bukowski's early publications, some veering into parody. One such flippant reaction was by Ron Offen, poetry editor of the *Chicago Literary Times*, when reviewing *It Catches My Heart In its Hands* in September 1963. "Once there was a poet in the City of Angels who was the embodiment of one of Blake's devils....After years of unconscious labor that seemed like seconds, the poet was told by his mentors that he could rest because they had enough material for a new sacred book...And he held the book up to the Good and Holy expecting them to cringe as the devils of old when threatened with the cross and was amazed when they fingered the book with obscene fascination". It concluded with a Buk-style 'Note Found Stuffed in an Empty Fifth of White Port'.[49]

More considered early reviewers were Jack Conroy, Thomas McGrath, and Kenneth Rexroth who included *It Catches...* in a *New York Times* Book Review article on 5 July 1964, headlined "There's poetry in a Rugged Hitchhiker". Robert Creeley briefly mentioned *Run with the Hunted* when reviewing for *Poetry Chicago*. He observed its "very open speech, and common sentiments and references....The starved, the poor, the bewildered, the dragged, sullen reality of usual life does not want, nor not want, to be a poem. The work is still to be done".[50] Writing in the same magazine, Dabney Stuart (later editor of the academic quarterly *Shenandoah*) was more straightforward in his dismissal of *It Catches...*:

> About the world Bukowski feels forced to say *ché sara, sara*; to say that about language is a capitulation of another sort, unwise, uncreative. The American language, as Bukowski hears it, can be nailed to paper rather easily...If Bukowski has arrived at the door to something great, he has knocked very lightly for entrance...Escapists don't write great poetry.[51]

This was reacting to the claims made by J.W.Corrington, who had praised Bukowski's language, "devoid of the affectations, devices and mannerisms that have taken over academic verse....What Wordsworth claimed to have in mind [i.e. "a selection of the language actually used by men"], what William Carlos Williams claimed to have done, what Rimbaud actually did do in French, Bukowski has accomplished for the English language".[52] Corrington also reviewed *It Catches...* under the title 'Charles Bukowski and the Savage Surfaces', in *Northwestern Review* during the Fall of 1963. In it he identified Bukowski's "concern for surface - for the color, texture and rhythm of modern life...his consistent presentation of physical minutia[e] of seeming inconsequence". This recording of life's ordinary details persisted throughout, and is marked in Bukowski's mature works. Corrington also noted "his pointed avoidance of...the 'social implications'" and "refusal to become trapped in the cerebral" as other hallmarks of "the savage quality, the surface dynamism of his poetry". He concluded: "however little thought Bukowski may give to his writing, he has mastered the literary lessons of the past century", placing him in a mixed tradition of Whitman and Mallarmé, Jeffers and Lorca.[53]

Another advocate was Hugh Fox, originally from East Lansing, Michigan. In 1968, his *Charles Bukowski: A Critical and Bibliographical Study* appeared from Abyss, a small press in Massachussetts, while he was teaching at Loyola College in Los Angeles. The study inevitably now reads very much as a product of its own era, with excitable prose and interjections of hippy lingo. But it did have a scholarly function, describing some already out of print publications and listing the earliest publishing events of Bukowski's career, with a bibliography of magazine appearances. Fox's observations are fine so far as they go, and interesting even when wide of the mark. For example, he attributes Bukowski's death-centered, existential concerns to an "Eastern-European slant...a kind of slavic nihilism that completely rejects everything that forms the American Way...a dark negative world-view" He identified Bukowski's love of the comically incongruous, defined by him as a cross between Hollywood gag writers, the Marx Brothers, Jack Benny radio scripts and Kafka.

Fox noted the pervasive sub-Surrealist imagery in the early works, commenting that in spite of Bukowski's claimed fidelity to 'reality', it is "always escaping its rules and procedures", and swelling to "fantastic dream proportions". He called him Henry Miller's successor on the American literary scene, "just as iconoclastic, as sentimental, as profane - and as full of life and reality". He made one comment that Bukowski would not have liked, calling him "the apotheosis of Beatnikism". He raised an aesthetic issue shared with the Beats, remarking sensibly that "'spontaneous' is a relative thing, and the really important thing here is not the conflict between spontaneity and re-working, but the ability Bukowski has of producing so much careful verse so rapidly and with so little reworking".[54]

In conclusion, he crowned Bukowski "King of the meat and cement poets" (that is, Blazek, levy and company) who were "a continuation and extension of the reality-opening aspects of the Beats without moving into their psychedelically altered sense of wonder and beauty....The day will come, of course, when he will move out of the floating underground, grow roots and be accepted like Rimbaud, Baudelaire, Whitman or Henry Miller".[55] It was a very worthwhile effort, but as ever, Bukowski was not happy. Correspondence shows him writing to Gerard Dombrowski of Abyss, complaining that "THE POEM-MESSAGE or FORCE was completely overlooked....that's what Fox is - a shadow of Buk...[one of] the Bukowski copyists" (3 January 1969).

The listings information provided by Fox was immediately superseded by Sanford Dorbin's *A Bibliography of Charles Bukowski* (1969). Dorbin, then a librarian at the University of California, Santa Barbara, carried out a scrupulous job of work for Black Sparrow. This recorded Bukowski's already numerous magazine appearances up to September 1969, with details of variant editions and publishing circumstances, as well as reviews, critical commentary and ephemera. By then, the pivotal event in Bukowski's career had already happened. The origins of the Black Sparrow Press go back to the mid-1960s and the first meeting between Bukowski and John Martin, at the home of John Thomas. This was later characterised by Bukowski as "Mr Rolls meeting Mr Royce". Martin at that time was "the manager of an office furniture supply company and... a collector of rare books".[56]

Martin printed a series of broadsides, single page poems on fine quality paper. The first of these, 'True Story', appeared during April 1966 and a further six followed over the next year. Joe Wolberg (writing in *Oui* magazine in 1980) quoted Martin as saying that these first broadsides were not for sale. "I had nobody to sell them to. I think I did thirty in each edition, but this, amazingly, was very encouraging to him".[57] Martin's business acumen, and his knowledge of the book market, that collectors would be prepared to pay premium prices for quality signed or limited edition books by Bukowski, made for the success of Black Sparrow. As Hugh Fox saw them, Black Sparrow books were "not as extravagantly artistic as Loujon Press products, but classy....Martin makes money with his books, but he also gives value". [58]

By 1968 the press was ready to do its first full-length Bukowski book, *At Terror Street and Agony Way*. The book carried a typically provocative author's preface: "Though I began writing poetry at the age of 35, some of my critics claim that I have already too much. So I have taken to painting, cuckoldry and increased beer consumption". It was dedicated to John Thomas, and "for John Martin who took the chance and for John the Baptist for no reason at all".[59] Thomas had rescued the poems by typing up the manuscript from a tape that he had made of Bukowski reading. The originals - a likely story - had been thrown out with the garbage. A recent memoir of their high times together appears in *Bukowski in the Bathtub* (Raven Press, 1997), edited by Thomas' wife Philomene Long. *At Terror Street*...appeared in an edition of 75 hardcover and 800 softcover copies, with further de-luxe signed copies. Fortunately, they sold.

Bukowski was still reluctant to take one necessary step towards becoming a freelance author earning a living; doing paid public readings. He had received offers as far back as 1963, but as he was in full-time employment there was no economic incentive. He clearly felt the same way even by 27 February 1968, when he wrote to Carl Weissner: "rumours on town hall reading of Bukowski, Corso, Micheline...impossible. didn't you know I have made it known for forty years that I don't read publicly? I have just turned down a reading, with fee, at Univ. of Southern Calif. Festival of the Arts. I never read in public, don't intend to unless it means the difference between starving in the gutter and starving in a closet....I have turned down fees of from $200 and $700 and told them to go screw....I am not an actor, I am a creator, I hope".

Bukowski's breakthrough to international publication came in 1969 when he was included with Harold Norse in the influential Penguin Modern Poets series. The volume was completed by Philip Lamantia, regarded by admirers as a visionary Catholic poet, and by others as an authentic American Surrealist. He had been a youthful protegé of André Breton during the war years, and was later associated with the Beats in San Francisco. The selection was taken from Bukowski's now out of print books, the poems being surrealistic ('I wait in the white rain'), or didactic ('Counsel'). At about the same time his prose was making a breakthrough. Essex House, a North Hollywood publisher associated with pornography, brought out a selection of his underground columns: "Yes...That's Right! *Open City's* Bukowski!...[an] erotic collection of his experiences and sense-impressions".[60]

His long years of apprenticeship and as an underground figure were coming to an end. A new more public phase was beginning. As a writer earning his daily bread, Bukowski could no longer afford the luxury of turning down readings. He had quit the Post Office. He could do this only with John Martin's financial guarantee, and a settlement of $5000 from his Post Office service. He did so with the name-recognition earned as the already notorious 'Dirty Old Man' of American letters. He was now out of his cage. He flew out on the wings of the Black Sparrow.

Linda King bust of Charles Bukowski, circa 1971

Chapter 3

The No-Holds Bard
1970-1994

Bukowski became a full-time writer-performer at a time when the citizens of the United States, particularly in California, were living through 'interesting times'. Protests against the Vietnam War, the Draft, and repressive government measures continued to gather support from students, activists and liberals, but also from wide sections of the middle class. Black Power, Women's Liberation and Gay Lib were growing into public awareness and influence. There was the beginnings of a definite change in the Zeitgeist, the naive hopefulness of the Hippie Era giving way to a more cynical public mind-set. The most popular poet-singer of the late 1960s in the U.S. was probably Rod McKuen - whose saccharine songs, poems and ingratiating performances are occasionally growled at in Bukowski's correspondence. It was, in retrospect, exactly the right moment at which a hard-bitten, rambunctious 'Dirty Old Man' of literature could find an increasingly receptive audience.

He was adjusting to life as a freelance author. Significantly, he chose to start his day's writing at 6.47 p.m., the time of his evening shift at the L.A. Post Office Terminal Annexe. Bukowski's bravado comes through in his usual portrayal of writing as "a good time", an act accompanied by smoking, drinking, and listening to classical music on the radio. But this association of writing with pleasure was again just part of his aura: the reality was that writing moved from being a spare-time pursuit to being his means of earning a living. The start time was a necessary gesture. He could not afford to be sidetracked into involvements which didn't pay. His 'apolitical' stance should be seen as a pragmatic, self-centered decision. As his columns in the papers show, he was certainly highly aware of the national state of political ferment, as protests against the expansion of the Vietnam War reached through the underground press to affect the literary/artistic community. He was no protester, no joiner of Civil Rights marches like Ginsberg, Mailer or Robert Lowell. While others were debating issues of politics and funding for the arts, Bukowski was getting on with his career. He began doing his first readings in L.A. bookstores and on campuses. *Chicago Review* in 1970 reported that Bukowski had "just completed a tour of the Western States", notably at Bellevue, Washington, an event which was recorded on film and audio tape.[1] He was also of course writing his first novel, *Post Office*.

Bukowski regularly reported on the progress of his new life to Gerald Locklin, then (as now) a Professor of English at Long Beach State University, whose own burgeoning career within little magazines and small presses was getting under way. He wrote to thank Locklin for having arranged a reading on campus: "no you don't act much like an English teacher - Corrington - Miller [Williams] vintage....your poetry showed that. I hope you and Ron K.[oertge] just don't flip over...With Bix Blaufus going into teaching, it now means that the three most promising writers I know are teaching. It's against the grain of my aged concepts" (uncollected letter, 22 July 1970). Bukowski had begun to get used to the idea of performing in public, and dealing with rowdy audiences. Later that year he told Locklin that "I read at The Bridge [L.A. bookstore] last night, and for a change they had an open and easy crowd, or maybe it was the heat...or everybody high, but it worked well....I don't even like to read, but I like to insist on survival...I am a literary whore. I've lucked it in the past couple of months at Cal. State, L.A.,UNM [University of New Mexico], West. Wash.[ington] State College. $225 at a couple of them, and I even got fucked - nice young clean stuff...so I'm on the treadmill" (uncollected letter, n.d., 1970).

During 1970, *Nola Express* brought out a tape of Bukowski reading, dubbing him 'King of the Hard-Mouthed Poets'. It makes interesting listening now, his voice somewhat higher and less authoritative than the rich baritone of his maturity later in the decade. It was also a home recording, entirely lacking the theatricality that Bukowski would later display before live audiences. The contents of the tape are very uneven, with minor classics such as 'Another academy' interspersed with scurrilous anecdotal pieces, 'The lesbian' and 'The night I killed Tommy' - the latter an account of sex with a prostitute in a roach-infested apartment, and definitely not for the squeamish. Most of the poems have not been subsequently reprinted by Black Sparrow, possibly because of their identifiable references to then-living people. 'Soup, cosmos and tears' is a humorous fantasy based on Bukowski's postal relations with a poet and painter living on the California coast. They apparently never met, though the poem describes an enthusiastic sexual bout! Sheri Martinelli (1918-1996), a 'Modernist Muse', had known Anais Nin, Charlie Parker, Marlon Brando, Ezra Pound at St. Elizabeth's Hospital, and later many of the Beats.[2] She enthusiastically reviewed one of Bukowski's early chapbooks in her astrological magazine *The Anagogic and Paideumic Review* in the early 1960s, gave his work a special issue, and they corresponded for some years. (When Allen Ginsberg visited Pound in Italy during 1967, he said to the aged maestro "I'd like you to give me your blessing to take to Sheri Martinelli - for I'd described her late history Big Sur, eyes seeing Zodiac everywhere hair bound up like Marianne Moore").[3]

Bukowski's readings' schedule hardly interrupted his myriad contacts with little magazines and underground papers, and the people running them. The literary magazine world now encompassed a wide variety of formats, from cheap and accessible mimeographs to those with fine printing. It had begun to get organised, through the efforts of Len Fulton, editor of *Dust* (1964-71), and the *Directory of Little Magazines*. Fulton was instrumental in fostering Bukowski's reputation, often featuring him in the *Small Press Review*. He was the founder of COSMEP (Committee on Small Magazines Editors and Publishers). Their first meeting had been held at Berkeley, near San Francisco in 1969. Attendees included several Bukowski contacts: Blazek, Harry Smith, Hugh Fox, and D.R. Wagner, the latter being editor of *Runcible Spoon* and a Cleveland associate of the recently-deceased d.a. levy. In retrospect, some have seen this move towards collectivity as a retrogade and conservative step. John Bennett, long-time editor of *Vagabond*, expressed in a *Chiron Review* interview during 1994 the view that "[The] small press scene, before the infamous Berkeley conference in the late 60s that spawned COSMEP, was dominated by balls-out renegades with a blood lust for life. Things declined after that...people became concerned with packaging and distribution".

The next conference was significantly bigger, held at Buffalo, New York, between 11-14 June 1970. It was fully covered in a special issue of Alan de Loach's *Intrepid* # 21/22. A host of small press activists attended, including William and Ruth Wantling, Allen Ginsberg, Robert Creeley, and figures such as maverick academic Leslie Fiedler and George Plimpton of *The Paris Review*. The conference was predictably divided between those who wanted genuinely 'alternative' cultural structures and those who were entrepreneurs. Between total rejectionists of any government subsidy for little magazines and those who thought that a federal dollar in their pockets was a dollar not going to further the war effort. Lawrence Ferlinghetti did not attend, but sent an open letter, stating that he as an individual and City Lights as a publisher would never accept government money. Acceptance of state subsidies made it clear that "the avant-garde in this country is not necessarily to be equated with the political left, and certainly not with the radical left". William Wantling observed to de Loach that "it was amazing how often the subject of money arose and how hung up everybody was about it".[4] In the event, the Nixon Administration carried out a policy of funding institutions rather than magazines. Bukowski's attitude to such wider social/ political issues can be judged by his actions. He accepted a grant from the National Endowment for the Arts in 1972 - the only such award he ever received. So much for Bukowski as a Saint of the Permanent Opposition.

Bukowski's public profile was becoming more visible, and he was increasingly asked to endorse publications by young writers. One of these was for *Invitation to a Dying* by Al Masarik, published by John Bennett's Vagabond Press in 1971. Masarik was a Korean War veteran (as William Wantling had been). Bukowski's preface is interesting in that it indicates again his attachment to the culture of the 1930s-1940s. He compares the current situation unfavourably with then: "I feel that the breakoff of real poetic talent began with World War II and that it never returned. What the causes were (are) I don't know. But from [then]...up to 1971 it has been a very barren time for poetic production, not only that form of production but, I feel, creation in other art forms and originality outside of the art forms".[5]

Bukowski's poems began to turn up in some surprising places, magazines associated with the avant-garde and with the literary mainstream. *Unmuzzled Ox*, for instance, was edited by Michael Andre in New York from 1971 onwards. It was a publication very much bound up with the New York School, the Beats, and poetic experimentalists, yet Bukowski appeared in #1 (with a cover by Richard Crumb, later to be an illustrator of his works) and five times between 1971-76. *The American Poetry Review* was edited by founder-editor Stephen Berg from 1972 onwards; its newspaper format and large circulation to libraries has given it wide currency. In 1975, Bukowski poems appeared, in volume 4 # 2.

A crucial element in Bukowski's rise was his increasing vogue in Europe, particularly in Germany, France, and Britain. Bukowski's poems had first been reviewed in *Satis*, a Newcastle little, back in 1962. His first appearance in mainland Europe was in a Belgian magazine, *Labris* (from Trier, 1966). Several poems had appeared in issues of the West Hartlepool magazine *Iconolatre*, edited by Alex Hand during 1965-1966. Further interest in Bukowski was registered during the early 1970s by the Cardiff-based *2nd Aeon* which regularly carried poems and reviewed his books. John Tripp enthused about *Mockingbird Wish Me Luck*, hailing its author "the high priest of the disinherited". He continued, "the ferocity, humanity and wise old bull humour burst the pages....Bukowski's [is] a process of 'de-Disneyfication', kicking the Mickey Mouse out of our heads".[6]

Editor Peter Finch, reviewing *Erections...* called Bukowski "a talespinner of the finest fashion", but also noted the repetitiousness that characterised stories mostly centered around women, drinking, and horseracing. The issue also reviewed Len Fulton's *Small Press Review* # 16, a Bukowski Special which concluded "He now bestrides his narrow underworld like a West Coast colossus".[7] Another significant publication of the 1970s British scene to regularly feature and comment on Bukowski, as well as those associated with him, was Peter Hodgkiss' critical magazine *Poetry Information*. Within a few years, however, Bukowski's novels at least were being reviewed in the heart of the British literary establishment, the *Times Literary Supplement*, and the arts pages of the national press.

But by far the most significant phenomenon for Bukowski's future earning capacity were sales in West Germany during the 1970s. This was largely due to the efforts of one man, Carl Weissner, who became his German translator, agent and lifelong friend. Through him, Bukowski's work gained access to mainstream publishers, and widespread distribution. Weissner had been a research student in the States during the late 1960s, initially studying Charles Olson's 'Maximus Poems' on a Fulbright scholarship. He and Bukowski had corresponded since 1966, when Weissner set up his own mimeographed magazine *Klactoveedsedsteen*, so called after a Charlie Parker tune. It was styled after the model of Jeff Nuttall's *My Own Mag*, which he later recalled as "probably the craziest and most adventurous mimeo mag of those years". Weissner visited New York, guest editing an issue of Allen de Loach's *Intrepid*, documenting and recording the avant garde, meeting Allen Ginsberg, Ray Bremser, Jack Micheline and Ed Sanders. In the Summer of 1968 he stayed on the West Coast with Jan Herman, editor of *The San Francisco Earthquake*, and visited Bukowski in Los Angeles.[8]

Returning to Germany, Weissner worked as an editor for J. Melzer Publishers, and spread the word about the Bukowski phenomenon. His first such translation for J. Meltzer, in the Spring of 1970, was *Notes of a Dirty Old Man*; it was apparently well reviewed, even in the conservative newspaper *Der Spiegel*, but only 1200 copies were sold. Weissner next translated *Post Office*, again with limited impact. Confounding the publishing truth that contemporary poetry doesn't sell, Bukowski's big impact in Germany, the land of his birth, manifested itself with a volume of poems, stories, correspondence and photographs selected by Weissner and published in 1974 by MaroVerlag, a small press in Bavaria. *Gedichte die einer schrieb bevor er im 8. Stockwerk aus dem Fenster sprang*; the title was borrowed from the 1968 Litmus chapbook *Poems Written Before Jumping Out of an 8 Story Window*. The book sold over 70,000 copies in

Germany by the end of 1977, and marked his ascent to bestseller status there. After this breakthrough, his stories and novels had sales in the hundreds of thousands in the latter 1970s and early 1980s, leading to television documentaries, a feature in *Stern* magazine, and an interview in German *Playboy*.

Weissner's life and professional activities as an editor and translator have been bound up with Bukowski, though he has translated the Beats, Denton Welch, Bob Dylan, and Gerald Locklin, and many other American authors, for German language editions. He was credited as co-editor, with Gerard Belart, on an L.P. recording for the poetry international festival, held in Rotterdam, Holland (20-24 June 1972). Its selection reflected Weissner's taste and contacts: Ray Bremser, Ted Berrigan, Ginsberg, Ed Sanders, John Weiners, Carol Bergé, Diane di Prima, Jim Silver and John Giorno were recorded live. Bukowski was represented by earlier recordings, 'A report upon the consumption of myself' and 'Something for the touts...'. The back cover's biographical blurbs carried a typical statement from a Bukowski letter: "the years that I have worked in slaughterhouses and factories and gas stations...do not allow me to accept the well-turned word for the sake of the well-turned word. There must be more for me or I am just another suicide in a cheap room or in the alley or in the sea or in the gas cloud. I do not treat my work as holy or necessary except to myself..."[9]

Despite - or perhaps because of - Bukowski's notoriety, the basics of a future academic industry on his work were quietly being assembled. The first university archive to receive Bukowski's correspondence from this period, roughly 1968-1973, was at Santa Barbara. Bukowski pleaded with his major correspondents for the return of letters, so that he could sell them for $5000; most, though not all of them, responded. This material, letters from and to Bukowski from writers, editors and fans, is largely unpublished. The archive contains letters on personal and professional matters from Doug Blazek and John Bennett, David Antin, and Frances Smith. Fan letters are also included. Another early archive of correspondence and other material was established at the University of Arizona at Tucson, acquired from the bookseller Jim Roman of Scotsdale, Arizona. The material dates from 1973 onwards, and includes letters from J.W. Corrington, Neeli Cherkovski (then Cherry), and the anthologist Don M. Allen. Since then, several other niches for Bukowskiana have been established in various locations throughout the States. Seamus Cooney, editor of the Bukowski letters for Black Sparrow, lists eight institutions, from Brown University in Providence, Rhode Island, to the Samuel Peters Research Library in Shreveport, Louisiana.

Alongside this accumulation of reputation one can set the numerous interviews given by an allegedly reclusive author from the early 1970s onwards. They certainly helped build up his public image in readers' minds. Bukowski was like Céline in at least this one sense: his interviews are deliberate myth-making, containing numerous half-truths as well as endless refinements of well-known positions. His deadpan pronouncements use the interviewer as a comedian would a 'straight man'. His first-ever interview had been given to Arnold L. Kaye of the *Chicago Literary Times*, published back in March 1963. Its preamble described Bukowski as looking like a retired junkie, with "sad eyes, weary voice and a silk dressing gown". Asked how much of his work was "frankly autobiographical", Bukowski flippantly replied, "Almost all. Ninety-nine out of a hundred, if I have written a hundred. The other one was dreamed up. I was never in the Belgian Congo".

Questioned about whether living in Los Angeles affected his writing, his response was that "It doesn't matter where you write so long as you have the walls, typewriter, paper, beer. You can write out of a volcano pit. Say, do you think I could get 20 poets to chip in a buck a week to keep me out of jail?". Kaye finally asked him about the role of the poet "in this world-mess", and he responded resignedly, with a sigh: "the role of the poet is almost nothing...drearily nothing. And when he steps outside of his boots and tries to get tough as our dear Ezra [Pound] did, he will get his pink little ass slapped". As a parting shot, Bukowski reflected that "Mickey Mouse had a greater influence on the American public than Shakespeare, Milton, Dante, Rabelais, Schostakovich, Lenin and/or Van Gogh. Which says 'what?' about the American public. Disneyland remains the central attraction in Southern California, but the graveyard remains our reality".[10]

Bukowski was interviewed several times in the underground press, invariably adding to his aura of dangerousness. 'An Evening with Chuck Buk' appeared in the *L.A. Free Press* (July 23 1971), with interviewer Don Strachan characterising Bukowski as "a pulpy receptacle of bad karma, self-pity and vengeance". A seemingly *laisser-faire* attitude to drugs and drink, in keeping with the self-indulgent spirit of the age, was indicated: "I guess anything that lets you get out of your head, it's good to take it". In a sour and bullying mood, Bukowski "started explaining to Linda King [his then girlfriend] the logic of committing suicide until she got upset".[11]

By far the best and most wide-ranging interview that Bukowski ever gave was in 1974 with Robert Wennersten, appearing in Alan Ross' *London Magazine*. Bukowski's comments on his writing methods and attitudes are illuminating, as are the hints on the psychological background of his work. Bukowski refers to an itinerant phase of his life, the immediate post-1945 period. "I've done my travelling...at one time I had this idea that one could live on a bus forever: travelling, eating, getting off, shitting, getting back on that bus. I had the strange idea that one could stay in motion forever....Of course, I deliberately went to New York broke. I went to every town broke in order to learn that town from the bottom....I got a bottom view, which I didn't like; but I was more interested in what was going on at the bottom".

This investigation of the Lower Depths was, accordingly, much more a deliberated act than Bukowski otherwise liked to acknowledge. It makes him more of a George Orwell figure than a genuine down-and-out. Another important conclusion to be drawn is that his search for identity as a person and as a writer was realised only when he arrived back at his adoptive home city, Los Angeles. His subsequent work was nevertheless informed by this period of travelling, by his knowledge of "what was going on at the bottom". Bukowski further remarked to Wennersten that "I can't write except off a typewriter. The typewriter keeps it strict and confined....I've tried to write long hand: it doesn't work....No machine-gun sounds, you know. No action". He listed his early heroes, and his current attitude to them: "Auden was pretty good. When I was young and I read, I liked a lot of Auden....I liked that whole gang; Auden, [Archibald] MacLeish, Eliot...but when I come back on them now, they don't strike me the same way...They say good things, and they write it well; but they're too careful for me now....I admire Conrad Aiken very much....Ginsberg...writes a lot of good lines....I hit the Library pretty hard in my early days [reading] J.D. Salinger, early Hemingway, Sherwood Anderson... but they all got bad".[12]

Bukowski even found time to run his own magazine for two years, from early 1969 to February 1971. This desire had been foreshadowed in a letter to Steve Richmond in June 1966, a *jeux d'esprit* enclosing The Toilet Paper Review, a parody of typical little mag contributions he said he'd put together in 20 minutes, with its motto "We Don't Give a Shit". This spirit extended to the magazine itself, titled, after some negotiation, *Laugh Literary and Man the Humping Guns*, where he was assisted by Neeli Cherkovski. The first issue contained two Bukowski poems; the second had letters; the third had a story. It lasted for three issues and was really an opportunity to annoy the so-called 'college professors' who submitted material in all seriousness. Bukowski claimed that before returning rejected manuscripts, he and his assistant smeared them with raw eggs, soaked them in beer and set them on fire. "We had one subscriber", Bukowski later told a reporter from the *Los Angeles Times Magazine*, "I was very proud of him".[13] But the enterprise did have a worthwhile offshoot, *An Anthology of L.A. Poets* published by Laugh Literary in 1972, which was co-edited by Bukowski, Cherkovski, and Paul Vangelisti, editor of *Invisible City*.

One of the poets included in the latter anthology was a striking young woman, Linda King, referred to in poems and letters as "the tigress". A talented sculptor, she became a little magazine poet under Bukowski's tutelage, and they enjoyed a joyous if stormy relationship for several years. They first met at a reading in late 1970, and their interaction impinges strongly on his work of that decade. She is a powerful presence in the early sections of the novel *Women* (1978). The 1972 collection *Mockingbird Wish Me Luck* is dedicated to her, "for all the good reasons". It contains poems directly about or addressed to her, including 'The shower', 'Power failure'. 'The split', and 'The answer'. They collaborated on a chapbook, *Me And Your Sometimes Love Poems* (1972), writing alternate poems, which was brought out by Black Sparrow in an edition of 100 signed copies. Republished in 1994, with Bukowski's drawings, by her own Kisskill Press, it is a fascinating document in many ways.

Linda King's brief preface states that it was put together when she and Bukowski lived in separate apartments at 5124 DeLongpre Avenue. Aside from two included in *Mockingbird...*, 'This is the way it goes and goes...' and 'Have you ever kissed a panther?', the poems have not been reprinted. King's verse was widely published in little magazines, notably Joan Jobe Smith's *Pearl*, and she also produced her own, *Purr*. As well as the *Anthology of L.A. Poets*, she also appeared in Edward Field's important anthology *A Geography of Poets* (1979). The collection tells the story of their relationship from both sides of the story, with hints as to why it eventually concluded. It opens with her poem 'Dirty' - a reference to his bathroom and to his persona. Linda King's poems are passionate, loosely-written, musing on incidents. Bukowski's are cooler, more ironic, answering and complementing hers. The first poem by Bukowski describes sitting while his head is being sculpted, kissing her, then being interrupted by her small daughter.

she picks up the tools again -
get that smile on, she says,
get that devil's smile on, come on!
('When the devil came on out for love')[14]

Bukowski as a devil, with connotations of horniness, is a theme pursued throughout. 'Love song' shows the affair rapidly ripening, with fairly explicitly-described cunnilingus, "children screaming outside.../ [at] 5 p.m. in the afternoon". But soon conflict and the time both spend writing starts coming between them:

our love-making is a reading of the heart, unveiled;
then you phone and speak of my novel
as if I had betrayed you
('For a suspicious lady')[15]

There are splits and reconciliations, as in 'I can see what built Paris'. The collection ends with her 'Hooked', and him observing "2 people in unbearable contact", as they make love. The poems in the chapbook are by no means classics, but collectively it is more than a poetic snapshot album. It anticipates the pervasively sexual themes and explicitness of *Love is a Dog From Hell*, a rehearsal for one of Bukowski's great books. After all, the women in the latter collection are those that Bukowski met on the rebound from Linda King, and on the reading circuit. She stimulated his creativity, and made him feel almost comfortable with writing about sex. But quite rightly for a strongly feminist artist in her own right, Linda King was by no means content to be simply a male writer's muse. Both coming into and going from Bukowski's creative life, she hugely enhanced it.

One of the West Coast magazines which consistently championed Bukowski during the 1970s was *Second Coming*, edited by A.D. Winans from San Francisco. Volume II # 3, published in January 1974, was a Bukowski Special (as was a 1977 issue), bringing together tributes to his work from little magazine editors, writers and activists. *The Outsider* had done this eleven years earlier, but this time brickbats were included as well as praise. Bukowski was now a nationally-known and widely notorious figure. He was attracting disciples and detractors in equal measure; some of the latter had previously been his followers. Bukowski was fine when dishing out the literary low blow but was highly sensitive when it came back in his direction. The male contributors to the issue were, however, mostly long-time Bukowski admirers: Cherry, Norse, Micheline, Jerry Kamstra, Richmond, Fox, Guy Williams, Locklin, John Kay (editor of *The Mag* in Long Beach) and G.J. Melling from New Zealand.

The female contributors were somewhat more acerbic. Alta stated, in resolute lowercase, that "just because bukowski writes well, & indeed helped 'humanize poetry', which was one of his self-stated goals, does not mean that i can quietly read his poetry as if he is not insulting me, & waging war on women, because sometimes he is". Linda King was more garrulously personal in her article 'To think I Fell in Love with a Male Chauvinist': "The first time I heard Charles Bukowski read poetry, he also read a short story he'd just written called 'Six Inches'. It's a story of a woman who shrinks her man down to six inches and finally uses him as a penis. The story made me laugh, but it also felt like an insult". Ann Menebroker observed that "Everyone loves him or hates him. He is a controversial subject...I never knew he was going to get this big".

Hugh Fox called Bukowski is "the prophet of the run-down, shoddy, dilapidated, rusting, blowing-away, sagging American reality that is the way most of it REALLY is". Steve Richmond claimed, with an element of hyperbole, that "Bukowski...enjoys playing King Devil....His life is based on continued creation.... He is the Balzac of today moving constantly back to his typewriter as if it were a fountain of spirit". Jerry Kamstra described Bukowski's stories as "wrenched out of his own ulcerated guts, flung onto paper between bouts of delerium tremens and alcoholic fantasy, and stamped with that peculiar L.A. madness". Gerald Locklin contributed rueful recollections on the perils of organising Bukowski readings on the campus at Long Beach. Easily the most extravagant panegyric came from 'street poet' Jack Micheline (a.k.a. Harold Silver, or Brooklyn Jack): "He is an American postage stamp, a screamer, a mark, a submarine. He gave me a dollar and kept ten for himself. Horses up his ass! Horses up his ass forever! He is the longest shot that ever came in, a highly intelligent and dangerous animal who has written seven of the finest poems in the English language today....His shade is down on De Longpre and on the boulevards of Paris his shades are down".[16]

Winans himself has since published an interesting volume of memoirs and self-justification, *The Charles Bukowski/ Second Coming Years* (1996). He rightly points out the many contradictions, sensitivities and petty jealousies within Bukowski's character, a mix of insecurity and bravado; and occasional wisdoms. Bukowski's variously combative relations with peers and disciples are detailed, and Winans concludes that Bukowski was "not the hard boiled person he claimed to be".[17] Winans has had a long involvement with magazines and small presses, as well as giving many readings and workshops in prisons. His North Beach associates included Bob Kaufman, Ben Hiatt and Kell Robertson. He shared with Bukowski the experience of working for the Post Office, in San Francisco. He was editor-publisher of the magazine from 1972-89, also publishing chapbooks such as *7 On Style* by William Wantling. A member of the COSMEP Board during the mid-1970s, he later resigned on a point of funding principle.

Winans attended the several successful readings in San Francisco that Bukowski gave around this time, including at the City Lights Theatre on 14 September 1973. This was recorded and subsequently released as 'Poems and Insults!' on an L.P., and 20 years later on CD format (with the exclamation mark removed, befitting more sober times). The reading was organised by Joe Wolberg, then manager of the City Lights bookstore, who was at one time engaged on what would have been the first biography of Bukowski. Wolberg's sleeve notes make an engaging plea to the listener:

> Bukowski lives in the underbelly of America with the whores, pimps, gamblers, bouncers and bums of Hollywood. From his one-room [it was actually three-room] apartment off Hollywood and Western in the red-light district of the City of Broken Dreams he sculpts the characters of the streets, bars, brothels and racetracks with his old Royal portable....Listen to his poems and his insults as over 1,000 did in San

Francisco. Decide for yourself if he is not one of the greatest literary voices we have today.[18]

The reading itself is lively, sometimes rambunctious, with many of the poems ('The sex fiends', 'Piss and shit') humorously provocative. The evening's proceedings show that Bukowski now organised his material well, alternating moods between scurrility, pathos, sentimentality ('The world's greatest loser') and more reflective pieces such as 'Law'. The latter is a surreal fantasy with a political subtext; dogs, horses, and then humans being hung in the trees, "because it's the law". He had learned how to deal with audiences, keep them enthralled and entertained. A series of readings took place in Utah and Michigan during November 1974; the Michigan reading paid $500 plus airfare, food and drink. He cheerfully told Carl Weissner: "Cost 'em a grand to hear me sing" (7 November 1974), with a crowd of 700 packed "asshole to asshole". Bukowski was starting to hit his stride as a performer. He had even begun to enjoy the antagonism that he provoked in his audiences, whether from feminists or drunken hecklers. Yet he also was wary of being typecast. He informed Joan Jobe Smith about a forthcoming reading on his 55th birthday, that he didn't want to get "sucked into a stance, an image....I don't want to get picture-framed too much so will probably shift tonalities, angle of bullshit, so forth. I would like to think that I'm more clever than the mob which wishes to destroy C.B." (uncollected letter, 4 July 1975).

Bukowski was still appearing in the *L.A. Free Press*, California's premier counter-culture paper. His *Notes...* column was there throughout 1974-75, and #598 (31 October 1975) was a Buk Special Issue. A Bukowski Symposium was recorded at their premises that year, with Ben Pleasants as moderator; on the panel were Gerald Locklin, Steve Richmond, Ron Koertge, and surprisingly enough - Bukowski himself. A group photograph in the paper showed them lined up against a brick wall, as Steve Richmond recalled, like subversives waiting to be shot. The conversation itself ranged widely, touching upon Bukowski's restoration of narrative: "you brought short stories and novels to poetry. A lot of your stuff is really stories", said one contributor. Ever the pragmatist, Bukowski replied that "I don't concern myself with what's a poem, what's a novel. I just write it down - it either works or it doesn't work. I'm not concerned with 'this is a poem, this is a novel, this is a shoe, this is a glove'. I write it down and that's it. That's the way I feel about it".[19]

But his time with underground papers was ending. Bukowski was bored with appearing in them; he had remarked as an aside in the Wennersten interview that he couldn't think of one paper that had "meant anything, shook anybody". They had served their purpose. He began publishing stories in sex magazines which paid well, such as Larry Flynt's

Hustler, starting in 1976, an association continued until the mid-1980s. Interviewed in German *Playboy* later in the decade, he was still too downmarket a literary figure to appear in the U.S. version. (Though it is pleasing to imagine Bukowski being thrown out of the Playboy Mansion for insulting Hugh Hefner or, equally likely, for drunkenly groping the girls). During the early 1980s he published stories in at least nine issues of another porn magazine, *Oui*. Bukowski's breaking down of boundaries between the literary and the non-literary proceeded apace. His poetry and prose had begun to attract comment even in magazines such as *Harper's* (March 1975). In it, Hayden Carruth was still equivocal; "Whether or not Charles Bukowski's 'poems' are actually poems is open to legitimate debate, even after the loosening up of our ideas about poetic form that has occurred in the past ten or fifteen years".[20]

Rolling Stone, a hippie magazine moving into the mainstream, also reported on the growing Bukowski phenomenon. An eight page feature by Glenn Esterly, 'The Pock-Marked Poetry of Charles Bukowski' (17 June 1976) described a reading in Long Beach before 400 noisy students and its aftermath, and included several poems and photographs. It described Bukowski "clad in an open-necked shirt, tattered American Graffiti-era sport coat and baggy gray pants", having vomited in the parking lot before the reading. But when he is on stage, "W.C. Fields has been reincarnated as a writer":

> On the humorous lines he reads drolly, stretching out certain syllables for emphasis in his mortician's voice and managing to get the same inflections into the spoken word as he has on paper. Despite his often professed dislike for readings, he seems to be enjoying himself now....As he ends, most of the students rise to give him an ovation....The applause continues as he walks away and, obviously pleased, he suddenly turns back and leans over the microphone. For just a moment, his guard comes down. 'You're full of love', he says, ' - ya mothers'.[21]

The article continued by interviewing Bukowski at home, a three-room furnished bungalow in a section of Hollywood heavily populated with massage parlours, porn movie theatres and fast food outlets. It ran through events in Bukowski's life yet again (as many magazine features persisted in, seeing his works as inextricably bound up with his life). There were sympathetic comments on his current state of play by Long Beach editor Leo Mailman, Linda King, TV producer Taylor Hackford, and by Gerald Locklin. After this picture of Bukowski interacting with others, it ended by emphasising his essential solitude.

Certainly Bukowski enjoyed attention and the high life, with air fares and expenses paid and increasing fees for performances. He informed Joan Jobe Smith that he had just done "a gig in Pitt[sburgh] for one grand plus air [fare]. luckily, I was on and the crowd response was high-pitched and continuous...one of my better warblings. next stops Tallahassee, Iowa City and N.Y. City....the best part about readings is FLYING there and back, stoking up on vodka 7's and living in old hotels, new motels...free ice and morning madness. maybe I'm a fucking trouper after all. I just lift a beer bottle and the crowd goes crazy" (uncollected letter, 22 April 1976).

As all experience was grist to his writing mill, Bukowski wrote about the experience of doing readings, usually with humorous cynicism. His enjoyment, reflected at times in his correspondence, rarely comes through in any of these poems. In 'Poetry reading' from *Mockingbird Wish Me Luck* (1972), the narrator has "sweat running down my arms", feels "desperate trembling/ lousy".

and I used to think
that men who drove buses
or cleaned out latrines
or murdered men in alleys were
fools.[22]

He has many other forgettable pieces about the experience of doing readings, such as 'On the circuit', 'On and off the road', 'The hustle'. One of the more entertaining is 'This poet', a minor exercise in the time-honoured practice of *epater les bourgeois*. It is formally unusual, the text being squeezed into a tight column down the page, running many of the words together and dividing lines for visuals in the manner of e.e. cummings, an early Bukowski favourite. The poet in question has been on a binge for several days before doing a reading at a university. Once on stage, he is sick into a grand piano.

I know this
poet: he's ju
st like the re
st of us: he'l
l vomit anyw
here for mon
ey.[23]

Bukowski's drink-fuelled antics were tut-tutted at, his chutzpah secretly admired. He rarely read with other poets or at benefit events. A notable exception was a 1974 Santa Cruz reading with Ginsberg, Ferlinghetti, Corso and Snyder, to raise funds for Americans in Mexican jails. (Bukowski was not entirely self-centered: he had also read at a benefit for the ailing poet and painter Kenneth Patchen in July 1971). His regular readings on the circuit, at nightclubs as well as on campuses grew ever more combative, hostile and wearing. One such event during 1976, at the 'Troubadour' club in Los Angeles, brought him the first contact with Linda Lee Beighle, his future second wife. He was still capable of eccentric acts; in *Koff* #3 in 1978, alongside three poems appeared a nude photograph of Bukowski posing as 'Mr February'. Peter Mickelson of *Chicago Review* remarked about his changing status. "Charles Bukowski, who ten or fifteen years ago was regarded as an illiterate drunk, is now practically a national hero".[24]

A 1978 interview with Karl Shapiro contained an interesting verbal snapshot of Bukowski. Shapiro had recounted a rueful anecdote. One of the two interviewers responded: "The idea of Bukowski using the word 'vulgar' is priceless. He gives readings and a lot of people you'd never associate with poetry come to the readings in leather jackets, carrying six-packs of beer and bottles of whiskey, to egg him on, and he sits there and belches through a reading".[25] The word 'vulgar' of course can mean either 'crude' or 'popular': Bukowski's performances fulfilled both meanings. He very rarely read outside the U.S., but did two at around this time, showing his Rabelaisian, larger-than-life public self at or near his best.

The travelogue-fiction *Shakespeare Never Did This* (1979) embellishes the details of Bukowski's foreign adventure, and telescopes together two separate visits to Europe. (Evidence, if any more were needed, that Bukowski's works are very far from unmediated autobiography). The trip to Paris was in September 1978, where Bukowski was thrown off the popular television programme 'Apostrophes' for being drunk. The earlier trip to West Germany began on 8 May of that year for 3 weeks, Bukowski and Linda Lee Beighle flying to Frankfurt, partly to see his elderly Uncle Heinrich in Andernach-on-Rhine. Also accompanying them was the German-born photographer Michael Montfort, whose pictures greatly enhanced the City Lights publication. Montfort subsequently became the premier Bukowski collector, with an amazing cornucopia protected at his Hollywood home. Montfort documented Bukowski at the track and at home from then on, taking the photographs at the 1985 wedding.

The reading in Hamburg was given, according to Weissner's account, at an old scruffy concert hall, "the centre of the alternative scene". It was apparently at the suggestion of Christoph Derschau, a young poet and self-styled 'son of Bukowski'. Bukowski's reputation was such that the chance of seeing 'Charles Bukowski in Der Markthalle' attracted an audience of 1200, including fans from Sweden and Denmark, with hundreds being turned away. Weissner remembered later that the crowd were mostly "young people, the kind you would see at a Joe Cocker concert....And there were the usual hecklers, some vociferous women's libbers among them, Hank trading insults with them in perfectly good humour".[26] Bukowski's account concentrates on the performer's necessary build-up from nervousness to a heightened state of ease:

> I took a drink from each bottle as I pushed forward. As I got closer to the stage the crowd began to recognize me. "Bukowski! Bukowski!". I was beginning to believe that I was Bukowski. I had to do it....I tasted the wine, pulled my poems and books out of the satchel. I was calm at last. I had done it 80 times before. I was all right. I found the mike. "Hello", I said, "it's good to be back". It had taken me 54 years.

Bukowski goes on to comment on his perception of cultural differences. In the States, "especially in the night clubs where I competed against rock groups", they wanted "poems that made them laugh", whereas the German audience appreciated more serious work. "Again the German crowd was different: they had my books. In the night clubs most of them brought in paper napkins to be signed".[27] This more sympathetic attention to the writing brought out one of Bukowski's greatest performances. The evening ends with 'One for the shoeshine man', before he tells them "Das ist alles" ["that's all"] amid wild applause.

A Vancouver reading, at the Viking Inn during October 1979, was also recorded for posterity. Bukowski followed established patterns by now, usually expressing a cheerful cynicism about the money that the audience had paid to see him: his standard line was that he would not pay to see *them*. He encouraged hecklers, burped, alternated scurrilous asides, humorous with serious poems. He threw in a few American put-downs of Canada on this occasion. Bukowski did not respect the integrity of the poems, frequently breaking off from reading to exchange insults. When a young woman calls out for him to read from *Burning in Water*... he replies brusquely "No, I hate that shit". His readings had become theatrical performances, exercises in giving the audience what they were expecting. His fee was by now $1000 plus airfare and expenses; and for this he was a professional King Devil, sometimes pretending to be drunker than he was. His opener, 'The secret of my endurance', sardonically comments on his financial success, his house and BMW. It satirises those readers who didn't want him to change and evolve, who expected him to stay with his old skid row subjects.

The second half of the evening was more serious. Bukowski ticked off the audience for getting restless, and talking when he is trying to read. But he still abused the crowd as "soul-suckers". He remarks "I hate poets and I hate poetry", and puts down one of his peers: "You think I'm Allen Ginsberg? Leading you somewhere?". In a well-worn phrase, he told the audience, "when the wine is done, the reading is done". There is a nostalgic air to some of the poems, particularly those concerning the movies he watched during his youth: ('Schubert'), the Depression years ('The lady in red') and 'The recess bells of school'. The evening ended with his farewells being drowned out by classical music.[28]

Within a year or so of that event, he had given up doing readings altogether. He no longer needed the money, and the exhausting experience of flying, performing, and fending off groupies (now that he was with Linda Beighle), became too much for him as he passed sixty. He told Gerald Locklin (2 August 1981) that he had turned down $2000 for a reading. Later in the decade he refused a reading in another letter to Locklin (16 October 1988): "I've always considered readings to be vanity trips for those who need instant response". Near the end of his life he wisely refused an offer of $10,000 to do two readings in Amsterdam. But he amazed a small audience at a San Pedro coffeeshop by reading there (presumably for free) in the early 1990s.

In Britain during the 1970s, his novels were being reviewed. By Valentine Cunningham, an Oxford don, in the *TLS*, and by the celebrated newspaper columnist Bernard Levin, who enthused about *Post Office* in *The Times*, in a piece titled 'America's Ginger Man'. Levin waxed lyrical, calling it "so hard-boiled you could crack a tooth on it...an unfalteringly entertaining account of a man trapped in a kind of Catch-23....The truth is that behind the mask of brutal and drunken fecklessness, there is a good and even gentle man....yet even as he [Henry Chinaski] whirls along on his booze-fuelled progress down his very special *via crucis*, there is a gleam amid the rubble".[29]

The Film Industry had begun to seize upon Bukowski. Despite living for almost all his life on the doorstep of Hollywood, with documentaries being shown on local TV stations in the early 1970s, this was pioneered by European film-makers. Jean-Luc Godard used a story in his *Sauve Qui Peut (La Vie)*, a.k.a. *Every Man for Himself*. Marco Ferreri's *Tales of Ordinary Madness* starred Ben Gazzara and the delectable Italian actress Ornella Muti, and was enthusiastically reviewed by no less than the doyenne of film critics, Pauline Kael. The Belgian Dominique Derruderre made a low-budget movie out of several stories in the mid-1980s. The French director Barbet Schroeder cajoled Bukowski into writing a screenplay - partly because of their friendship and partly because of $10,000 - which eventually found finance from the Cannon Group to become *Barfly*. As ever, Bukowski's attitude was sceptical: see his sparkling satirical novel *Hollywood* (1989) for a lightly-fictionalised look at some of the personalities involved.

Despite growing international success by the beginning of the 1980s, Bukowski remained surprisingly raw and insecure about his standing. In correspondence, he regularly abused magazines whose pages remained closed to him. When Joan Jobe Smith told him that the *Paris Review* had taken one of her stories, Bukowski shot back with "The Paris Review? I would never dare submit to that literary fag bevy of inbred snobs...." (uncollected letter, 15 July 1981). However, he remained loyal and encouraging to magazine editors who asked him for work. He also had a long memory. In 1991, after a break in communication of ten years, he sent her magazine *Pearl* eight poems.

Successive poetry collections became increasingly retrospective, nostalgic, approaching self-parody, as in *You Get So Alone...*(1986), or marked time, as with the early uncollected poems in *The Roominghouse Madrigals* (1988). But *Septuagenarian Stew* (1990), issued in the year of Bukowski's 70th birthday, was a widely acclaimed return to form. For the first time a Black Sparrow volume mixed poems with stories, a natural combination. Its 80 poems and 20 stories conducted a thematic tour through all the most obsessive territory of his life and writing. This was not just repackaging material at a lower intensity. The poems reflected movingly on painful relations with women and a brutal father; survival as a bum and autodidact writer in low-rent L.A.; gambling, drink, and anarchic sex. Above all, it focussed upon contemplation of death and ageing, defiant insistence on freedom and continued creation.

By now, his readers expected and got few surprises from book to book. Bukowski's marvellous way with narrative is in evidence throughout. Poems of several pages' length are handled with short lines and dialogue, wisecracks and asides. He achieves a memorable terseness and finality in 'The movie critics'. It looks back on parental arguments, concluding that as a family they had nothing in common

in or out of
the movies

and
it never
changed from
that

and
now
it never
can.[30]

Nostalgia tinges some of the poems, such as 'The burning of the dream', concerning the destruction of the old L.A. Public Library. Bukowski's worldly-wise, unsparing eye for the pathos as well as the ridiculousness of human foibles is, however, intact. A valedictory air is apparent in the final section of poems, which grapple with illness ('Pernicious anemia') and intimations of death: "it's going to happen: the drinks/ toll for everybody" ('The last drink'). Even his typewriter, the weapon with which Bukowski fought time and mortality all along, is simply "feeding a/ closing space". The book is really a rehearsal, leading on to the greater achievement of *The Last Night of the Earth Poems*.

Indications of Bukowski's increasing stature and 'respectability' had begun to appear. One was Lionel Rolfe's *Literary L.A.*, which had given him a derisory single mention in its original 1981 edition. Reissued in 1991, he was allotted twelve pages, and had his photograph on its cover. The first Ph.D thesis, my own *The Poetry of Charles Bukowski*, was accepted by the University of Hull in 1990. The first full-length biography, *Hank*, by Neeli Cherkovski, appeared in 1991, in editions from both Random House and Black Sparrow. Bukowski was unimpressed by the book, telling Locklin that "Neeli...gave it his best but his best wasn't very good" (1 May 1991). To balance this, Bukowski had certainly praised the excellence of Cherkovski's previous book, *Whitman's Wild Children* (1988). The first critical study heavily informed by literary theory and politics appeared in 1994: Russell Harrison's *Against the American Dream: Essays on Charles Bukowski* was published by Black Sparrow.

A feature on Bukowski appeared in the *Los Angeles Times Magazine* (22 March 1987), predictably focussing on his late success story, being taken up by Hollywood via *Barfly*: "Mickey Rourke and Faye Dunaway are starring in a movie based on his life". He fed their reporter the usual line: "'The wine', he explains, 'does most of the writing. I just open a bottle and turn on the radio, and it just comes pouring out....It's a free lunch. A free dinner. I don't know how long it is going to continue, but so far there is nothing easier than writing".[31] The actor Sean Penn interviewed him for Andy Warhol's *Interview* magazine in 1988. Warhol's long-time friend and assistant Gerard Malanga incidentally took several outstanding portrait photos of Bukowski over the years, including one in his recent retrospective book *Screen Tests, Portraits, Nudes 1964-1996*.

By the time of his death in March 1994, Bukowski had been for some years the best-selling poet in the world, and the most widely-read contemporary American author in translation - a fantastic achievement. The obituaries were many and varied, though his local paper in San Pedro, *Random Lengths*, perhaps exaggerated with its headline "The Whole World Mourns the Death of a Poet". The reporter noted that "after 1980 his appetite for meeting people who liked his work grew short indeed...[especially when at] 'Sacred Grounds', the coffee house that was Bukowski's sometime haunt. In his very last days his resolve in this matter began to relax. A birthday party was held last summer [1993] at Vinegar Hill Books in Bukowski's honor and, much to the surprise of everyone involved, 'Hank' attended. It would prove to be the final public appearance of any kind for Mr Bukowski. However, local shop owners who had contact with 'Hank' remember him as a gentle, quiet man who preferred not to be bothered with his celebrity....Bukowski was laid to rest in Green Hills Cemetery on March 14. A memorial poetry reading...[was] held at 'Sacred Grounds' at 8 p.m. on Monday, March 21".[32]

Obituaries appeared in many broadsheet newspapers in America, notably the *New York Times* ("Bukowski was a bard of the barroom and the brothel, a direct descendant of the Romantic visionaries who worshiped at the altar of personal excess, violence and madness") and the *L.A. Times*. In the U.K., *The Times, Independent* and *The Guardian* all published significant obituaries. In the latter, Christopher Reed noted Bukowski's statement on how a notorious reputation had helped his writing career: "'I got my act up...I wrote vile but interesting stuff that made people hate me, but [also] made them curious about this Bukowski'". Lionel Rolfe in the *L.A. Village View* called him the 'Reluctant Saint of the Dispossessed', who chose to chronicle the dark side of the City of the Angels: "Bukowski transformed the darkness with the hard light of his honesty and humour".[33] Stephen Kessler memorialised Bukowski - and his own contacts with him - in the *Mendocino Outlook* (April 1994). He recorded Bukowski's advice that "the main thing about writing is to write, not to talk about writing", and concluded "His work is a beacon for those who would honestly face the wounded beauty of their lives and turn it into a battle-scarred art".[34]

It took Bukowski many years to gain a wide reading public. But the fact that his career evolved within little magazines, small presses and underground newspapers, was greatly beneficial, both to its dissemination and longevity. His critics, advocates and detractors did not need to be paid to do his P.R.; they freely promoted his mystique of No Compromise and Outsiderdom, his antagonistic image. His Long March to success on his own terms was precisely because Bukowski did not, and did not have to, compromise his work in order to satisfy pre-existing mainstream publishers. In doing so he avoided the self-destructive potential of early fame in America, or the conforming pressures exacted by agents and editors on successful authors. He didn't need to worry about literary prizes or acceptability. He had his two main publishers in the U.S., and others overseas. Most of all he had an army of readers. Bukowski liked to say, with characteristic insouciance, that his favourite fan letter was from a prisoner in jail, who told him "yours are the only books that are passed from cell to cell". He recognised that he had eventually achieved an enviable circumstance: "famous elsewhere and writing here" as he put it in a 1988 interview.[35]

With Bukowski's death, and in reality for some years previously, his revels were indeed ended, his turbulent life rounded with a sleep. (Despite his regular badmouthing of Shakespeare, he enjoyed the odd humorous self-comparison, not least in the title of his 1979 travelogue). But he had done his work, carved "from his own marble" as he told Jon Edgar Webb back in the early 1960s. In many ways Bukowski was in tune with the changing spirit of his times. His works subversively challenged the boundaries of literary taste and decency in the 1960s and 1970s, using the underground press. During the conservative 1980s, his subjects were his own financial success, and the increasingly ugly Reaganite society around him. All these factors gave him an ever-increasing vogue in Europe and in the States. It gave him, after decades of effort, the "great audience" for poetry which was the embodiment and fulfillment of Walt Whitman's challenging demand.

Chapter 4

Reactions To Modernism and The Beats

> but to me, the twenties centered mostly on Hemingway
> coming out of the war and beginning to type.
> - 'The last generation'[1]

Bukowski began to be formed as a writer in the mid-1940s, after the heyday of Modernism but while most of its major figures were still alive. But his true career began a decade later, as we have seen, by reacting against Modernism's disciples in academia, the New Critics and their associated magazines. In this push against perceived orthodoxies he was typical of his artistic generation in America, not exceptional; and his generation included the Beats. Collectively, theirs was yet another attempt to put 'life' back into art. They reached back to Whitman, and to those American Modernists not yet completely absorbed by academia, notably William Carlos Williams, and arguably Henry Miller. But they also looked to 'dissident' figures: to some of the deceased Surrealists, Céline, Artaud, and even the then-imprisoned Ezra Pound. The impact of Surrealism - especially as popularised in poetry by bardic performers such as Dylan Thomas - on the American avant-garde was also being washed through their works. Bukowski's inherent romanticism was crucially affected by his reading of the American Moderns, foreign dissident authors, and all this ferment created by the Beats. But his development differed from the Beats in a number of respects: he picked up on an anti-Modernist, even conservative figure, Robinson Jeffers. As ever, Bukowski's approach was mixed, intuitive, non-theorised. Jeffers' pessimistic loner philosophy of 'Inhumanism', his narrative poetry that included dialogue, were what Bukowski needed.

Bukowski's relation to Modernism is necessarily both for and against. He was inspired by Modernists who were also literary nationalists, and followed them in rejecting the cultural elitism of the Anglophile T.S. Eliot and his followers. Chiefly important for Bukowski's poetry were Williams' advocacy of the American language; cummings' witty typography; and above all the structural model provided by Hemingway's early prose. Bukowski takes certain Modernist techniques into his poetry, simplifies and popularises them; and later sends them up, adding humour to the mix. His wartime reading at the L.A. Public Library was vital. Yet this was no dogmatic process; in a 1974 interview, Bukowski let slip the names of some of his early, rather surprising heroes - Conrad Aiken, W.H. Auden, even Aldous Huxley.

To take one instance, Ezra Pound; at first sight an unlikely Bukowski affinity. Indeed, he regularly condemns *The Cantos* as an example of elitist art divorced from an audience, characterising them, accurately if reductively, as "full of dead languages/ newspaper clippings/ and love scenes from St.Liz" ('Horse on fire').[2] But admiring him as a repository of intelligence about writing, Bukowski often alluded to Pound in his letters, which themselves sometimes imitated E.P's eccentric epistolary manner and are similarly full of writing advice and capitals. This liking for Pound persisted, and in 1986 he contributed to a Pound tribute published by Limberlost Press. He had earlier told the poet and editor Joan Jobe Smith, then a tyro, that "if you write poetry and have not read Ezra...it seems a strange situation. He's probably been the greatest influence on modern poetry". (uncollected letter, 10 March 1975).

A month later, he further advised her that "Pound, Hem, Gertie [Gertrude Stein] did teach us how to LAY DOWN THE LINE, it was, is, important and good, but damned if they had any humour or EMOTION. Basically, they were arid, basically the literature of the centuries has been arid. What we need is the line that allows emotion without Hollywood sentimentality" (uncollected letter,10 April 1975). Thus Bukowski clearly identified where he wished to differ from Modernism's high seriousness, and this is reflected in his work. A symbolic clincher: 'He wrote in lonely blood' refers to a "lovely girl" (the painter, poet and editor Sheri Martinelli) who had befriended Ezra Pound during his years of incarceration, and even approached Jeffers on the West Coast but was turned away. The speaker observes that if she comes to see him, he'll turn her away too;

"after all,/ who wants to follow old/ Ez?".[3] Certainly not Bukowski - he was an unashamed populist, demanding accessible idioms, and entirely lacking wider cultural or political ambitions.

When reading Bukowski's verse in bulk one is struck by the sheer number of references, often irreverent, to Modernists in all the arts. 'The last generation', published in 1982, unfavourably contrasts the contemporary situation with that of the singular figures of the 1920s, treating them with affectionate familiarity. 'Them and us' fantasises a bunch of the Moderns arguing out on the Bukowski family porch. Even a novelist whose narrative complexity Bukowski would seem to have little time for, William Faulkner, is occasionally alluded to. 'As I lay dying' (itself a quote) recalls "myself 20 years old,/ reading Faulkner". And the humour of an episode in the title poem of *The Days Run Away like Wild Horses Over the Hills* comes from the hard-drinking, recently-deceased novelist being confused with a jockey by "the rummy downstairs":

'you're in a bad mood', he said.
'sure', I said, 'haven't you heard? Faulkner's dead'.
'Faulkner? wasn't he a bullring jock? Pomona Fairgrounds?
Rudioso? Caliente? you knew the kid?'
'I knew the kid', I said
and then walked on upstairs.[4]

Modernism in early 20th Century Anglo-American literature involved a revolution in artistic techniques. The uses, for example, of montage to juxtapose differing narratives (as in Faulkner's novels, or Hemingway's *in our time*); collage, where materials such as correspondence (*Paterson*) or Chinese ideograms (*The Cantos*) are incorporated; and palimpsest, a novel such as *Ulysses* being written on top of an existing narrative, 'The Odyssey'. The typewriter, as wielded by cummings, became a tool to direct lineation. A number of these devices are invoked, parodied or sent up in early Bukowski poems; if rarely in his strongest work. For instance, a 1960 *Hearse* broadside, 'His wife, the painter', juxtaposes the conversation between a couple with the bitter internal monologue of one of them, and includes details of works by Daumier, Corot and Orozco. 'Sunflower' combines surreal imagery with palimpsestic layering:

good night
sea elephant
good night
Greta Garbo
good night
steam shovel

good night
spaghetti and beer[5]

    This sends up the ending of 'The Game of Chess' section of Eliot's *The Waste Land* ("good night, sweet ladies", etc) which is itself echoing Ophelia's last words in *Hamlet*. Another parodic echo of *The Waste Land* intrudes into 'An argument over Marshal Foch': "outside the crickets were chirping like/ mad: Foch, Foch, Foch, Foch..." (cf. "Twit twit twit/ Jug jug jug jug jug jug"). There are various poems with a Cummings-like free range of typography, one a fairly dire depressive piece inelegantly titled 'The hairy hairy fist and love will die'. There is probably a future thesis to be written on Bukowski's uses of the typewriter, but in general his works keep to a left-hand margin. And in his mature practice, his line endings vary: anything from one or two-word lines to the full width of the page, as the limit of the typewriter is reached.

    William Carlos Williams insisted that a 'new measure' should come from American speech, with lines divided and spaced so as to indicate rhythmic breaks in spoken language. He observed, "where else can what we are seeking arise from but speech, from American speech as distinct from English speech...from what we hear in America". The Williams slogans "no ideas but in things" and "speaking straight ahead" were of general use to Bukowski, as to other members of his literary generation. Williams' constant urging of rejection of English verse forms and the intellectualising dominance of the Anglophile T.S. Eliot bore fruit. Williams urged that poetry should be "brought into the world where we live...out of the clouds and down to earth....Using common words in a rare manner will advance the cause of the poem wonderfully".[6]

    The uses that subsequent poets have made of this have been very various, as the critic Stephen Fredman has pointed out: "the lines of Whitman, Pound, Williams, Olson, and Creeley are all available to poets in this tradition as distinct formal possibilities; these various poetic lines carry along with them characteristic American poetic stances, from the operatic or oratorical to the meditational or notational".[7] Robert Creeley, Allen Ginsberg, Frank O'Hara, Robert Duncan, and Ed Dorn can all be regarded as Open Form poets, writing an energised, often scrupulously observed, verse that draws upon the sounds and contours of American speech. They produced distinctively different work from this raw material. Bukowski should be regarded as in this tradition of using the American language. In a 'Poem to a man in jail' first published in *Second Coming* in 1974, he named the New Jersey paediatrician and referred to his project:

Poetry does seem to be getting better, more
human,

the clearing up of the language has something to
do with it. (w.c. williams came along and asked
somebody to clear up the language)
then
I came along.[8]

The Williams line does make a minor detour through Bukowski's early work, with several apprentice exercises in his mode. This debt has not gone entirely unnoticed; an article in 1987 by Jimmie Cain, Jr. argued Bukowski's Imagist roots, thus connecting him up to Williams and the experimental lyric tradition. 'I taste the ashes of your death' (published in 1959) is a prime if rare example, strongly reminiscent of Williams' vowel music. This one involves a Williams-like invocation of flowers. It records a moment of awareness as two images cross: an accidental soaking from a wet tree releases memories.

the blossoms shake
sudden water
down my sleeve,
sudden water
cool and clean
as snow -
as the stem-sharp
swords
go in
against your breast
and the sweet wild
rocks
leap over
and lock us in.[9]

Formally, this is a dance for words of one or two syllables. A backbone of internal rhymes is organised around what is most often a four-syllable line. This patterning is clearly not worked out by following any rigid syllabic grid, but played by ear. Alliterative and assonantal effects are evident throughout in the selection of 's' and 'c' sounds, with full rhymes and half-rhymes (rocks/ lock, against/ breast) laid out for listening pleasure. The poem itself is, however, a cul-de-sac. The romantic blossoms, snow, swords and sweet wild rocks were soon jettisoned in favour of a much harsher rub against existence.

Williams was a human bridge from the Modernist era to the 1950s Beats and Black Mountaineers, meeting and corresponding with numerous young American and British poets. He wrote the introduction to Ginsberg's

Howl and Other Poems (1956), though later said he was disgusted by it - not by its contents but by the long lines! He also wrote introductions to books by Jack Kerouac and - here is the Bukowski link - Harold Norse. Williams and Norse corresponded in the 1950s, with Norse telling him about his travels in Europe and his writing struggles. Williams urged him to abandon regular forms and take up the American idiom, "the language we speak in the United States....free from all influences which can be summed up as having to do with 'the Establishment'". This, Williams claimed, "pared to essentials, is the language which governed Walt Whitman in his choice of words".[10]

Bukowski took up the Williams' ideal of using the American idiom - more so than Norse, whose poems are more mannered and self-consciously 'poetic' than either of his erstwhile friends. Bukowski's poems contain much working class speech, as well as the sorts of 'errors' or ambiguities usually erased from written texts. Williams' art-speech is hardly taken, as he claimed, from the mouths of Polish mothers. Thematically, there are vast differences. Bukowski's view of the uneasy relationship between masculine sensitivity and aggression is far more basic. An early example would be 'I cannot stand tears' (1957), which is told by a painter lamenting the intrusion of a crowd into his previously untroubled landscape. They are standing around a goose with a broken leg; the guard's are the slangy expressions ("kiss my ass", "take it to the president"). Simple and brief as it is, 'I cannot stand tears' looks forward to his aggressive mature manner.

Bukowski's main access to Modernism is through Ernest Hemingway, the most accessible of them all, the prose technician whose works reached a popular audience. 'Papa' Hemingway's stripped-down but patterned language, his masculine role model and larger than life public image were all important to Bukowski. (That he saw Hemingway as an Oedipal father figure is seemingly confirmed by the story 'Class' in *South of No North* where a young man climbs in the ring and knocks Hemingway out). References to and identification with his mentor abound in poems of all eras, but especially early on. 'Parts of an opera, parts of a guitar, parts of Nowhere' describes a fight in an alley: "I took him quite/ easily and I felt like Hemingway'. 'Suicide' maintains that "Ernie tagging himself/ when the time was ready" was preferable to Robert Frost "licking the boots of politicians". And Bukowski constantly takes up the theme of 'style' in art and life, though he doesn't go as far: "when Hemingway put his brains on the wall, that was style..."[11]

Bukowski also at times echoes Hemingway's aesthetics of existential authenticity, maintaining that the artist must engage with the world, be eroded and shaped by it. Hemingway's preface to *The First Forty-Nine Stories* (1944) states that "In going where you have to go, and doing what you have to do, and seeing what you have to see, you dull and blunt the instrument you write with. But I would rather have it bent and dulled...and know that I had something to write about, than to have it bright and shining and nothing to say".[12] Even as late as 1973, Bukowski wrote that "the hard life created the hard line and by the hard line I mean the true line devoid of ornament".[13] This is pure Hemingway; perhaps even *Ham*ingway.

Again, influence by E.H. makes Bukowski very typical of his times: from the 1930s onwards there were legions of his followers. But he was no mere copyist or hero-worshipper. Bukowski poems may invade Hem territory, and treat subjects such as the bullfight, but take a very different, less heroic view. These are usually set in Mexico, such as the 1969 'Even the sun was afraid' published in *Evergreen*, which depicts a squalid end for the bull, tormented to death by Mexicans with "dirty behinds". In 'Brave bull', the speaker's sympathies are again with the animal: "I prayed for California, and the dead bull in man/ and in me". He published two more poems about bullfighting in 1961, the year of the exhausted Hemingway's shotgun suicide. 'The priest and the matador' opens with the bull's death: "his great head held no more terror than a rock". The speaker is estranged from the spectacle. In 'Side of the sun', a sonorously-phrased distrust of "the stale crowds" ends with a sour moral commentary:

generally the bull stands pure
and dies pure
untouched by symbols or cliques or false loves,
and when they drag him out
... the eventual stench
is the world.[14]

What Bukowski most importantly took from Hemingway was not subject matter, but structure. The prose art was to be a basis for his own in verse, specifically using an essentially Hemingwayan model of repetition with artful variation. Which of course makes "Gertie" Stein Bukowski's stylistic Grandma! In his Paris memoir *A Moveable Feast* (1964) Hemingway gave her at last some credit. "She had...discovered many truths about rhythms and the uses of words in repetition that were valid and valuable and she talked well about them. But she disliked...the obligation to make her writing intelligible [and] *The Making of Americans*....began magnificently, went on very well for a long way with... stretches of great brilliance and then went on endlessly in repetitions that a more conscientious writer would have put in the waste basket".[15] He also mentions *Three Lives* (1909). This has a deliberately simplistic tone, allied to a pattern of repetition and summary. This is from the first page of 'The Good Anna':

Anna managed the whole little house for Miss Mathilda. It was a funny little house....They were funny little houses, two stories high, with red brick fronts and long white steps. This one little house was always very full with Miss Mathilda, an under servant, stray dogs and cats and Anna's voice that scolded, managed, grumbled all day long.[16]

The rhythm of this banal narrative is insistent; the repetitions differ slightly each time they occur, and the trio of verbs in the final phrase has the effect of binding the passage together. Hemingway's first novel *The Sun Also Rises* (1926) was written at a time when he was still very impressed by Stein's experiments. Its structural pattern directly relates to *Three Lives*:

The fiesta was really started. It kept up day and night for seven days. The dancing kept up, the drinking kept up, the noise went on. The things that happened could only have happened during a fiesta. Everything became quite unreal finally and it seemed as though nothing could have any consequences. It seemed out of place to think of consequences during the fiesta. All during the fiesta you had the feeling even when it was quiet, that you had to shout any remark to make it heard. It was the same feeling about any action. It was a fiesta and it went on for seven days.[17]

Ezra Pound originally hailed Hemingway as an Imagist poet in the medium of prose. This passage suggests why: it has rhythmic effects usually associated with verse. It achieves this by the pattern of repetitions. The word 'fiesta' is repeated five times, occurring strategically in the first and last sentences; 'seemed', 'and', 'happened', are rapidly repeated, as are 'consequences' and 'feeling'. The phrase 'kept up' is used three times, while 'seven days' joins 'fiesta' to commence and summarise the action. The simple connecting word 'it' recurs eight times, and with increasing frequency towards the end. Hemingway's debt to Stein is there, but he obviously attains a much greater realism and narrative interest.

Now a more specific connection to Bukowski. Hemingway's early story 'Up in Michigan' can be compared to - in my view - one of the best poems of the 1960s, 'Something for the touts, the nuns, the grocery clerks and you'. The two works have structure in common, but very differing attitudes to death. Hemingway, traumatised in the First World War and by his much-loved father's suicide, was death-fixated; his characters have to continually prove their courage. Bukowski's characters are intent upon getting as much joy - drink, sex, art - out of life before inevitable death.

Hemingway's tale, which Stein found 'inacrochable' [obscene], tells of the clumsy seduction, a near-rape, of a love-struck waitress by a drunken hunter just returned from a successful trip. It is a fable of the hunter and the hunted, a perception of the ultimate desolation of human relations. The story moves through five sequential phases:

What Jim Gilmore does:
He bought the blacksmith shop....He was a good horse-shoer....He lived upstairs....He liked her face because...

What Liz Coates likes about Jim:
She liked it the way he walked.... She liked it about his moustache.... She liked it about how white his teeth were.... She liked it very much that he didn't look like a blacksmith.... She liked it how much D.J. Smith.... She liked it the way the hair...

How much Liz thinks about Jim:
Liz was thinking about Jim....Liz thought about him...She couldn't sleep well for thinking about him.... It was fun to think about him...

Liz's fear as Jim seduces her:
Liz was terribly frightened...She was so frightened .... She was frightened....She was very frightened...

What Liz does while Jim sleeps:
Liz pushed him..She worked out from under him.... Liz leaned over and kissed him...She lifted his head a little....Liz started to cry...[18]

While there are other sentence types dispersed amongst those listed, the unmistakable pattern is for short sentences to be grouped together in paragraphic 'stanzas'. The shift from one sentence type to the next takes place precisely at the point at which the repetitions are in danger of becoming distractingly dull. The mood of the narrative alters slightly as the changeover occurs. The final sentence in most of the paragraphs summarises what has gone before. As the critic David Lodge has pointed out, though Hemingway purged his style of metaphors he nevertheless "contrived to retain in it the emotive resonance of metaphorical writing".[19]

Bukowski's poem, probably written during his long lyrical month in New Orleans with the Webbs during the Summer of 1964, has a similar structure, though with more linguistic complexity. It moves through sixteen sequential phases, and can be schematized:

we have everything and we have nothing...
some men do it...
something at 8 a.m....
it's always early enough...

days with glass edges...
men who...
at a harbor...
or disgust or age or...
what do you see?...
sometimes the first...
the vacant lots are not bad...
trying to be red...
no wonder sometimes the women cry...
some of them want...
and if you go inside...
some do it...[20]

Each of these sentence types is repeated two or three times, and Bukowski departs from the Hemingway model in some ways. His poem has many more syntactic phases, sometimes parallel units within the same sentence, and the poem ends exactly as it had begun, with its most thematically potent statement, namely "we have everything and we have nothing". This is repeated, more or less entire, on five occasions and has several incomplete echoes: "and nothing, and nothing". These repetitions underscore the narrator's awareness of death's closeness everywhere in life, and the necessary distractions - wine, women and song - to dull this sure and certain knowledge. That death is omnipresent is of course an essential Hemingway theme: "all stories, if continued far enough, end in death, and he is no true story teller who would keep that from you".[21] (*Death in the Afternoon, 1932*). 'Something for the touts...' waxes eloquent on the subject of mortality:

the man you knew yesterday hooking
for ten rounds or drinking for three days and
three nights by the Sawtooth mountains now
just something under a sheet or a cross
or a stone or under an easy delusion,
or packing a bible or a golf bag or a
briefcase: how they go, how they go! - all
the ones you thought would never go.

Bukowski's poem builds up a compelling rhythmic momentum. It emphasises, however, not a stoic acceptance of death but relish for existence, seizing the moment. It embraces messy, sexy life. Hemingway's philosophy was more brutal and fatalistic. Life may be a losing game - even the resolutely unheroic Philip Larkin knew that - but the style of defeat is important to Hemingway's characters. Bukowski is much more of an unheroic survivor, telling jokes to cover the same perception of crevasses under existence. This pattern of repetition and artful variation is apparent throughout Bukowski's verse in all its phases. But latterly it was pared down and used humorously. This can be seen in a sardonic poem of the mid-1970s, 'Leaning on wood'. There are only three sentence types being used.

there are 4 or 5 guys at the racetrack bar...
there is a mirror behind the bar...
the reflections are not kind...[22]

The first statement is repeated, or has echoes, on four occasions. The second occurs twice, the third three times. Very little takes place. Three pieces of advice about horse race betting are given. The punters order drinks, stare at their "unkind" reflections, hear the race buzzer and leave to place their bets. With a lifetime's experience behind him, the narrator concludes

what shit. nobody
wins. ask
Caesar.

The quip is typical; a jokey reference to the Classics placed on the lips of a racetrack-goer. Its point is that "nobody wins". It is yet another echo of the phrase in 'Something for the touts...', one of the most resonant in all Bukowski's writing, that "we have everything and we have nothing".

But Bukowski the reader and critic of Modernism also learned from at least one noted anti-Modernist: Robinson Jeffers. During the 1920s-1930s, amazingly in view of his current neglect, Jeffers loomed almost as large as T.S. Eliot. He was then at the summit of his vogue, writing lengthy verse tragedies in a sonorous sub-Biblical style. His repute rapidly descended during the early 1940s to near-pariah status, partly because of his implicitly fascist politics, and because his style became outmoded. During his wartime reading, Bukowski must have absorbed Jeffers' highly-charged narratives such as 'Tamar' and 'Roan Stallion', as well as the many powerful observations of the natural world. Such was Bukowski's infatuation, which lasted well into his 50s, that he has poems about Jeffers in no less than six of his volumes. Jeffers' poems about animals and birds carry the imprint of D.H. Lawrence, who Bukowski also admired. Though Bukowski is very much the urbanite, there is a streak of sympathy for the natural world. As evidence, see all those poems about wounded dogs and especially cats; about crows piled up by Texas farmers as so much rubbish, and for nature working through its purposes. One Jeffers-type poem surviving into Bukowski's early maturity is 'The mockingbird', a fable-like observation of a bird teasing a cat all Summer. The cat is then observed walking "calmly" up the driveway with the bird in its mouth:

feathers parted like a woman's legs,
and the bird was no longer mocking...
but the cat
striding down through centuries
would not listen.[23]

Jeffers' stern neo-Nietzschean philosophy of 'Inhumanism' - the insignificance of humanity compared with the glories of the natural world - was challenging to the dominant liberalism and recently-triumphant forces of democracy. Jeffers, a long time resident at Carmel, on the California coast, is said to have derived it from personal observation of wildlife, especially birds of prey such as hawks. (He was a decided influence on the Yorkshire poet Ted Hughes).[24] Jeffers was increasingly out of favour when Bukowski seized upon critically-savaged collections *Be Angry At the Sun* (1941), which had included a masque about Hitler; *The Double Axe* (1948) even appeared with a disclaimer from its publishers disassociating themselves from certain poems. The New Critics had anyway virtually excluded Jeffers from the pantheon of modern poetry, another good reason to be interested, so far as Bukowski was concerned.[25]

In early correspondence, Bukowski refers to Jeffers as "my god", and told Jory Sherman that he had been the only man since Shakespeare to write the long narrative poem that doesn't put one to sleep. (1 April 1960) In December 1961, he wrote to the same correspondent: "Shit, I have a hero. I would like to sit in a room with Jeffers for 35 or 40 minutes". He never had the chance, as Jeffers died in 1962. A number of poems brood on his legacy. 'He wrote in lonely blood' in the early 1970s; 'The poets and the foreman' in *Dangling*...(1981), which states that "now I've gotten rid/ of Auden and Jeffers.../ and to be alone/ like this/ is the way/ of course". 'Jeffers' is conspicuous in *Septuagenarian Stew* (1990). 'Goodbye' in *War All the Time* (1984), says a symbolic farewell to a number of his early heroes, as does 'Someday I'm going to write a primer for crippled saints...' in *You Get So Alone*...(1987).[26]

The Bukowski-Jeffers affinity was clearly a mix of personal identification and the literary. Both were the hypersensitive, rebellious sons of sternly disciplinarian fathers. The effect that Jeffers had on Bukowski comes through in the powerful negativity of their view of America; for Jeffers it was "a perishing Republic". Their misanthropy at times encompasses the imperative note, and a didactic, denunciatory streak comes out in fairly stilted, ponderous poems of the 1960s such as

'Counsel' ("be not taken with the nearness of the minute/ or a beauty or a politic/ that will wilt like a cut flower"). It has its apotheosis in the pamphlet poem 'The genius of the crowd' printed by d.a.levy's 7 Flowers Press in 1966. Jeffers announced himself "quits with the people". Bukowski tried to outdo the old man in snarling at the bovine masses: "humanity, you never had it from the beginning".[27]

Bukowski was once again simply taking what he needed. He was no true disciple, no classical scholar as Jeffers was, and has nothing remotely approaching that heavy-handed grandeur of style, or Biblical and Classics-based works harping on fate, incest, violence and tragedy. No poems the length of 'Tamar' or Roan Stallion'; no overt symbolism. But Jeffers' poetic credo (published in 1928) was surely relevant: "I want it rhythmic and not rhymed. My feeling is for the number of beats to the line....The rhythm comes from many sources...[such as the] beat of blood...[and the] desire for singing emphasis that prose does not have".[28] Verse that is heavily-cadenced, irregular; often the scansion of lines cannot be determined exactly but remains poetic because of a natural 'ear'.

To return to Bukowski's language: within 'Something for the touts...' there are interpolations of surreal imagery ("days with glass edges", "signs in bullrings like diamonds hollering/ Mother Capri") and an illogical, dreamlike landscape:

up a road where a madman sits waiting among
blue jays and wrens netted in and sucked a flakey
grey....

there is the softsmoke feeling from urns
and the canned sounds of old battleplanes

Surrealism constitutes a fairly minor tributary in Bukowski's huge river of words, and is the enemy of his general lucidity. But it is a presence within it, and constitutes a shared feature between Bukowski and the Beats. Tinges of Surrealist language are most apparent in his early, more derivative verse: in 'Sunflower', or 'I wait in the white rain'. Its trace survives into many a poem of the 1970s, whose flat narration is counterpointed by a surreal simile or metaphor - usually for humorous effect. Bukowski probably first noticed Surrealism when it was becoming fashionable in America - even reaching Hollywood with Salvador Dali and Bunuel. If so, that again makes him typical of his generation. Ashbery, O'Hara, Duncan, Lamantia, Norse, and many of the Beats, passionately admired poets such as Paul Eluard, Phillip Soupault, Louis Aragon, Pierre Reverdy, Jacques Prévèrt and Henri Michaux. City Lights Books, and James Laughlin's New Directions, made available works by most of these to American readers from the late 1950s onwards. It is also possible that Bukowski may have absorbed second or third hand Surrealism through reading Edith Sitwell, David Gascoyne, and George Barker: he certainly read Dylan Thomas avidly.

Thomas made several American tours during the immediate post-war years and enthused a generation of young American poets with his performances. John Berryman hung around with the Welsh poet in New York bars; Lawrence Ferlinghetti recalled attending readings by Thomas in San Francisco: "his voice was so great, even though he was lushed up when he read".[29] (Does this sound like someone we know?). Bukowski's affection for Thomas comes out in name-droppings, and he regarded him as having been 'killed' by audiences - rather than by the reputed 32 straight whiskies. 'I am with the roots of flowers' has some echoes of Thomas' 'The Force that Through the Green Fuse Drives the Flower', which famously "blasts the roots of trees".[30]

As Kenneth Rexroth pointed out, Thomas was no formal innovator but a populariser of language first minted in the French and Spanish avant-garde. There were plenty of earlier U.S. avant-garde connections with this original Surrealism. Man Ray and photographer/ model Lee Miller had been involved with the Surrealist Group in Paris. Poet and publisher Harry Crosby wrote in a quasi-Surrealist mode. Charles Henri Ford, Henry Miller and Kenneth Patchen were very much interested in its methods. Even stay-at-homes such as Wallace Stevens or Nathanael West kept up with it in the pages of *Broom*, *transition* and *The Little Review*. Carlos Williams wrote for the American-based Surrealist magazines *Blues* and *View*. Many Surrealists themselves spent the war years in New York, and some settled permanently in the States.

Surrealism - like Bukowski himself, an offshoot of the First World War - derived from Pure Psychic Automatism. This was conceived as the inexhaustible, free-flowing reservoir of words and images dredged up from the subconscious mind, the source for them - as for Freud, with whom André Breton had corresponded - of the most important human drives. The Surrealists tried to tap into the subconscious by transcribing dreams, by Automatic writing, by playing free association games with words, drug-taking, the indulgence of fantasy. Breton outlined prescribed methods, perhaps with his tongue in cheek, in his 'First Manifesto':

> Put yourself in as passive, or receptive, a state of mind as you can. Forget about your genius, your talents, and the talents of everyone else. Keep reminding yourself that literature is one of the saddest roads that leads to everything. Write quickly, without any preconceived subject, fast enough so that you will not remember what you've written and be tempted to reread what you have written. The first sentence will come

spontaneously, so compelling is the truth that with every passing second there is a sentence unknown to our consciousness which is only crying out to be heard....Go on as long as you like. Put your trust in the inexhaustible nature of the murmur.[31]

The key word here is "spontaneously": a word also that intrudes on any discussion of Bukowski and the Beats' claimed writing methods. The unstructured play of thought is libidinal. Quasi-sexual predictability is apparent in a lot of second-rate Surrealist writings. The anthologist Edward R.Germain pointed out that these formulae quickly became established: " 'the - of the -': 'the craters of his eyes', 'the threads of her heart', 'the snakes of her hair', 'the lids of her windows, 'the houses of their blood', 'the key-hole of your eye', 'her thoughts of heat-lightning'".[32] Over-reliance on such imagery is found in the early works of American followers of Breton's such as Philip Lamantia. His verse of that period has not worn well - a criticism that also applies to Bukowski's (and Norse's) sub-Surrealist efforts included in the Penguin Modern Poets volume that they shared. In Lamantia's 'The enormous window', for instance,

Within closets filled with nebulae the blood shot eyes
swim upward for the sun
This world of serpents and weeping women is crushed in the violence
of a swamp large enough to contain
the enormous razor blade of the night[33]

Surrealist language was really just a detour in Bukowski's development. He was never the kind to sign up to artistic manifestos, or even to fully trust his own subconscious. Besides, by the late 1950s and early 1960s when he and others were borrowing from Surrealism, it was already old-hat. Bukowski does go on to exploit at least some of Surrealism's comic potential. For instance, 'Vegas', first published in 1961, sends up the sort of imagery that its narrator expects to find in "a poetry class". Hitch-hiking back from Las Vegas to Los Angeles, its narrator unwisely talks surreal gibberish to a laconic truckdriver:

I'm not going all the way to L.A., the truckdriver said.

it's all right, I said, the calla lilies nod to our minds and someday we'll all go home
together.

in fact, he said, this is as far
as we go.

so I let him have it; old withered whore of time
your breasts taste the sour cream of dreaming...[34]

He is let out in the middle of the desert. When an old Ford picks him up, he tells us in the punchline, "I kept my mouth/ shut". This lightly sends up an outdated poetic diction, but also attacks the notion that poetry's language should be divorced from, say, the speech of truckdrivers. 'A report upon the consumption of myself' does however have its surrealist inclinations disciplined, and its mobile rhythms and a dream-like, illogical landscape make it memorable.

the blue evening is cinched like old
muskets and the dangling sex rope hangs
as the tree stands up and calls:
July. and the dust of hope in the bottom of paper cups
along with small spiders that have names like ancient
European cities; cuckoo-spit and dross, heavy wheels;
oilwells stuck between fish and sucking up grey gas
of love and the palms up on the cliff waving[35]

This imagery has much of the 'arbitrary' nature that Breton would have endorsed. It allows the evening to be described as "cinched like old muskets". The dangling sex rope could be from a dream notebook, which hangs as the tree - another phallic symbol - stands up. "The dust of hope" is a phrase that could have been coined by any of the Surrealist bards. Small spiders have names like "ancient European cities, a distinctly odd simile. It ends with an authentically libidinal, surreal image as a building floats away, suggesting a giant condom - "they've blown up the YMCA like a giant balloon and/ sent it out to sea full of screaming lovely lonely/ girls".

Traces of Surrealist lingo that survive into poems of the 1980s are played for laughs. An ordinary restaurant scene in 'Table for two' is propelled into a realm where the bartender is like "a piece of silk/ tacked over a doorway leading/ nowhere". There is a grotesque carnival, as in a Fellini film, involving tap dancing midgets playing with tennis balls, and a weird dialogué with a foul-mouthed woman on a bar-stool. Another couple enters, a man with "a head like a pumpkin", a woman whose face "looked like a seal's" wearing a hat with a large wristwatch fastened to it.[36] But this is hardly a revelation of the horrors that lurk beneath the surface of ordinary life, just light satire. In Bukowski's early phase, his speakers are isolated in their world, and surreal language is used as a kind of shorthand for their alienation. In his maturity, Bukowski uses it as just one of his weapons, and usually for comedy. Aptly, since Surrealism itself can now be regarded, as the critic John Osborne's *bon mot* put it, as

"Modernism laughing at itself".[37]

Modernism contributes to Bukowski's poetic structures, and Surrealism can be found infiltrating his language at times. Which brings us to factors linking Bukowski to the Beats. But the likes of Corso, Ferlinghetti, and especially Allen Ginsberg, are far more adept at coming up with genuinely surreal imagery:

the crack of doom on the hydrogen jukebox...
who disappeared into the volcanoes of Mexico leaving
behind nothing
but the shadow of dungarees and the lava and ash of
poetry
scattered in fireplace Chicago[38]

Another common element was their veneration for certain dissident figures. As a general principle within the avant-garde, its internal 'politics' takes precedence over mainstream party politics. Thus the dissenting Jew Allen Ginsberg visited Céline, and later Ezra Pound in Venice - both convicted fascist collaborators - in their old age, and wanted their 'blessings'. But here is an immediate difference of approach, literally: Bukowski wasn't the type to seek his heroes out, uncomfortable even when visiting the hospitalised John Fante. Céline's major novels of the 1930s, *Journey to the End of the Night* (1932) and *Death on the Installment Plan* (1935), with their withering anti-bourgeois contempt and negative view of humanity's potential, are often deferred to by Bukowski. They helped form a kind of Existentialist-Beat mythology, namely that criminals, madmen, bums and whores, drug-addicts, live more 'authentically' than solid, tax-paying citizens. Bukowski echoes this in his works. In his life, of course, he was a solid tax paying citizen, as many of the Beats were not.

Bukowski's early characters feel estranged from the motivations of those around them. They brood in roominghouses behind pulled windowshades, "gassed or stoned/ or insulted by the days". In 'The day it rained at the Los Angeles County Museum' its speaker carries his anxiety around with him, aggressively keen to preserve his own inner space while inspecting "the propeller of an old monoplane".[39] He is conscious of the 'nausea' of existence, Sartre's *le Neant*, and Hemingway's *Najda*, the nothingness perceived as surrounding everyday life. For Bukowski, overcoming this is by action - drinking, sex, fighting, betting on horses - anything which heightens existence. His characters fight (as in the movie *Barfly*) in dark alleys behind bars. This embattled concept of existence is far less evident from the 1970s onwards. Céline's pessimistic recognition of a "universal sadness" in human existence is however one of Bukowski's most abiding themes; life as a continuing process of loss. Existentialism urged mankind not to waste precious and ever-diminishing days on God, but to live the fullest life possible between the parameters of birth and burial. Death is seen as an energiser of human activity, a contemplative spur for life.

Sex, eventual acceptance of humanity, the comedy of errors; all these lighten what one might portentously call Bukowski's existentialist ethos. He does not really follow Sartre or Camus in their ethical, intellectual, and politicised concepts, even if he jokily refers to them. Albert Camus, for example, is sent up in 'All right, so Camus had to give speeches to the academies and get his ass killed in a car-wreck' (*Chicago Review*,1970).[40] But neither does Bukowski go as far as Céline in denying validity to all human aspirations. Existentialism in Bukowski's work is stripped of its theoretical and intellectual ramifications, but forms a permanent underpinning of the ways in which his characters perceive the world.

It also supplies a link to the whole vexed question of Charles Bukowski and the Beats, who are clearly 'cousins' of a kind, but also antagonistic in certain ways. There is a connection through their mutual relation to European existentialism. John Clellon Holmes, a friend of Kerouac's, explained the term 'beat', and proposed it as a native American, non-theorised counterpart to existentialism. For whatever reason, Holmes largely omits Kerouac's further connotation of 'beat' as in jazz music. Beatitude, i.e. the search for spiritual enlightenment, was one aspect; another was that to be 'beat' also meant:

> not so much weariness, as rawness of the nerves; not so much being 'filled up to here', as being emptied out. It describes a state of mind from which all unessentials (sic) have been stripped, leaving it receptive to everything around it, but impatient with trivial obstructions. To be beat is to be at the bottom of your personality, looking up; to be existential in the Kierkegaard, rather than the Jean-Paul Sartre sense.[41]

Here Clellon Holmes identifies Beatness with the spiritual rather than the political dimensions of existentialism. He further claimed that the Beats were saying "don't talk to me about essence but show me what's happening". This last statement does relate to Bukowski: after all, he turned down a last chance to meet Jean-Paul Sartre when visiting Paris. By implication, Bukowski was also turning down theorised, intellectual and political approaches to literature; he preferred the subjective experience and individual witness to any notion of collectivity. This may account also for Bukowski's relative political quietism; he gave support during the 1960s to writers threatened by the authorities but never joined any marches. The Beats, by contrast, were social activists, often to be found involved with liberal causes, especially mid-1960s Civil Rights and anti-Vietnam War demonstrations, and latterly for gay rights.

'Bukowski and the Beats' is a subject already visited by numerous critics, and virtually another book in itself. Yet he seldom if ever featured in anthologies of Beat writing published during his lifetime. This was partly because he was never part of the in-group surrounding Ginsberg, and partly because, though older, he developed later than them. But he could and perhaps should have been included in retrospective Beat anthologies: many of his works exemplify Beat hallmarks of alienation, zany humour and disaffiliation from straight society. Moreover, Bukowski owed the Beats the inspiration to resume his writing career at all, after its 5 year publishing lapse from 1950-51. When Ginsberg, Kerouac, Snyder and others were being introduced by Rexroth at the Six Gallery in October 1955, Bukowski was just beginning, after his false start a decade earlier. He would certainly have heard about them, and he began publishing in little mags which sprang up to serve the Beat impulse during the late 1950s, notably Wallace Berman's *Semina*.

That Bukowski and the major Beat Generation writers enjoyed at best an uneasy relationship during their lifetimes is generally true. It depended: he disliked Kerouac's lyrical prose-poetry, and ignored Burroughs. But he was later on perfectly equable terms with Ginsberg and his poetry. As he informed Al Purdy in a letter dated 2 March 1965, "as a personality he works against me but as an artist he lays down a pretty good line".[42] They infrequently met, during the 1970s shared a reading platform at least once and, as Neeli Cherkovski records in *Whitman's Wild Children*, sometimes spoke on the telephone. He liked and then fell out with Gregory Corso, meeting him through the Webbs; and he recorded a ruefully admiring column about Neal Cassady's driving prowess for *Open City*. He was grateful to Ferlinghetti for providing an essential second string to his publishing bow, finding a home for those stories probably too strong for Black Sparrow. Among Bukowski's long-time friends were Jack Micheline, Harold Norse, and Neeli Cherkovski, all with personal and writing links to the Beats, who would have each supplied him with inside information on the Beat Generation.

And yet - the differences are perhaps more persuasive. Would Bukowski have sat up all night at a jazz club, or endorsed lifestyles of poverty, madness, mind-altering drugs (alcohol excepted), bisexuality, or regarded writing as a religious quest? Clearly not: he was both socially more conservative than they, and arguably more artistically radical. His work evolved over time, went through a stylistic evolution, whereas many of the Beats sprang nearly fully formed into prominence and stayed that way, endlessly repeating themselves. (Bukowski too went through years of self parody, but he did also have a great late phase, which none of the Beats really managed).

One of the energising forces in Beat writing, almost an essential, was love of jazz, bebop as practised by Charley Parker and Miles Davis. Bukowski occasionally says a good word for trad jazz, but his musical nirvana was found in the European romantic music of Beethoven, Brahms, Wagner and Mahler. His pleasures were 'square', essentially drink, women and the horses. And so, when Bukowski was referred to, usually by journalists, as "a late Beat Poet" or (worse) a "disciple" of the Beats, he objected. It may also have an element of the homophobic. Bukowski, despite his friendships with gays such as Harold Norse and Neeli Cherkovski, did not particularly want to be grouped with Ginsberg's friends and followers.

Certain critics have argued that Bukowski was 'truly beat' whereas many of the Beat Generation, some being conspicuous college dropouts from Harvard or Columbia, were really 'slumming'. Others have seen their opposition in class terms, Bukowski being the working man, the true proletarian. Bukowski's biographers have established that the latter was hardly the case. His German grandparents were solidly middle class, and certainly after the inheritance of a house from his unloved parents, the money from which went into a bank account, and his decade or so of employment in the Post Office, Bukowski was nowhere near skid row. His estate ended up being worth millions of dollars. By contrast, some of the fringe Beats, such as Bukowski's friend Jack Micheline, spent much of their lives in marginal circumstances or real poverty.

Bukowski referred slightingly to the Beats' sense of collectivity in his correspondence. He assured Jon Edgar Webb, however, that "the original Beats, as much as they were knocked, had the Idea. But they were flanked and overwhelmed by fakes, guys with nicely clipped beards, lonely hearts looking for free ass....Art can't operate in crowds" (1 October 1962). The divergences between them are clearly more than a matter of tastes; they had differing stances towards humanity. Bukowski was a loner, the Beats far more sociable. Photos very seldom show Bukowski with other writers; he is often standing solitarily in the kitchen of his East Hollywood bungalow, holding a bottle of beer. By contrast, think of the famous photo taken by Lisa Law in a San Francisco park in 1967, showing Allen Ginsberg exultant, arms stretched wide, during a 'Human Be-In', surrounded by laughing hippies.

But, as we have seen, his works certainly share some roots, and artistic ideology with the Beats. They tend to defer to children's innocence (cf. the numerous poems about his young daughter), or to the wisdom of madmen and other social outsiders (cf. 'The wild'). More importantly, they also share ideals about 'spontaneity' of composition, what Ginsberg, paraphrasing Kerouac, called "First thought, best thought". As the hostile conservative critic Norman Podhoretz defined it in 1960, "strictly speaking, spontaneity is a quality of feeling, not of writing: when we call a piece of writing spontaneous, we are registering our impression that the author hit upon the right words without sweating, that no 'art' and no calculation entered into the picture, that his feelings seem to have sprouted a tongue at the moment of composition".[43]

When Bukowski's poems really work, that is precisely the impression they succeed in conveying. His editors over the years have greatly assisted Bukowski; his great impact would hardly have been achieved without them, and their more conventional grasp of spelling and grammar. By Jon Edgar Webb's account during 1965, Bukowski typed his poems "straight out on the typewriter without rewriting....He doesn't even make a carbon".[44] The poems were then edited by Webb for spelling, grammar, and the occasional disputed word. More generally, over-reliance on autobiographical spontaneity is responsible for the record-breaking amounts of dross produced by Bukowski and the Beats when not on top form. True spontaneity only operates in Bukowski's correspondence, as Seamus Cooney, editor of the letters for Black Sparrow, has pointed out. The letters are (in the originals) fluid, emotive, scabrously funny and sometimes - notably to Doug Blazek - move into verse. As Cooney puts it, "The Bukowski letter...has something in common with the 'spontaneous prose' described by Kerouac in 1957 [in 'Essentials of Spontaneous Prose']....a kind of performance art, an improvisation [like]...a jazz soloist. The mood of the moment...is the essential subject matter".[45]

His poems are another matter. Contrary to his public statements and the general impression he liked to give, Bukowski's poems are far more than spontaneous. Certainly as published by Black Sparrow they were usually revised documents, products of Bukowski's second thoughts. Compare magazine texts of early poems and the texts as reprinted by Black Sparrow. There are frequent, at times significant - and sometimes insignificant - differences. Bukowski depended on his editors. All of his editors seem to have suggested changes in poems to Bukowski, with the possible exception of Marvin Malone. By his own account, John Edgar Webb regularly agreed alterations with the author. And Bukowski leant heavily on John Martin's expertise, and willingness to file everything sent to him: "[I] hope you'll keep filing my stuff for me....I have a rough draft which I sometimes keep and which I sometimes lose, and also many poems sent out are never heard from again" (25 August 1970). In a recent letter, Martin explained that "When Bukowski mailed off poems to little magazines in the 1960s and 1970s, he usually sent off a first version that was written just a day or two previous. Then before sending me a copy for our files, he would often 'clean up' that first version with future book publication in mind. Thus, many of the poems in books differ slightly from their original magazine publication. As a rule, the only revisions we would make would be to correct spelling and punctuation" (10 March 2000). This implies that Bukowski went in for self-censorship, at least so far as publication by Black Sparrow was concerned. (His prose works with City Lights are in general more extreme and sexually explicit). On at least a couple of occasions correspondence shows him asking Martin to destroy or disregard poems too harsh on individuals, and that Bukowski did not wish to offend.

This business of spontaneity and revision has consequences for his published works. The most significant volume in this regard to the changes made, compared with original magazine texts, is *The Roominghouse Madrigals* (1988). It would be tedious to list the alterations: suffice to say that the changes are often rhythmically for the worse, and sometimes alter the tone. Words and lines have been added or subtracted. These revisions generally 'smooth out' the roughnesses, or cut out obscenities, as in the *Olé* poems first sent to Doug Blazek. Bukowski states in the introduction to the volume that "The poems were sent out [to magazines] as written on first impulse, no line or word changes. I never revised or retyped. To eliminate an error, I would simply go over it thus: ########".[46]

Book versus magazine publication were thus slightly different things in Bukowski's mind. He had no real concept of the integrity of a 'final' text, trusting his editors to print what they saw best. But as regards the contents of a collection such as *Roominghouse*, there are definite losses. Some titles have been altered; slang and swear words are omitted; 'speech' indicators are in general regularised ("you" for "ya"), and there are some changes to syntax. To state the obvious, individual words do matter in a poem. Bukowski touched upon the sensitive importance of a particular word in a letter to J.W. Corrington (12 January 1962). He discusses Corrington's use of the word 'nigger' (Corrington himself being a Southerner, to whom the word would have been normalised). "I had the same trouble with the poem 'On a night you don't sleep' (see *Flower, Fist and Bestial Wail*) and I had to go with nigger because that is what he was....I thought if I put 'negro' then I am a coward". The word in the 1988 reprint reads: "negro", itself now an unacceptable term of course. To take a less-charged instance: the first line of 'Another academy' was for years, as recorded on taped readings, "How they can go on" (i.e. what endurance these bums have). By its publication in *Mockingbird Wish Me Luck* (1972) it had become "How can they go on" (i.e. why are they doing it). The poem contrasts down and outs in Hollywood with the bums of New York, who drink anti-freeze in the Winter, get warm and "graceful" for a moment, and then die. In the book's version this word is "grateful", clearly a more prosaic meaning.

To return to the Beats and Bukowski: they both espouse disaffiliation from the status quo in art and life - this was, as Kenneth Rexroth put it, the 'art' of the Beat Generation. Rexroth's 1957 essay pinpointed this state of 'revolt' among the young avant-garde, against the New Critics and their literary followers. They shared social/ political experience of America: a youth during the Depression, war, coming to maturity during the Cold War, McCarthyism, and social conformity engendered by the 1950s consumer boom. 'Howl' was essentially a 'Song of Myself' to wake up the deadening Eisenhower years, its address being about 'my generation'. Could Bukowski have written in such an ecstatic and public mode? No - and he presumed only to ever speak out of his own experience and on behalf of himself. Just as he lacked a concept of social change, and of the necessary collectivity, so Bukowski lacked a vision of spiritual change.

Then think of those stylistic opposites: the lyrical, prolix Kerouac and the terse, hard-bitten Bukowski. In print, Bukowski showed scant respect. For instance, two of the sections in 'Voices', in *Burning in Water*..., written around 1972-3, satirise Kerouac (a "bad writer") and Burroughs (seen as aridly pretentious).[47] Other poems, such as 'Tarot', an account of meeting Gregory Corso ("a very fine sort")[48], are warily positive about the man and steer clear of saying anything about the works. Yet there are early Bukowski poems which could easily have been written by Corso: 'A nice day', 'Sunflower', 'All-yellow flowers', for instance, all evidence for the Beats' general influence on him at that stage.

A 1974 interview with Gary Snyder observed that "the original meeting, association, comradeship of Allen [Ginsberg], myself, Michael McClure, Lawrence Ferlinghetti, Philip Whalen...Lew Welch...Gregory Corso did embody a criticism and a vision which we shared in various ways, and then we went our own ways for many years".[49] Curiously, Snyder omits his friend Jack Kerouac. But his use of the words 'criticism' and 'vision' signals that they were key concepts for the Beats. Charles Bukowski, unlike Ginsberg, was never trying to sell ideas, or influence people. (Though he did). He may share that psychological extremity which hallmarks truly 'beat' writing, their criticism of academia and mainstream society, their indulgence towards madmen or children, even their Whitmanic gesture towards those on the social margins. But crucially he does not share the 'vision', nor their exuberant, high-flown performances.

In retrospect, Bukowski's badmouthing of the Beats can be seen for what it was. He did tend to attack those whom he owed something to. Early jealousy of their fame, and occasional homophobia, gave way to more relaxed attitudes in his maturity. His statements were in keeping with an endemic distrust of anything collective, from politics to poetry. He equally disparaged the Black Mountaineers and the New York School poets. Bukowski was in some ways more socially conformist than the Beats - simply by maintaining a regular job at the Post Office for over a decade. But he was never likely to found or join an alternative kind of academy, still less become a teacher at the Buddhist Naropa Institute in Boulder, Colorado, the 'Jack Kerouac School of Disembodied Poetics'. By a delicious irony, however, the irreligious Bukowski was buried to the chants of Buddhist monks.

Bukowski's characters, which include 'himself', are sometimes *in extremis*, sometimes whimsically anecdotal, continually restating their dislocation, and existential alienation. They have a full experience of being (dead) beat. But as the critic James Campbell observed, while Kerouac's and Bukowski's characters have in common "a feeling and experience of rejection", the latter's "do not seek to compensate that rejection by recourse to a spiritual philosophy".[50] Bukowski found the transcendent only ever located in bottles. He was once again close to Hemingway, in a refusal to countenance anything he cannot, as it were, eat, drink, or fuck.

As with Modernism and its subsidiary Surrealism, Bukowski proved an acquisitive talent. He took just what he needed and satirised the rest. The Beats themselves, for all their emphasis on anarchic individualism, in effect operated as a literary group, with Ginsberg as kingpin and cheerleader. They were a self-supporting Whitmanic brotherhood. Bukowski never could be part of that: as he told Jon Webb, art does not operate in crowds. Besides, he himself wanted to be kingpin. But posthumously at least, he has been co-opted as a member of the Beat Generation, and his work certainly stands comparison with the best of theirs. Bukowski does not have any single poem or novel as 'great' and culturally pervasive as 'Howl' or 'On the Road'. But his eventual *Selected Poems* will be far more impressive than any of the Beats except perhaps Ginsberg. Moreover, I would contend that Bukowski's poems seem far less dated than theirs. The Beats speak of a now historical era, the Cold War and its aftermath. A final observation: Bukowski and the Beats grew to resemble their adoptive cities of Los Angeles and San Francisco. One a haven for loners, the other with a cosmopolitan sociability and a cooler climate. Situated on the same coast, they are 400 miles apart, and - earthquakes permitting - always will be.

Artwork by David Hernandez

Chapter 5

Three Essential Collections

The Days Run Away Like Wild Horses Over the Hills
Love is a Dog From Hell
The Last Night of the Earth Poems

Every Bukowski fan will have their own personal favourites among his numerous poetry volumes: these are mine. They seem to me to be simply the best, the most entertaining as well as profound. The Loujon *Crucifix in a Deathhand* (1965) is also a great collection, and has the added attraction of marvellous production and artwork. Most of it is included in the early selected poems *Burning in Water, Drowning in Flame* (1974), but it is not available in entirety except via rare book dealers. Any of these collections would introduce new readers to Bukowski's virtues, vices, and aggrandizing manner. Collectively they illustrate the two types among his Black Sparrow books. Some are selections reprinting earlier work; relatively few were developed as integrated wholes.

The hammered-home words in Bukowski's poems would remain the same even if 'Charles Bukowski' was the pseudonym of a little old lady with a rich fantasy life. But would they have the same impact? Certainly not - for most readers, and certainly for the fans, his poems need their author standing behind them, and standing by his words. Their contents, the lack of inhibition, all go together with Bukowski's posture as a rugged, big city individual concerned with preserving personal integrity in the face of an indifferent or hostile world. Bukowski's poems are artefacts, stories - which may deny their fictional, rhetorical status, but cannot escape it. Bukowski's work is deeply personal, but by no means always autobiographical. To take one simple example: when Bukowski writes "I have lived in England/ and I have lived in hell...", this is no reportage. He never did come to England. I was once excited to read an advert in *Time Out*, circa 1980, 'Charles Bukowski at the ICA' [Institute of Contemporary Arts] in London, but it was cancelled.

Another early poem begins: "I found a loose slab outside the icecream store,/ tossed it aside and began to dig...", and goes on to tell a tall tale ('The best way to get famous is to run away').[1] Much of his work is sheer storytelling, fantasy, enjoyable irrespective of whether anything described actually happened. However, many incidents and characters within the books are certainly based around real people and events, reflecting on his life and times. Reading pleasure is deepened by knowing something of this personal background, and his published correspondence is well worth reading alongside the poems.

Each of these three collections has their own special characteristics. *The Days Run Away...* is a romantic, elegiac compilation of mainly early works, ending in the radical/ hippy circles of the late 1960s. *Love is a Dog...* is the torrid almost-diary of a late-blooming Don Juan discovering his sex appeal and increasing notoriety; explicit and funny. *The Last Night...* puts the reader on the shoulder of a man staring at a computer screen for the first time, and at the prospect of his own extinction. It tells us about the dimming of the creative passion by illness and encroaching death, but is itself defiant creativity. Each is very different, full of compelling - and some great - works. These are at least some of Bukowski's Greatest Hits, the nucleus of any future *Selected Poems*.

THE DAYS RUN AWAY LIKE WILD HORSES OVER THE HILLS (1969)

A highly significant book in his career, it was directly linked to the start of Bukowski's life as a full-time writer, and also provides a retrospective of his career up to then. Romantic, exuberant, by turns sentimental and satirical, it is filled with sidelights on Bukowski's lovers, friends, small press associates, and ends with poems about his beloved young daughter Marina. Published by Black Sparrow on 30 December 1969, it was being prepared for publication as his years as an employee of the Post Office were thankfully coming to an end. Bukowski actually gave his first public reading, at 'The Bridge', a bookstore off Hollywood Boulevard, on 19 December of that year, using galley proofs of the book.

Largely compiled from his early chapbooks, it was assembled with the assistance of Sanford Dorbin, the librarian at Santa Barbara who had just completed *A Bibliography of Charles Bukowski* for Black Sparrow. While a number of poems, particularly towards the final pages, date from 1968-69, the majority were originally published in magazines between 1956 and 1964. (Original publishers are henceforward given in brackets). While the title poem is listless and episodic, the title has established itself as an elegiac phrase of some resonance. The phrase is, for instance, carved into a stone tablet on the California coast near San Francisco, and been used in newspaper headlines. The book, uniquely for Black Sparrow, features the author photo on the back cover - a set-up shot by Sam Cherry (father of biographer Neeli) showing Bukowski clinging rather insecurely to a train carriage, in the pose of a 1930s freight-hopping hobo. Its dedication is 'for Jane'; that is Jane Cooney Baker (1910-1962). She was the great love of Bukowski's life, his major muse, who died - of cancer and cirrhosis of the liver, according to biographer Howard Sounes - on 22 January 1962, aged 51. At the heart of the book is the sequence of poems written for his lover, following the grieving process from numbed realisation of her death to the funeral and the pain of memories.

Given that the collection mainly consists of early work, there are some inelegant romantic lyrics. There are apprentice efforts such as 'These things' (*Quixote*, 1956) or 'All-yellow flowers' (*Compass Review*, 1958). The latter rather obliquely describes observing a dead body being taken away - perhaps his father - and yearning feelings about a girl with golden hair: "it's autumn, it's trees, it's telephone wires,/ and she sings some song I can't understand, some High Mass/ of life". (Bukowski was himself a very lapsed Catholic, a status he shared with John Fante, though he doesn't make much of this). The poem does have one intriguing reference, to 'Arturo' - no doubt 'Arturo Bandini', hero of Fante's novels. Characteristically, the book revolves around women. Many of these are unnamed, unspecified, but always being observed, their sexual power being felt by male narrators:

girl in shorts, biting your nails, revolving your ass,
the boys are looking at you -
                      you hold more, it seems,
than Gauguin or Brahma or Balzac
('Plea to a passing maid')

Another generalised physically spectacular woman is conjured up in '18 cars full of men thinking of what could have been' (*Southern Poetry Review*, 1965). She is:

all rump and breast and dizziness running
across the street.

she was as sexy as a
green and drunken antelope and...
the girl was built
all around all around...

But many of the women are identifiable. 'Down by the wings', for example, refers to the New Orleans poet and painter Kay Johnson (a.k.a. kaja), a long-time resident of the 'Beat Hotel' in Paris. Other poems are about important women in Bukowski's life: Barbara Frye ('My wife the painter'), Frances Smith ('Poetess' - "for S.S.V." - she used the pseudonym S.S. Veri) and their infant daughter Marina ('birth', 'Kaakaa and other immolations'). Pre-eminently, there are five poems about Jane written between 1962 and 1965, grouped together. Strangely, the poem immediately before them, 'I taste the ashes of your death' (*Nomad*, 1959), seems connected to the sequence, though because of its publication date cannot be about her. (It may relate to either of his parents, who both died in the late 1950s). The poems about his former lover are 'For Jane: with all the love I had, which was not enough -', 'Uruguay or hell', 'Notice', and 'for Jane'. The impact of her death is alluded to elsewhere in the book, in "I thought of ships, of armies, hanging on...', "the woman who had given me these fish/ was now dead 6 months".

...I even have her voice on tape,
and she speaks some evenings...
a photo and a piece of tape
is not much, I have learned late
('Remains')

The Jane poems describe the emotional cycle of feeling, from numbness at her death ("I call God a liar"), to the funeral, and depressed memories. Some, written years after the event, are still fairly raw; others are calmer:

in this room
the hours of love
still make shadows...

I kneel in the nights
before tigers
that will not let me be.

One of the Jane poems, 'Notice', incidentally confirms Bukowski's early reading of W.H. Auden. It is strongly reminiscent of Auden's lyric

'Stop All the Clocks', published in 1936, which was given wide currency by being read out in the film *Four Weddings and a Funeral*.

Stop all the clocks, cut off the telephone,
Prevent the dog from barking with a juicy bone,
Silence the pianos and with muffled drum
Bring out the coffin, let the mourners come.

Let aeroplanes circle moaning overhead
Scribbling on the sky the message He is Dead...
My noon, my midnight, my talk, my song;
I thought that love would last for ever; I was wrong.[2]

Bukowski's poem is a much cruder free verse rendition, ending:

take the lavender kisses from my night,
put the symphonies out on the streets
like beggars,
get the nails ready...
burn the enthralling paintings,
piss on the dawn,
my love
is dead.

Bukowski's early speakers approximate to the same type: they are alienated loners, detached observers of humanity, cynical about the actions of men and voyeuristic about women. Sometimes they are revealed as artists, relishing their estrangement from the 'beastly bourgeois'. In 'What seems to be the trouble, gentleman?' (*Satis*, 1962), the speaker is a tough-guy who slaps "a screaming chippy" around, uses other slangy idioms (ass, broad, god damned), and is at home with dubious women and classical music. He has on

the 2nd movement of Brahms' First Symphony
and had my hand halfway up the ass
of a broad old enough to be my grandmother

He is used to "the fuzz" banging on his roominghouse door. Three people are attacked within the poem, including the narrator. It would be stretching things to call it a rebuke for police brutality, or an endorsement of male domestic violence; the tone is too flippant. What it enacts is opposition to bourgeois morality, the values of solid citizens. The next morning, he tells us, he is in a prison ward, hardly worried about being late for work. This piece tells more about Bukowski's poetic identity than about disputatious relations between men and women. This is a poet of the Lower Depths, proclaiming his marginality, familiar with the Classics as with brassy barstool hustlers. He is, like a latter-day Whitman, no stander-aside from humanity's seamier side.

Even by this early stage, Bukowski was intent upon forming a distinctive self-image in reader's minds, encouraging readings of his work as unmediated autobiography. He very often makes these gestures explicit, naming their speaker or main characters. In later career Bukowski shows much greater willingness to enter the text as 'Henry Chinaski' - hero of his novels - or 'himself'. The poems themselves are meant to be seen as stemming from the author's life in a direct, almost diary-like way. Early on Bukowski's imagination is most free-ranging when the speaker is not specifically named, or tied to the author, but acts simply as a storyteller. In some of his best works, even the sex of the narrator is unclear; in perhaps one-third of these early poems there is no indication of gender.

Yet the easy assumption that Bukowski, or his later persona 'Chinaski', is, or pretends to be, the narrator of all his poems is demonstrably false. In *The Days Run Away*... Bukowski uses a range of identifiable personae, voices that are distinctly not that of an urban author. Some are in the voice of a hobo or daylabourer, as in the bitter 'Poem for personnel managers', or the comical 'Scene in a tent outside the cotton fields of Bakersfield'. Bukowski thereby presents a range of bottom-view perspectives on art, life and society. His personae include the female masks of bar-stool floozy ('Did I ever tell you?') and landlady ('When Hugo Wolf went mad'). Other voices adopted are as cartoon cowboy ('What a man I was'), boxer ('The loser'), Sunday painter ('Peace'), flop-house manager ('The moment of truth'), football coach ('Yellow') and jailbird ('Riot'). Whatever Bukowski's motivations, the use of personae - a device used in much more mannered ways by Pound, Eliot, Bunting, Yeats, Robert Browning and further back - also indicates his early relative literariness.

One of the first poems published in his resumed career, 'Did I ever tell you?' (Harlequin, 1957), recounts the many men in a woman's past. Bukowski may well have had Jane Cooney Baker in mind when writing this monologue. Her experiences range over a garrulous seven and a half pages, too long to sustain interest, even with her many wisecracks and comic asides:

Ralph was the only one, I think,
who ever loved me,
but he didn't appreciate the finer
things:

> he thought that Van Gogh used to pitch for
> Brooklyn and that George Sand played
> opposite Zsa Zsa Gabor

This is characteristic Bukowski: he habitually makes great play with culture-heroes, actors and actresses (the 19th Century woman novelist 'George Sand' a malapropism for the villainous smoothie George Sanders) placing them in the mouths of social outcasts, low-life types, sportsmen, relishing the comical incongruity. 'L. Beethoven, half-back', portrays the composer as a tough-talking football player. By doing so, Bukowski sends up the usual gap between high art and 'the man in the street', satirising both the public's ignorance and artistic pretentiousness. 'Peace' (*Quicksilver*, 1960) is told by a painter, whose activity outdoors is disturbed by uncomprehending members of the public (as is the even earlier 'I cannot stand tears'). Two hunters, probably poachers, out shooting come to look at his canvas, and criticise it. The angry painter tells them to go away and look at Picasso and Rembrandt, Klee and Gauguin, listen to a symphony by Mahler, and only then should they return.

> what the hell's wrong with
> him? the one guy
> said.
>
> he's nuts. they're all nuts,
> the other guy said. anyhow,
> I got my ten doves.
>
> me too, his buddy said, let's
> go home: we can have them
> in the pan
> by 2:30.

This is more a deflation of the artist's values than of the hunters'. After all, eating is even more fundamental than creativity. The persona as a painter enables him to satirise both sides. Further within the poem is an implied criticism, not of the artists named, but of advanced art's status within society, separated from most ordinary people, and beyond the educational grasp of a large sector. The painter urges the men to go away and let him get on with his art: this is the artist's position. But he also urges them to let their lives be enriched by art - as unlikely as that is.

Sporting personae, whether boxers, baseball players or racetrack punters, in Bukowski's world are almost invariably failures. This identification with losers is handled in a variety of ways. In 'Yellow'

(*Iconolatre*, 1966), spoken by a tough American football coach, he appears to be an overbearing advocate of the success-orientated ethos of the sport and, by implication, American society at large. The coach tells us about 'Seivers', a former star running back who has lost his nerve following an injury, and is now "gun shy as a/ squirrel in deer season". The coach can't stand to see a man "jaking it", (that is, cheating) lacking the guts to do battle again. Seivers tries to answer back, and the coach, advocate of collective macho values, punches him to the floor. (This was of course written well before America became the litigious society it now is. These days Seivers would simply hire a smart lawyer and sue for multi-millions). Seivers starts to cry. The coach's final remark is that "guys like Seivers" will end up washing dishes for a dollar per hour, "and that's just what they deserve".

Bukowski's portraits of masculinity are, however, never unambiguous. Through the coach in 'Yellow' he seems to endorse physical courage; it and economic success or failure are linked. American football functions as a microcosm of American society. Bukowski's use of the coach's voice may appear to endorse machismo. But American footballers are a male gang, a collective responding unthinkingly to orders. They are precisely the kind of conformists, essentially corporation men, that Bukowski is forever criticising. Here the persona enables him to have a side-swipe at the competition ethos of Capitalism, and its effects on individuals, though not from an ideological viewpoint. Bukowski is not advocating socialism or any other ism, simply taking a look at the human cost of the current system.

From the big winners of American football to the losers in the competition ethos of American society, in 'The moment of truth' (*Dare*, 1966). This is told by a skid row roominghouse manager in Detroit, one of whose residents has committed suicide by taking rat poison. His fellow bums mourn him. The manager's reflections are brutally cynical about the value of human lives at the bottom of the economic heap:

...and I told them: "all right, all you monkeys
clear the god damned halls! you hurt my eyesight!"...
you should have seen the rest of them disappear:
death doesn't matter a damn when you need a place to sleep.

The manager regards the pathos of Benny the Dip's plea as just another con-story: clearly a likely scenario. Human feelings are outweighed by their concern for survival. Putting these views about the down-and-outs into the mouth of a worldly wise manager again makes them ambiguous. This is no call for overturning the system, however: the bums, as with the daylabourers in 'Poem for personnel managers' are resigned to their lot. The poem reinforces mythologising of skid row, the place where all illusions about existence are stripped away, where even basic humanity, sympathy for the deaths of others, is emptied of meaning. In one sense, the last thing that one finds on skid row is the truth. Many can only bear to look at the truth of their existence - as we all do at times - through the bottom of a beer or wine bottle. The man stretched out on the pavement or in the shopping arcade may be a victim of the economic set-up, but he is no rebel and no philosopher. He can't afford to be.

Bukowski's narrators are constructed by the text, of course, and not the other way around. In later volumes, and ever more markedly, there is a continuity of the speaker's identity from poem to poem in such a way that the books seem to stem from the life of their creator-narrator rather than being detached artworks. This is part of Bukowski's progressive dropping of literary devices. He is unmatched at giving the impression of autobiographical immediacy. Further, Bukowski's texts are designed to appear to have been 'spoken'. This is true of classic American literature, from *Moby Dick* to *Huckleberry Finn*. Bukowski's poems include many colloquialisms, slang terms, vernacular idioms, obscenities, malapropisms, ungrammatical constructions, and aposiopesis [sudden breaking-off in speech] - all attributes of common talk usually excised from written texts. Such storytelling tactics obscure the most obvious aspect of literature - that it has been written. Though his poems succeed in giving the imprint of American speech, they are - thankfully - nowhere near a transcription of actual talk, which is by its nature highly repetitive, digressive and unstructured. Wordsworth aimed at using "a selection of the language actually used by men". "Heightened speech" was Yeats' definition of poetry. In a U.S. context, think of Whitman, Carlos Williams, or Allen Ginsberg. Then think of how much closer to the American vernacular Bukowski's poems are than theirs. It indicates his Romantic roots as a writer, and a nationalist American literary heritage. Bukowski uses the energy of spoken language. All his strategies are designed to give an air of spoken ease rather than educated discourse and literariness.

Bukowski early on realised that the traditional poetic tools of what Eliot termed 'the Auditory Imagination' - regular rhyming and rhythmic effects, assonance, and alliteration - were alien to his talents and purposes as a writer. Some examples can be found while he was still experimenting and had not yet found confidence in his own stylistic freedoms. 'I taste the ashes of your death' and 'Hooray say the roses' for instance use assonance and internal rhymes, but one would be hard-pressed to find such effects being used after the mid-1960s. It would be unrewarding to read Bukowski for his delicacy of utterance or 'musical' qualities!

Instead of these literary devices, some of his traits were appropriated from popular culture: comedy techniques, undoubtedly imbibed from the movies and radio shows. Bukowski's poems often contrast 'unlike discourses', which have a long tradition in American comic writing, from Mark Twain to Woody Allen. These arise from the incongruity of two contradictory narrative modes. Louis D. Rubin, writing in the 1970s, argued that in this tradition, the "vernacular perspective, set forth in opposition to the cultural, the literary - is the approved American mode of humor". (Very often we find Bukowski following not usurping native traditions). Twain's humour frequently exploited collisions between the literary and the low-life, as when in *Huckleberry Finn* those strolling players, the Duke and Dauphin, travesty the "to be or not to be" speech in *Hamlet*. Other humourists who exploited this were Josh Billings, Don Marquis, Ring Lardner and James Thurber. Lardner was a Hemingway favourite, while Thurber was the man for Bukowski. His drawings, especially on Bukowski's correspondence, are crude but very Thurberesque, usually showing small men menaced by large women, birds or dogs.

There is precisely the same comedy of incongruity at work in the significantly-titled 'A Literary Discussion'. A boozy, randy bard is drinking at the home of pompous critic 'Markov' and his wife. The contrast is between word and action, between the verbose self-justifications of the critic and the poet's direct access to life.

I would rather, says Markov, entertain a ditch-digger or newsvendor
because they are kind enough
to observe the decencies
even though
they don't know
Rimbaud from rat poison.

my empty beercan rolls to the floor...

This familar put-down can be taken also as a comment on literature itself, which Bukowski time and again emphasises must have life in it, and not be merely word games. The poet says very little, only eight words, and these are addressed not to the critic but to his voluptuous wife:

I had one of her breasts out.
it was a monstrous
beautiful
thing.

Bukowski typically condemns rhetorical, 'poetic' flourishes, and endorses straight-talking. His comedies of unlike discourse reinforce the linguistic and cultural assumptions (or prejudices) on which his writings operate. They also tie in with his treatment of machismo, which is invoked, only to be sent up. Of course, comedy's success depends more upon good timing than good material. In structural terms, the comedian seeks to manage tension, so that when this is released, the audience's pleasure is maximised, and laughter results.

In *The Days Run Away...* there are numerous instances of the control of comic tensions: in humorous punchlines and deliberate anti-climaxes. In 'No grounding in the classics', on the narrator's couch sleeps "a wine-soaked whore" who has fallen asleep while "politely" listening to Beethoven's 9th Symphony. When she awakens,

just think, daddy, she said,
with your brains
you might be the first man
to copulate
on the moon.

Here, the generative force is built up to by a banal listing of ordinary details before a zany ending. The joke depends upon 'the street' confronting 'culture', her view of the (sugar) "daddy" compared to her usual clients. Again, these are street level perspectives on high art, and their comical collision. At this early stage, the identification of the narrator is with the persecuted artist, as in 'When Hugo Wolf went mad-' (*Epos*, 1959) which gives us his landlady's reductive view of the great German composer of *lieder*:

...that rotten son
of a
bitch has dummied up his brain, he's jacked-off
his last piece
of music and now I'll never get the rent...

The collection also contains some lengthy rambling narratives, which tell us about the author-narrator's anarchic life in the present - Bukowski later on does this very much better. One largely unremarked aspect of the book is its element of topical satire. 'The seminar' ("dedicated to my betters") is cast in the form of a diary by "Howard L. Peter, Univ. of L." attending a poetry Summer school. It is relevant to note that Bukowski's early critical advocate J.W. Corrington taught at the University of Louisiana in the 1960s, but by the end of the decade they had fallen out. More generally, the piece sends up Beat slogans and Olsonian 'Open Field' poetics, and the teachings of Allen Ginsberg and Robert Creeley. Bukowski and Creeley had a lifelong mutual antipathy; and he liked to refer to

Ginsberg, who was 6 years younger than himself, as "a nice old bore". Amazingly, Bukowski's published correspondence shows that years later, in 1981, Ginsberg offered him 2 weeks' teaching at the Buddhist Naropa Institute in Boulder, Colorado![3]

Continuing in the vein of satire, naive would-be radicals are debunked in 'The underground' (*Wormwood Review*, 1968), which is again a comedy of unlikeness, based loosely on Bukowski's *Open City* involvements. At a meeting called to discuss advertising as well as revolution, he finds himself experiencing what was known as the generation gap:

the girl next to me said,
"we ought to evacuate the city"...

I said, "I'd rather listen to Joseph Haydn"...

when I got back they were talking Revolution.
so here I was back in 1935 again,
only I was old and they were young...

A brief memoir by Michael C. Ford, editor of the 1970s magazine *Sunset Palms Motel*, 'I Met Hank in 1968' incidentally indicates the real event that the poem alludes to. Ford dates the meeting as taking place in October 1968, at the *Open City* office "practically in [L.A.] City College's backyard". Bukowski attended it by chance: he had come along to drop off his weekly column. It was a planning meeting for the disruption of the upcoming Democratic Party convention, and present were the then-radicals Jerry Rubin, Tom Hayden and Abbie Hoffman.[4]

The book does reflect the times that it was written in, at least in its final section. The continuation of the war in Vietnam is prominent. As a young man, Bukowski had avoided military service by being declared 4-f (i.e. psychologically unfit). He appeared in several anti-Vietnam War poetry anthologies, notably *This is Vietnam* (1968) edited by Walter Lowenfels the editor of *Mainstream*. 'On the fire suicides of the Buddhists' has an epigraph - itself a rarity in Bukowski's oeuvre - from Mme Nhu, about the motives of these anti-war protests. The sobriety and flatness of 'Communists' and 'Poem for the death of an American serviceman in Vietnam' indicate that his imagination was simply not engaged.

Politics in a more general sense is dealt with in 'Ivan the terrible'. It shows that Bukowski's inherently anarchic approach to politics could be liberating, subversive, and funny. It fully answers Whitman's plea that poetry should cheer up slaves and horrify despots. The despot that the work cuts down is not the tyrannical Russian tsar - who has been safely dead since 1584 - but Communist Party art policy in Russia. It opens with a banal recitation of Ivan's physical details, his acts of sadistic cruelty, such as might have been taken from an official history. A long thin progress down the page enables ironies to be savoured. The last 13 lines shift abruptly from past to present, lurching into the surprise end to such a development:

last summer
they removed his
skeleton
from the Arhangelsk Church
in the Kremlin
to make a
life-like
bust

now
he's almost done
and looks like
a 20th century
bus driver.

The hilarity of the clinching simile does not just satirise L.A. bus drivers. It makes a point against Soviet artistic doctrine (topical at least in 1965) and collectivising forces in general. The Soviets, enforcing the doctrine of 'Socialist Realism', have deliberately commissioned "a life-like bust" to make Ivan into a symbol, possibly to draw parallels between his uniting of Russian territories by force and their own. The eye of the poet has seen the ludicrous result of such a policy, that even the arch-individualist Ivan has been transformed into an ordinary Joe - a distortion, like Gerasimov's portraits of Stalin as the smiling protector of the Russian peasantry. The poem is not a defence of Ivan but of individualism itself, specifically the artist's freedom from having to toe the Party line. After all, the Russian avant-garde in the 1920s largely self-destructed under official patronage and political pressure.

The resolutely apolitical 'Footnote on the construction of the masses' (*Wormwood Review*, 1968) is, I would claim, is one of Bukowski's great short poems. Unusually regular in cadence, it has 'poetic' flourishes, recording the narrow confines of human lives with unsentimental clear-sightedness. It is didactic: people are young, or old, or in between, "and nothing else". These statements are counterpointed by fanciful imagery - flies wearing clothes, atom bombs crying - then restated, leading to a conclusion buttressed by internal rhymes:

the few who are different
are eliminated quickly enough
by the police, by their mothers, their
brothers, others; by
themselves.

all that's left is what you
see.

it's
hard.

Could Samuel Beckett or Philip Larkin have stated this negative view of humanity's potential any better? Certainly no barer or harder statement exists in their lexicon. All in all, *The Days Run Away...* is still a fresh reading experience, and remains one of Black Sparrow's best-sellers. It hits most of the chords from elegy to celebration, satire to sentiment. It encapsulates the 1960s, but resists datedness. With its publication, he moved from the private world of writing to a much more public career as a reader-performer. With this book, he really started to 'become' the Charles Bukowski of legend.

LOVE IS A DOG FROM HELL (1977)

There has been nothing in poetry like *Love is a Dog From Hell* since the Earl of Rochester was at his priapic, satirical peak in mid-17th Century England. This is the most liberated, outspoken, Dionysian, and sexually explicit of all Bukowski's collections - there is usually more 'bad language' than anatomical descriptiveness in his works. It has much material in common with *Women* (1978). The novel was completed just as this volume was being published. They are like two halves of the same work, with real-life characters appearing under differing names. *Love is a Dog From Hell* - a trademark melodramatic title - records half a decade of readings and love affairs. Most of the poems were written in the period 1975-76 when he was becoming successful, both in his career and love-life. Sex became a Bukowskian territory. In 1976, Bukowski was interviewed by *Hustler* magazine, one of two sex magazines - the other being *Oui* - that regularly published his stories. In 1977 he was interviewed by German *Playboy*.

His reading career also was, literally, taking off - he told a correspondent in May 1976 that he would be "flitting round the country" for most of the month. His standard fee then was $500 plus air fare and expenses. (It would later be considerably more). The collection's themes are *Carpe Diem*, and love on the run, relishing existence at its most freewheeling. A gargoyle stares from the front cover, a suitable image for this 20th Century Rake's Progress. It is also the despairing diary of a trapped man, an ageing roué. Sex here has no tragic consequences - certainly no horrible diseases - except occasional jealous rages and the inevitable end of love affairs. The writing is at times so palpable that it is like hearing the downstairs neighbours fucking, laughing, fighting, and then fucking again.

The book is very much of its time. The 1970s, in Western society, was a decade of excess and conflict, its sexual ethos being post-Pill and pre-AIDS. Having said that, the book already seems less explicit, more romantic, than it did at the time. Freud's concept of the male artist's motivations, striving for sexual as well as artistic success, seems to be borne out by this collection. Bukowski himself was in his prime, at the height of his bravado and attractiveness to women. Tall and large, with a leonine head of hair, he had an increasing income, increasing fame and notoriety. With a battered Volkswagen to drive, and liberated from a workaday routine, he was finally in his element.

Earlier feelings of alienation, childhood traumas, skid row perspectives on life, art and death have been banished. Retrospection is rare: the book records an anarchic, highly-sexed present life. There are continual sexual bouts, fights with women and between them, arguments and reconciliations: "here's a cock/ and here's a cunt/ and here's trouble" ('This then-'). At the heart of the book - once again - is a sequence of poems written for and about a particular woman. This is the section 'Scarlet', detailing Bukowski's real-life infatuation with a strikingly beautiful red-haired woman, Pamela Miller, a.k.a. 'Cupcakes', (reputedly so-called because of the shape of her breasts, a.k.a. 'Tammie' in *Women*). She was in reality a young mother, a former 'Miss Pussycat' of 1973, an 'exotic dancer' (that is, a stripper). She is depicted in both fictions, enticingly but unflatteringly, as a pill-popping part-time hooker. Though names are changed, virtually all the characters are based on people moving in Bukowski's orbit at the time, lightly fictionalised. Georgia Peckham-Krellner, a woman friend of 'Cupcakes'; his neighbours Brad and Tina Darby; and Linda King, his lover of the early 1970s.[5]

This was the first of Bukowski's truly large, capacious collections, well over 300 pages, and the zenith of his access to 'unacceptable' areas of the self. It contains numerous self-recordings of libido and unashamed bad behaviour. Masturbating in his car while watching a young woman; sexual interest in pubescent schoolgirls lolling on park benches, and even worse.

when I got back there was a letter from a

lady in Eureka. she said that she wanted me
to fuck her until she couldn't
walk anymore.

I stretched out and whacked-off
thinking about a little girl I had seen
on a red bicycle about a week ago.
('Waving and waving goodbye')

Love is a Dog... is a truly obsessional book, vehicle for a rampant ego, a man urgently making up for lost time, conscious of time running out. Yet it is also at times touched by love and feeling, emotional beyond the satisfaction of appetite. It is formally no orgy, being carefully organised into four sections. Bukowski's use of narrative is by now almost total. Few if any poems are identifiably lyrics. Authorial distancing has been laid aside - this book is presented as autobiography. (Though it is more profitably read as fiction).

The first section opens with a succession of worldly-wise views of sexually adventurous women; one-night stands with "bedroom damsels" and "goddesses" (oddly antique phrases, far from hippy jargon of 'groovy chicks' and 'babes'). The opener concerns a 32 year old 6ft tall blonde who usually prefers smooth "unscratched boys/ with faces like the bottoms/ of new saucers":

Sandra looks very good in
long gowns
Sandra could probably break
a man's heart

I hope she finds
one.
('Sandra')

The sex is not entirely cynical. There are tender episodes: "later we lay locked like human vines". But this is Bukowski's own Midsummer Night's Sex Comedy, with himself sometimes wearing asses' ears. Another flirtatious woman falls down inside her own sexual organs and vanishes:

it was like an alarm clock
dropping into the
Grand Canyon.
it banged and rattled and
rang and rang

but I could no longer
see or hear it.
('Sexpot')

In the next poem, he is energetically recovering from an affair that had "gone badly":

(I'm fucking the grave, I thought, I'm
bringing the dead back to life, marvelous
so marvelous
like eating cold olives at 3 a.m.
with half the town on fire)
I came.
('One of the hottest')

Bukowski's 1950s lover Jane - whose memory this extract may allude to - was in reality a decade older than he was. In this book all the women involved are younger, usually by decades. After a reading, in bed with an anonymous young woman, he remarks "it's like a party -/ two trapped/ idiots". So much for poetry groupies. (Are there any? Male poets in general lack sex appeal, being mostly middleaged and obsessional by the time they come to prominence. Poets run way behind even mediocre rock and reggae musicians when it comes to attracting women. There are exceptions of course, from Byron to Ted Hughes).

A persistent stylistic trait over the years is that Bukowski slips in a consciously 'poetic' line to counterpoint flat demotic description. This mellifluous line is often chopped up, as in 'Trapped': "she is a/ child/ and a mannequin/ and/ death". And he always notes the elegiac passage of time: "our marriage book, it/ says./ I look through it./ they lasted ten years./ they were young once..." ('The drill'). The collection almost entirely takes place in the fictional present, with memory - so pervasive in other collections, which grow increasingly retrospective from *Dangling in the Tournefortia* (1981) onwards - seldom intruding. There are some recollections: of living with "fat Marie" in New Orleans; and 'An almost made up poem', tenderly recalls a correspondence with the deceased painter and poet Kay Johnson.

But existence is for now, as Larkin put it, a quite unlosable game. 'The end of a short affair' is a jokey piece on current sexual attitudes, satirising the aftermath of an energetic sexual bout. The lady friend leaves, then calls him up:

the phone kept ringing.
I picked it up.
"hello?"

"I LOVE YOU!" she said.

"thanks", I said.

"is that all you've got
to say?"

"yes".

"eat shit" she said and
 hung up.

love dries up, I thought
as I walked back to the
bathroom, even faster
than sperm.

The punchline ends on the word "sperm": one can imagine this as a Lenny Bruce monologue, the words "shit" and "sperm" still carrying a minor frisson when sounded out loud. The build-up is long enough to carry the information needed, but short enough to escape boredom. The comedy also comes from the brevity of the responses, which deflate the woman's expectations of reciprocated 'lurve'. Bukowski also favours the deliberate anti-climax. One great example is 'Cold plums', whose first lengthy verse paragraph is an account of a banal monologue by a woman about a drapery shop, a "sad story" full of dull details, while the plums are shared in bed. The brief second paragraph shifts abruptly, as the unnamed woman shows herself not so dull after all:

Then she bent down and began sucking me off.
the windows were open and you could hear me
hollering all over the neighbourhood
at 5.30 in the evening.

But Bukowski is prone to over-use the device, as with punchlines. Far less effective is 'Rain or shine', which moves at its ending into fantasy, just to send up a then-current catchphrase. A couple, presumably tired of fucking, visit a zoo and see some bored, over-fed and lethargic vultures. They move onto the next cage:

a man is in there
sitting on the ground
eating

his own shit.
I recognize him as
our former mailman.
his favourite expression
had been:
"have a beautiful day".

that day, I did.

As a comedy device, punchlines and anti-climaxes have their limitations. Some of the real masters of American comedy, W.C. Fields or Phil Silvers, hardly ever used them, or if they did, tended to throw the punchline to a gag away. Rather than try to hit audiences with a knock-out blow, they preferred a relentless verbal assault containing running-gags, tall-tales, non-sequiturs, wisecracks, quick-fire quips, one-liners and fracturings of language and logic. Bukowski's finest comic narratives, pre-eminently 'Fire Station', are indeed written by a real comedian, with the whole range of devices being used. But there is no grand set piece comedy narrative in this book, which would detract from its diary-like intentions.

The sexual atmosphere of the book gets ever more riotous. Encounters are sparked off by readings, by phone calls, by women arriving on his doorstep. There are fights and jealous arguments. Oral sex and masturbation becomes as common as in, say, *Hustler* or *Oui*. But crucially - and this distinguishes these texts from pornography - these are rendered humorously. Bukowski's work is nowhere near as sexually extreme as the genre of 'erotica'/ pornography, not even of the well-written literary kind. (He was certainly no antecedent of Pat Califia, the lesbian pornographer of *Macho Sluts* fame). Titillation is generally absent from *Love Is a Dog From Hell*; there are too many grotesquely funny details.

it was sticking up there and we were both
looking at it.
"ah, come on," I said, "my girlfriend fucked
2 different guys this week and I'm trying to
get even."

...I want to WATCH while you beat that thing
OFF! I want to see it shoot JUICE!
('Trying to get even')

There is yet more bad behaviour. 'This poet' vomits into a grand piano before reading at a university. 'What they want' summons up a parade of artist-victims from Vallejo to Lorca, Pound to Artaud, sneering at the public as "dreary/ admirers of carnivals". Male bravado is presented as wisdom: "you've got to fuck a great many women/ beautiful women/ and write a few decent love poems...remember that there isn't a piece of ass/ in this world worth over $50/ (in 1977)" ('How to be a great writer'). 'The price' opens with its narrator drinking "15 dollar champagne" with "Pam and Georgia", presented as two hookers: "you want me, says Pam, "it/ will cost you a hundred". (An article in *Beat Scene* # 22 by photojournalist Joan Levine Gannij gives further information about the extraordinary Georgia Peckham-Krellner, describing a photo session at Bukowski's place during 1975). The 'price' is by implication marriage, domesticity; the narrator says that he cannot ever pay that "again". It counterpoints Bukowski's perennial diatribes about the intrinsic unfaithfulness of women. 'Pam' reappears shortly to take centre stage.

This third section, 'Scarlet', is in more senses than one the heart of the book. There are self-comparisons with Roman poet Catullus, presumably his poems inspired by equally fascinating and unfaithful 'Lesbia'. (Bukowski versions of Catullus would have been great to read, but he was never that kind of poet). It tells the man's story of the affair, from the first meeting, first sex, from rapture to rupture, with growing involvement on his part and frustration: "after the cock gets swallowed/ the heart follows". Various adventures, splits, reconciliations, occur; there is a trip to New York's Chelsea Hotel where Scarlet, totally high on drugs, nearly falls out of the window. Her needs are for money, pills, feeding her speed habit. She is presented as an archetype of her predatory sex: "and as that woman saves you/ she makes ready to/ destroy". ('Red up and down') Sex is indeed everywhere, but only as overcoming Scarlet's essential indifference.

I continued to rub the cunt.
"you want an apple?" I asked.
"sure," she said, "you got one?"
but I got to her-
she began to twist
then she rolled on her side...
and my fattened cock entered
into the miracle.
('Like a flower in the rain').

Scarlet is encapsulated by her slim appearance - "barefooted/ dressed casually/ except for huge ear rings/...all 112 pounds of her....200 years ago they would have burned her/ at the stake" ('Huge ear rings').

shark-mouth
grubby interior with an

almost perfect body,
long blazing hair...

she runs from man to man
offering endearments
('A killer')

Depression and disillusion follow. This pain is rendered, jokily, as part of a wider malaise: "that's what I get for kicking/ religion in the ass./ I should have kicked the redhead/ in the ass/..." ('Melancholia'). The end of the affair includes the inevitability of this: he is three decades older. He alludes to his wartime generation and national origins:

I feel like German troops
whipped by snow and the communists
walking bent
with newspapers stuffed into
worn boots...
('The retreat')

The sequence concludes pathetically with him leaving books and messages, near weeping, vainly searching for her, "a confused old man driving in the rain" ('I made a mistake'). However, the last section shows the poet-hero back in the sexual saddle, exorcising obsessions with the female. He observes schoolgirls on bus stop benches, "looking tired at 13 with their raspberry lipstick". In the middle of a reading, a woman announces that she wants to fuck him, and is taken away by security: "one can never be sure/ whether it's good poetry or/ bad acid" ('My groupie').

But there are other things in life than sex to be concerned with. '$$$$$$', a.k.a. 'I've always had trouble with money', opposes the bohemian life of bars and drinking to routinised work. (This is also the theme of the novels *Post Office* and *Factotum*, both products of the 1970s, but fictionalising earlier periods). Hard-up fellow-workers are progressively pissed-off by a devil-may-care attitude to money when he arrives for work, "forgets payday", and keeps finding cash about him. (Bukowski gives a hilarious reading of this poem on the 'Live in Hamburg' audio tape, recorded in May 1978).

"my God, I'm RICH...I don't even need
this job..."
...they believed I had
plotted the whole thing
just to make them

feel bad...

A brief visit from a fan of Henry Miller, who asks "how come you flog off/ so much?", brings a deadpan statement on the link between the sexual impulse and creativity:

it's the space, I said,
all that space between
poems and stories, it's
intolerable.
('Dead now')

In 'The place didn't look bad' further all-too-human details are added: after ejaculating, he is handed a rag "stiff with other men's sperm". He wipes off surreptitiously on the sheet, "as she put Mozart on". As ever, whoredom is romanticised, and he drops off his latest book of poems to his "favorite", imagining that they'll give the girls "some laughs":

they are whores without
souls
and they are magic
because they lie
about nothing.
('The girls at the green hotel')

The collection ends with one of Bukowski's great poems, a most moving piece, 'One for the shoeshine man'. It reads like a Whitman-like address to readers, and an acceptance of humanity, far from previous sneering. A self-penned obituary, written years before it was needed, it returns to the lyrically reiterative style of earlier years, with the same or similar constructions leading successive lines ("the balance...the luck...the miracle...the gift...the peace"). It captures an uplifted state of mind, "as you needle through traffic". Music, the handmaiden of pleasure, in all its forms, is celebrated: "anything that contains the original energy of/ joy". Even depression, "the deep blue low/ yourself flat upon yourself" is accepted, knowing "the lilting high that always follows". "Marilyn" [Monroe] and "Jackie" [Kennedy], "before they got her Harvard lover" are named; and Chopin "with his bag of Polish soil". Almost uniquely in Bukowski's work, it invokes the spiritual, "that which helps you believe/ in something else besides death". The central image is an old black man, Beau Jack, shining shoes - a symbol of past glories - a former boxer who has frittered his money, his life away, and accepted it all:

humming, breathing on the leather,
working the rag
looking up and saying:
"what the hell, I had it for a
while. that beats the
other".

In the last section he directly addresses readers: "the best of you/ I like more than you think". It ends with further acceptance of the "justice" of life. That Bukowski's most life-enhancing collection should end on an elegiac, valedictory note is perhaps appropriate. He lived and wrote prolifically for another 17 years, but never again would Bukowski be so positive, so concentrated in the present moment. His collections from *Dangling in the Tournefortia* (1981) onwards become increasingly retrospective and introverted. *Love is a Dog...* brings an extrovert phase in his life and work to a close. Within a year of its publication, Bukowski had started living with his future second wife, Linda Lee Beighle, in an apparently contented monogamy. A year or so after that he had given up doing readings, no longer wanting the attention or the groupies. But this collection shows how it was during the 1970s in America; great fun while it all lasted, before AIDS brought the sexual revolution crashing down.

THE LAST NIGHT OF THE EARTH POEMS (1992)

This was the last collection published during his lifetime, and his last great book, in my view. But it was also a new beginning, his first written on a computer, after a writing life of pounding a typewriter. The machine, a Christmas gift from his wife, greatly assisted this late flood of creativity. He confirmed as much to Fred Voss: "Thanks [for] the good words on LAST NIGHT poems. Almost all of them came off of the computer in 1991. I feel I peaked with these and now I could be going down the other side. We'll see". (uncollected letter, 1 May 1992) Though certain poems date from 1988, it was mostly written in a burst of energy after recovering from a serious illness, tuberculosis - initially diagnosed as pernicious anemia - that had struck him at the end of the 1980s. The book was squeezed in before the onset of his finally fatal leukaemia. It has the sombre pressure of a man looking into the abyss of non-existence, and with an effort of will revisiting his subject matters one last time. It also has unexpected moments of comedy. But in general it reviews and summarises a lifetime, which lies behind poems preoccupied with the past, and with his present existence as a financially successful writer - who at times feels he can no longer write. Melodramatic to the end, 'Death is smoking my cigars'.

At just over 400 pages, with 160 poems, it is the size of many a more cautious author's *Collected Poems*. The computer did indeed allow him even greater prolificness than usual. He had told Gerald Locklin, in a letter dated 1 May 1991, that he had written hundreds of poems since January, "a shitty gushing effusion". The book is an extended statement; endlessly reinterpreting memory and anticipating death. Contemplation and memory stands in place of the previously irreverent approaches to writers, literature and sex. Even the previously inspirations of his work no longer work:

I
no longer
read
I no longer
breed...
and when I see a sexpot on the street I
only see
trouble.
('Mugged')

The book's long sombre journey toward death does have a few flashes of the old iconoclast. 'The idiot' recalls being a child clasped to the bosom of kind schoolteacher Mrs Gredis "of the long silken/ legs", giving him "the most wonderful/ hard-ons/ of any eleven year old/ boy/ in the city of/ Los Angeles". 'Batting order' puts Bukowski's favourite writers into a baseball team - echoing 'L.Beethoven, half-back' from many years earlier. There is a bombastic letter from a filmmaker in the Hollywood area, with an idea for a movie about "an alcoholic Satan" leaving Hell to meet up with "old buddies" Richard Burton, Errol Flynn, Idi Amin - and Chinaski:

he needs to look up a mortal worthy of
drinking with him (YOU)
....drinking Mezcal and playing Russian
Roulette with Satan while 2 big fat chicks
are slapping each other with Salamis.
('An invitation')

This time, the invitation is declined. Bukowski's speakers have always claimed emotional honesty. He observes a rapidly declining creature, himself, almost constantly ill, "a 70 year old white man/ with a face like/ Frankenstein" ('Bright red car'). After five decades of typing and more than forty books and chapbooks, *The Last Night...* finds Bukowski well into his twilight phase of gruff philosophising: "the words will never/ truly come through for any of/ us" ('Sitting with the IBM'). A detached critic might feel that some of the poems could be 'improved' by judicious cutting, to reduce redundancy, even sentimentality. That judgement seems quibbling compared with the slow drama, the page by page consciousness of approaching death. Living with and living out his subject matters, Bukowski is simply not that fastidious. His stance remains open and inclusive, lineation a matter of chopped-up units, or "hard-driven lines". Some of the poems have long lines, reaching the edge of the page, and others have a skeletal one or two words per line. Reiteration is used, at times in a doom-laden Jeffers-like manner, as with 'In the bottom of the hour'.

The book opens with that typically L.A. experience, the traffic jam. It takes place on "that Harbor Freeway south through the downtown/ area....motionless behind a wall of red taillights". The experience of being stuck there, sucking in exhaust fumes, listening to the radio's world news, induces "a strange whirling" in the head. He imagines all the other drivers equally battling their compulsions, "as we wondered/ whose clutch was burning/ out?":

we were like some last, vast
final dinosaur
crawling feebly home somewhere,
somehow, maybe
to die.
('Jam')

The dinosaur image becomes a leitmotif throughout the book, persisting through to the quasi-prophetic 'Dinosauria, we', and the last poem, 'In the shadow of the rose' ("photographing your/ dinosaur dream"). Consciousness of impending extinction is striking home. This is not just an individual, but the death of a whole way of life - the concreting over of the orange groves of his youth, the burning of the L.A. Public Library, the sweeping away of familiar neighbourhoods. Faced with impending loss, the mind clutches hold of memory, becomes overwhelmingly retrospective. Following 'Jam', the narrator returns to his youth during the 1930s: L.A. City College, a lousy job, his early reading - Aldous Huxley, Knut Hamsun - while dividing time between the bars, libraries, and hock [pawn] shops.

Sex itself is now nostalgia, as in 'Before Aids': "so many high-heeled shoes/ under my bed/ it looked like a January/ Clearance Sale". A drunken threesome with two hard-bitten whores is summoned up ('Hunk of rock'). He returns to 'Dinner, 1933', the agonies of a meal with his parents. 'Those mornings' snapshots rats in New Orleans roominghouses. There are intermittent returns to the present, in tributes to his editor John Martin, and to a racetrack parking attendant. 'Poetry contest' is lightly satirical. Bukowski's correspondence shows, remarkably enough, that in 1992 he agreed to judge just such a contest, for *Explorations* (safely at long range; the magazine came from Alaska), partly at his wife's urging.[7]

The second section (of four) opens with an intimation of suicide ('Going out'), salutes to Jack London and Eugene O'Neill, and a put-down of Lorca. Then it is back to the past: the memory of trying to sell Christmas trees in a blizzard, ducking in and out of a bar ('No sale'). The past is a strangely familiar foreign country peopled by landladies, cowed fellow workers, women, his parents, and others "long gone along the way". Bukowski's customary elegizing approaches the 1930s Los Angeles of his youth, "when it was a short ride to the orange/ groves". Sentiment is set alongside remembered bitterness: "humanity/ you sick/ motherfucker" ('This'). Photographs of Hemingway and Céline are described, and he still spits contempt for the "soul-sucking" folk who approach at the racetrack or call on the telephone. In a riposte to Carl Sandburg, "it is The People, No/ then and now" ('A rejoinder').

He is "waiting for death/ like a cat/ that will jump on the/ bed", thinking about his wife finding his dead body ('Confession'). The poems discuss illness, creative - and sexual - impotence. He has treatment for a minor skin cancer. He is conscious of "the next to last line/ and then the last" ('In the bottom of the hour'). He experiences writer's block "after over/ 5 decades/ of typing". He has tuberculosis, "and the/ antibiotics dull the/ brain"...."I've got to do a/ Lazarus/ and I can't even/ shine/ my shoes" ('Upon this time').

I look like a man in a death camp.
I
am...

I sit in bed and wait for the whole thing to go
one way or the
other
('Ill')

The violent society around him impinges via the radio and television. Things are getting uglier, less free in many ways: "today they shot a guy who was/ selling balloons at the/ intersection" ('Balloons'). "Los Angeles has been burning for/ weeks" ('Heat wave'). The mind returns again to the 1930s, in 'We ain't got no money, honey, but we got rain', about the incessant rains of the Depression years, over eight and a half pages. A long-dead high school teacher is summoned up, a score settled. Then at last the depressed mood breaks, the tone changes into fantasy, to reinterpret his parents' perspective on his writing ambitions. 'Them and us' puts the heroic generation of American Modernism - Hemingway, Pound, 'Wally' Stevens, T.S. Eliot, 'Gertie', Faulkner - out on the front porch of the Bukowski family home, arguing together:

"they are talking garbage," said my
father, "they ought to get
jobs"...
"and he", my father pointed to me,
"wants to be like them!"

'Luck was not a lady' nods to a number in 'Guys and Dolls' - reputedly Bukowski's favourite musical. (References to the show are scattered throughout his works, notably at the end of 'Fire station' when the narrator gets into a game of darts with Harry the Horse, a name drawn from the Damon Runyon world). The star of the movie version, Marlon Brando, is also satirised early on in *The Last Night...*, as 'The greatest actor of our day'.

A final suite of poems opens with a vision of apocalypse, a quasi-prophecy of the destruction of Los Angeles by pollution and war. In another return to an earlier manner within his career, it is a Jeffers-like indictment of modern America:

we are born into this sorrowful deadliness...
the sun will not be seen and it will always be night...
rain will be the new gold...
the last few survivors will be overtaken by new and hideous diseases...
and there will be the most beautiful silence never heard...
('Dinosauria, we')

In an abrupt shift of tone, he then facetiously worries about his newly-acquired word processor:

will this machine finish me
where booze and women and poverty
have not?
('My first computer poem')

He contemplates 'The damnation of Buk', his life as a successful author, able to pay $30,000 in cash for a black BMW. The bartender at Musso's/ remembers me when/ I was/ in rags" ('Inactive volcano'). A septuagenarian existence has mellowed down to typing and drinking wine while listening to classical music, the company of his wife and cats; going to the racetrack, aware that he is running out of days. This realization has always fuelled Bukowski's work; it is here brought to its ultimate expression. It means occasional portentousness, as in the terminal connotations of the book's title. Essential locales remain, but transfigured by memory, the remembrance of times passed.

These late works constitute a poetry of flattened and direct statement, experience and language having been worn-down like teeth. They still reflect his reading style, with lines rushing down the page. But by this time, Bukowski had long since given up readings in public. The feeling throughout the book is that this is a narrative ending in death, as all stories must, according to Hemingway's *Death In The Afternoon*. Bukowski too views death as a suitable denouement to some of his works. Underlying these late poems is the sense that death, the one inevitability, is also a necessary termination: the task has been fulfilled. In this sense at least, *The Last Night...* is the culmination of his career. And as so often, Bukowski made a positive out of a negative. The collection gathered some of the best reviews of his writing life, especially from major critical publications. There was not much time left to him, but he continued despite the onset of leukaemia to submit poems to magazines, and to correspond with sympathetic editors, particularly William Packard of *New York Quarterly*. He produced *Pulp*, and a good deal of material to be issued posthumously, but this collection was his final integrated effort in poetry. A wonderfully intense communion with the self, it largely consists of monologues, and is deeply sunk in memory. It shows throughout Bukowski's ungodly durability and heroic sense of purpose. Only death could stop him writing.

Photograph of Gerald Locklin by Vanessa Locklin July, 1998

Chapter 6

At the Movies and the Racetrack

"We have our heroes, you know - John Dillinger, Humphrey Bogart, even Clark Gable....Cagney, yeah."
C.B. interview with Michael Andrews, 1980.

It would be an exaggeration to suggest that Bukowski spent most of his time when young watching movies or even, in his maturity, going to the racetrack. But these undoubtedly colour and flavour his work; they are where much of the 'action' takes place. Those early Hollywood movies are, I contend, the major source of his characters. And the racetrack is a quintessential Bukowski setting, one of those that best define his gritty poetic world. The latter functions for Bukowski as a grand metaphor for life and writing, as well as being where he juiced himself up with observation for his evening's writing tasks. The drama of the track - triumph and tragedy, winning and losing - also suggests the link between Hollywood Park and Hollywood. This is implicitly made throughout his works, which literally ended up with the Film Industry. His rhetoric was of course often otherwise, antagonistic to Hollywood values of sentimentality and crass commercialism. But occasionally he did give cinema back-handed compliments, as when in *Shakespeare Never Did This* he remarks that he prefers bad movies to art galleries. His early immersion in popular cinema was vital in his later fictional construction of male and female identity. Further, he takes much of his own persona of laconic, worldly-wise masculinity from role models at large in the cinema of the 1930s-40s. The movies and the track offer not just romance and escapism but, for Bukowski, lessons in and material for his writing. And together, they frame the whole much-vexed question of his perceived 'sexism', which is more culturally mediated, ambiguous and complex than it appears to be.

Indeed, probably the most commonly-expressed negative reaction to Bukowski's work concerns its apparently bull-headed sexism, and the raucously insulting terms frequently used within it to typify women. There is a persistent harping on female infidelity within his novels, stories and poems. Feminist reaction has often been scathing, when it has bothered to notice his work at all. Even his admirers have problems with this "waging war on women", to recall Alta's phrase. Bukowski was not as flamboyantly indifferent to feminist criticism as he liked to appear. He did, for instance, reply at length to a letter of complaint from Lynne Bronstein about one of his stories in the *L.A. Free Press*, responding with twelve numbered points. He wrote to the editor that the story "was about pretentiousness in art. The fact that the pretender had female organs had nothing to do with the story in total" (15 November 1974). He and his younger critics were to some extent talking at cross purposes. Bukowski's literary and sexual ethos was formed during the Depression and the War years; his attitudes appeared increasingly old-fashioned, patriarchal, and, yes, sexist, as times changed. The era in which Bukowski came to prominence, from the late 1960s onwards, was of course also that of the emergent Women's Liberation Movement, many of whose most radical figures were active in the same underground papers on the East and West Coasts. The clash of values between them was inevitable.

On the personal level, Bukowski himself was strongly supportive and 'in favour' of female artists. He married a little magazine editor, and was later deeply involved with the strongly pro-feminist poet-sculptor Linda King. He corresponded with and generally encouraged a range of women editors, writers and artists, from Sheri Martinelli to Ann Menebroker, Kay Johnson, Joan Jobe Smith, and many others. Almost all the most significant women he was involved with were connected with the arts. Yet the female characters in his early fictional world - the racetrack whores, brassy barstool hustlers, unfaithful lovers, rapacious landladies and the like - are undeniably an extremely reductive portrayal of one half of the human race. Here again, Bukowski's work evolved; his later collections move away from the hardened denizens of roominghouses and bars towards portraying a combative but essentially contented domestic life with wife and cats. Moreover, there is in general a far greater sympathetic dimensionality to Bukowski's portrayal of women than in, say, Henry Miller or Norman Mailer's works. There are numerous strong-minded women who are very far from downtrodden doormats. Even those supposed 'anti-female' insults are, by the contemporary standards of so-called 'gangsta' rappers, very mild indeed. Only some of Bukowski's work is based on social observation, the 'realism' that many fans and commentators have found. A major component in his work is American cultural mythology: and this comes out in the free play of larger-than-life male and female sexual stereotypes and archetypes.

Bukowski's humour, garnered from movies and popular radio shows during his youth, makes his work more divided, ambiguous and harder to pin down ideologically than other male authors who recycle machismo in literature. The function of this humour at times reinforces stereotypes, and at others gloriously explodes them. He is by turns subversive and reactionary. Thus, he does at times put down female artistic creativity, and makes demeaning connections to their sexuality. But his male chauvinism is by no means as monolithic as his detractors have maintained. Part of the 'problem' is terminology, and statements like "wait on the word. She's more faithful than any woman". Properly viewed, this says more about his devotion to writing than about women, who were essential to him. At other times an equation between women and writing is made; this male construction of poetry as 'female' is of course a traditional poetic trope. But he is apt to call poetry, a.k.a. the Muse, "a whore" who will leave and go to another man. This tendency is expressed in terms designed to wound real-life women:

you don't use words like
you use bodies.

the word won't betray.

this ribbon moving now
is more real than what
we had.
('Note upon the end of an affair')[1]

There is sexism in Bukowski. 'The price', for instance, makes a direct link between the economics of marriage and of whoredom. Worldly-wise cynicism about romantic love is pushed to humorously insulting extremes; as when the narrator of 'Ants' is asked for advice about 'the female' by a tearful friend -

listen, I said, meeting a bitch is an accident,
having one leave you is a basic reality,
be glad you're coming up against

basic reality...

Even more dubious is the way in which domestic violence is represented as just part of the natural order of things, as in the title of 'And the moon and the stars and the world'. This narrator takes late walks at night, and sees wives fighting off "their beer-maddened husbands", describing this as "good for the soul". Bukowski's early speakers are themselves by no means free of violence towards women. In 'And what seems to be the trouble, gentlemen?', there is a Bogart-like slap for a screaming "chippy". 'The colored birds' observes a couple in "a highrise apt. next door" and their ugly argument over two birds in a cage. The narrator hears screams, and concludes:

...he usually only beats her at
night. it takes a man to beat his wife night and
day. although he doesn't look like much
he's one of the few real men around
here.

The use of the ambiguous phrase 'real man' alerts us to an ironic dimension. Bukowski has plenty of poems which debunk male pretensions, sexual and otherwise. And unlike many contemporary novels and movies, there are no serial killers or stalkers in his fictional world. There is one poem only which comes to mind, treating the subject of ultimate male violence against women, ('He even looked like a nice guy'). With deadpan irony it details the cutting up of a woman's body by a psychopath.

Bukowski's best collections are structured around specific women. One of the most touching aspects of his treatment of women is that, sexism notwithstanding, throughout his career he wrote still-grieving poems about Jane Cooney Baker. Her spirit is actually summoned up best not in elegy but in comedy. Its finest fruit is in the highly sexist but also highly comical 'Fire station', which is worthy of Phil Silvers' Sgt. Bilko. Bukowski had a special affection for the novels of Carson McCullers; and he claimed to have once written a ten-page tribute to the blues-rock singer Janis Joplin, which he had to destroy because there was "too much love" in it. His poetry is full of admiring lines about women; and sensitive, not to say sentimental, tributes to movie actresses such as Marilyn Monroe, Jayne Mansfield, and Brigitte Bardot.

A poem in a 1987 collection even manages to insult women while significantly invoking their movie archetypes:

Being drunk at the typer beats being with any woman
I've ever seen or known or heard about

like
Joan of Arc, Cleopatra, Garbo, Harlow, M.M. or
any of the thousands that come and go on that
celluloid screen
('This')[2]

With the possible exception of Joan of Arc - portrayed by Ingrid Bergman in a mid-1940s production, who was publicly castigated for her marital infidelity - each of the names in this extract traded upon their sexuality. Bukowski's misogyny when returning obsessively to the subject of women's sexual unfaithfulness is at least partly cultural, derived from Americana. Is it any 'worse' than in, say, classic Country and Western songs like 'Your Cheatin' Heart' by Hank Williams? Or 'Ruby Don't Take Your Love to Town' by Kenny Rogers? Bukowski's explanation for using derogatory epithets like 'whore' was at times confused and confusing. He told one of his numerous female correspondents, Veryl Blatt, that "in a sense, I am a romantic; I mean when I call a woman a whore, I mean, in my language, a woman who loves one man...I also use 'whore' to mean 'death' which is also, in a sense, 'love' to me" (2 April 1966). He was seldom interested in debating ethics; he generally denied that artists had moral responsibilities for their activities at all. Bukowski told John William Corrington that "a man's either an artist or a flat tire and what he does need not answer to anything, I'd say, except the energy of his own creation" (1 February 1961).

More aspects of Bukowski's treatment of women emerge as we go to the movies, which permeated his artistic soul to a much greater extent than he ever admitted, emerging in a variety of ways. Of course, Bukowski's art is not 'cinematic' in technique - no tricksy cross-cutting or very few montage effects - but emotionally the movies contribute a good deal. Hollywood was for him his youth, and the first artist-hero he strongly identified with was John Fante's 'Arturo Bandini'. In the novel *Wait Until Spring, Bandini*, this headstrong would-be writer spends much time, as did the young Bukowski, enjoying "the drugged enchantments" of the movies. Fante, a screenwriter for many years, sometimes deliberately conflates the place Hollywood - a suburb of Los Angeles, with low-rent areas during the time that he himself lived there - with the unreal showbiz/movie world. Bukowski echoes this cynicism. In a poem in the *Transatlantic Review* (July 1998), 'The Hollywood hustle', these associations function as a given, as the speaker encounters successive bums trying to get money. A related but far more effective satire on Hollywood is 'Another academy', which alludes to the award of an Oscar to the dying John Wayne, only to subvert its illusory values.

Most commentators have taken Bukowski's statements at face value, stating that he "hated" the movies, or that "Bukowski very rarely went to movies" (Seamus Cooney). He himself assured Carl Weissner that "movies don't do it for me" (3 April 1978). But when one goes back to the context of Bukowski's impressionable early experiences of the movies, and the studio conditions that obtained then, a much qualified picture emerges. In the 1930s, a world without television or instant international communications, the motion picture industry had a massive cultural importance to the American viewing masses. Then as now, the fundamentals were sex appeal and action - or as studio boss Harry Cohn put it more colourfully, "it's cunt and horses". Movies involved dreams, aspirations, desires. Even the arch-critic Céline noted, in *Journey to the End of the Night*, celluloid dreams that "waft upwards in the darkness to join the mirages of silver light". The talkies were a recent phenomenon, making movie stars at once more human and seductive; popcorn had arrived as the cheap movie-snack of choice. While the Depression closed around one-third of picture houses, those that remained were ever more inventive in attracting customers.

Before the Hays Committee sanitised film products in the mid-1930s, the studios responded to the desperate times with some socially subversive movies, challenging smug assumptions of the day. Vibrant archetypes, Little Caesars and Blonde Bombshells, predated Snow White and later stereotyped celebrations of folksy small-town America. In violent gangster movies such as *The Public Enemy*, James Cagney's character observes that going to school meant "learning to be poor". The Marx Brothers spread the spirit of genuine anarchy; W.C. Fields sent up American family values; and stars such as Mae West, Jean Harlow and Marlene Dietrich brought an unprecedented level of sexual innuendo and provocation to the screen.[3] ('Betty Boop' was their cartoon contemporary; her small baby later replaced by a more moral small dog). Émigré directors such as Fritz Lang tackled explosive social issues in *Fury*. Bukowski will certainly have seen many of these movies, with and without his parents, and enjoyed - like the masses - a surrogate existence in which he spoke like Bogart, postured like Flynn, and had women who vamped like Dietrich. All this fantasy material is amply reflected in Bukowski's poems from the 1960s onwards - their characters, their dialogue - and becomes ever more noticeable as Bukowski nears the end and becomes subsumed in memory.

Bukowski himself - like Hemingway, another sceptic of the studios so far as his own works were concerned - ended up with many contacts within the film industry, and even made a cameo appearance in *Barfly*. While he insisted that "the old movies were best", his second wife Linda Lee Beighle, an enthusiastic film-goer, would have kept him in touch with current movies. She herself apparently performed a minor role in *Death Wish III*. Their friends such as the photographer Michael Montfort, the director Taylor Hackford, moved in movie circles. Sean Penn arranged for Hank and Linda to attend a number of premieres, as well as those made from his own works. References in his poems to then-current movies are surprisingly common. During his 1979 reading in Vancouver, Bukowski read an uncollected poem, 'The Alien', indicating that he had seen that sci-fi shocker, the first in the *Alien* movie trilogy. The title of 'Close encounters of another kind', about going to the movies with a girlfriend, clearly alludes to a Spielberg movie of the mid-1970s. His later portraits of domesticity even include watching, on television, bad movies: about Alexander the Great, or Japanese monsters, as in 'Fall out'.

Judging by his work, his 'favourite' movies were of the gangster genre, though he cites in interviews a whole gamut of films from the 1930s onwards, from the highly commercial to the eccentric. These ranged from Billy Wilder's *The Lost Weekend* (1945) starring Ray Milland, a portrait of a desperate alcoholic that summoned up a hazy romance with booze, and which won several Oscars; to David Lynch's enigmatic *Eraserhead* (1980). An often-expressed liking for the musical *Guys and Dolls* was surely reinforced by seeing the 1955 movie version starring Marlon Brando and Frank Sinatra. He sometimes discussed movies in his correspondence, such as Francois Truffaut's *The Man Who Loved Women*. As a speculation, he might have even have enjoyed Federico Fellini movies: his parade of male grotesques and pneumatic females surface in Bukowski's imagination, usually at the racetrack.

Bukowski lived most of his life on the doorsteps of Hollywood. His much-maligned parents, at least to judge from 'The movie critics', were keen film-goers during the Depression, typical of their times in escaping economic woes with a cheap dose of escapism. In 1935, for instance, a cinema ticket cost only 15 cents. Bukowski insisted - in keeping with his increasing tendency towards retrospection and nostalgia - that these, 'The old movies',

were best, the French F. Legion
every man with a bitch and the Arabs charging down
on white parade ponies....
And the ones with the boys flying around in the Spads
full of wire and one plat. blonde who seemed to symbolize
everything...[4]

In the posthumous collection *Betting On the Muse* (1996), it is more specifically 'The World War One movies' that "were best". It goes on to describe the aerial dogfights between Spads and Fokkers in them which thrilled "we kids". Further details from the experience of going to the movies in the 1930s are summoned up:

outside the movie theatres they displayed
parts of a Spad, a huge wing, a
propeller, and at night there was a
searchlight probing the skies...[5]

Another poem about aerial combat, cast as a childhood fantasy, is 'Dagwood and Blondie' - the title refers to newspaper cartoon characters of the 1930s-40s. French Foreign Legion movies, such as *Beau Geste* or *The Four Feathers*, were another favourite of his youth, and are represented in several poems. Clearly, watching movies marked his imagination. There are literally dozens of invocations scattered throughout his collections. Movie stars are used as a kind of shorthand for an entire vanished era. 'Lilies in my brain', for instance, alludes to Chaplin, Laurel and Hardy, Clara Bow, and "the rest". 'Drunk again, and wondering, wondering' has a quixotic line about curtains "like the/ sadness of an old Garbo film...". In 'The race', "you've aged like a punk in a movie" immediately brings to mind gangsters, perhaps *The Maltese Falcon* when Bogart tells one of the hoodlums that "you're taking the fall, punk". 'To hell and back' has a line "like the/ tough guys in the movies". An ironic revisitation of the old Hollywood occurs in 'A great show', based upon the experience of going to see the dying John Fante in the Malibu Motion Picture Hospital. We are told that they have one of the "original Tarzans" there, heard yodelling for his Jane. If Bukowski wrote reportage - which he seldom if ever does - he might have mentioned the actor's name: the most famous, Lex Barker, or Elmo Lincoln, the first screen Tarzan in 1918. He instead notices the "touch of/ the brave and dramatic in/ the air". The patients continue acting, as aged parodies of their former selves, with

dramatic gestures...
senatorial tones; they had
fierce blue eyes,
white, carefully cropped beards,
deliberate enunciations....
old dolls, once beautiful
now toothlessly munching
soft toast, poking at
peaches.[6]

In Bukowski's range of references to Hollywood, he usually refers to the most popular movie stars, the ones with the most charisma: there is nothing esoteric about his movie poems. He uses these stars for elegiac observations on the fleeting nature of beauty and the ravages of time and death. One example is 'For Marilyn M.': Marilyn Monroe "brought us something,/ some type of small victory". Some of its lines recall a rather better-known elegy for Monroe, the Elton John/ Bernie Taupin song 'Candle in the Wind'. Perhaps Taupin (who started out as a poet) had read Bukowski?

your sure body lit candles for men
on dark nights,
and now your night is darker
than the candle's reach[7]

Several other tributes to or elegies for female movie stars occur. There is an oddly comic one, 'Like that', about Jayne Mansfield (or rather her "unbelievable body" - in 1957 her vital statistics were 40-19-36). The piece describes mortuary attendants sewing her head back on, following decapitation in a car accident, and saying "what a waste". A rather striking work published in the 1968 Warhol/ Malanga *Intransit*, 'Poem for Brigitte Bardot', concerns one of the volatile star's several suicide attempts. This can perhaps be dated to shortly after her 26th birthday in 1960, when she took sleeping pills and slashed her wrists, only to be found outdoors and rushed to hospital. These details are reflected in the poem, which seems to indicate that it came directly from newspaper accounts. Indeed, in the *Memoirs* of her former husband, the director-Svengali Roger Vadim, he points out that at the time "the foreign press was not to be outdone. In the United States, John F. Kennedy was campaigning against Richard Nixon; the UN was in an uproar over France's first atomic bomb; but for more than a week, Brigitte's suicide attempt was front-page news".[8] The poem, romantic and quotidian, opens with coronets "alive with the fire of wine" and ends with a "cigarette and cucumber sun". As so often with Bukowski, the subject is addressed with familiarity, as 'Brig', her problems sympathised with. Her story is contrasted with the narrator's own life, one of physical pains, the eggshells of breakfasts, and shopping trips.[9]

Cinematic sources can also be identified for his male characters, and his dramatisation of their attitudes. Bukowski chose his masculine role models from the stock available via literature and the movies, having psychologically rejected his own father. Screen stars of the period provided appealing templates: Bogart, Cagney, W.C. Fields. Of course, Bukowski actually owed his movie loves to his parents. 'The movie critics' is an intriguing work, which refers to arguments between his parents about the merits of film actors. Wallace Beery is his father's favourite, and two unnamed French actors, one probably Maurice Chevalier, his mother's. Beery was perhaps best-known for playing a ruthless businessman, opposite Joan Crawford, in *Grand Hotel* (1932). Another of his big hits was *The Bowery* (1933), with George Raft - another Bukowski favourite - and

Jackie Cooper, a story of New York in the 1890s.

"what a disgusting
man!" my mother said.

"he's no
phoney", said my
father...[10]

The exchanges in the poem seem to favour the father, even though the speaker claims to have had nothing in common with his family "in or out" of the movies. Images from the 1930s, real life gangsters and their movie equivalents, stayed with Bukowski, becoming entwined, even confused, in his own mind. As he remarked in a 1980 interview with Michael Andrews, "We have our heroes, you know - John Dillinger [gunned down coming out of a gangster movie], Humphrey Bogart, even Clark Gable....Cagney, yeah".[11]

'The lady in red', its title referring to the woman who supposedly betrayed Dillinger to the FBI, nostalgically revisits the Depression, naming its heroic gangster figures - their exploits widely covered in the press - and calling it "a glorious non-bullshit time". The poem begins by blaming a woman. Bukowski's male speakers express hostility to women, and appeal to the latent misogyny of the reader, with a range of abusive epithets for women as 'whores', 'bitches', 'shack jobs' (women cohabiting with men, but not married: clearly an archaic usage these days, but not in the 1940s). Such types - seldom individualised - are always willing to trade on their sex appeal. His men, however disreputable, are laconic and worldly wise. In 'I love you', the narrator finds his woman in bed with a man. Despite her protestations, he knows that "this is the way love works", and "we all sat/ there drinking the whiskey and I was perfectly satisfied".[12]

The intrinsic faithlessness of women is a perennial theme. Sometimes this is presented in the form of a quick gag - of the sort that might have been heard in movies or on the radio - as in 'Hello, Willie Shoemaker' (the title indicating the racetrack destination of its about-to-be fired narrator):

and he said, Kid, I hear you been takin' Marylou out,
and I said, Just to dinner, boss,
And he said, Just to dinner, eh? you couldn't hold
that broad's pants on with all the rivets on 5th street[13]

Bukowski has more than his fair share of dross on this subject. In 'Hot', a mailman rushes to collect and deliver his quota of mail, in order to get back to his woman. Delayed, he arrives to find a note propped up on a purple teddy bear, complaining that "I wated until 5 after ate" and threatening that "somebody will love me". The note is spelled phonetically. He sets off to comb the bars in search of her, whether to embrace or to hit her is not made clear. Sexual innuendo operates feebly: the van engine, bathwater, the woman herself, all being "hot". When Bukowski's inventiveness deserts him, the stereotypes are untranscended.[14]

A much more extreme 'solution', self-mutilation, is the subject of 'Freedom', meaning male freedom from desire for women. First published during 1964, this luridly improbable scenario concerns a man whose woman frequents lowdown bars. He drinks at home. When she returns, with that "special stink again", the man takes out a butcher's knife. Instead of attacking her, however, he castrates himself in front of her, carrying the testicles "like apricots" and flushing them down the toilet bowl.

not caring now whether she left or
stayed....

and one hand holding and one hand lifting he poured
another wine.[15]

Similarly, in 'True story', a man is found wandering along the freeway "all red in/ front", having cut off his "sexual machinery". He is called a "one man Freedom March". These sexually masochistic works bring to mind Hemingway's story 'God Rest You Merry Gentlemen', in which two doctors talk about a young boy's demand to be castrated. When this is refused, the boy - torn between religion and the demands of his adolescent flesh - cuts off his own penis.[16] The impotence of war-wounded Jake Barnes in *The Sun Also Rises* is also relevant. He desires Brett Ashley, is tortured by this state and by her flaunted affairs.

Hemingway and Bukowski are hardly unique in suggesting the ambivalence of male sexual attitudes to women, veering between disgust and desire. Interesting from this point of view is 'Making it', which again concludes at the movies. The piece encapsulates the subject matter of his *Love Is a Dog From Hell* phase, but much more negatively. Physical discomforts and consequences are emphasized at the expense of pleasure, and women are referred to only by their initials.

at the most intense and passionate
moments
I wished that I could be that
lonely fellow again
sitting in a movie house with

my bag of popcorn
as all about me
couples sat
side by side
together.[17]

A brief comparison between Bukowski and Henry Miller is necessary. Miller's male characters are relentlessly libidinous, often light-headed from starvation. Women are reduced to orifices and cyphers, frequently tricked, robbed, and abused. Prostitutes are always to hand, and under-age girls are willing to take on males' fantastic urges. His *Tropic* books were long banned in the U.S. - one reason why Bukowski almost never mentions them. He probably couldn't get hold of copies during his book-consuming youth.[18] With the exception of *Love Is a Dog From Hell*, Bukowski never reaches those levels of sexual frenzy. Miller liked to claim that his books were not 'about' sex but about self-liberation. The pioneering feminist critic Kate Millett long ago pointed out in *Sexual Politics* that in his books female identity was restricted to an exclusively sexual being.[19] This seldom happens with Bukowski: numerous ordinary domestic details intrude. But there are some overlaps. In Miller's world, the ideal woman is the prostitute, who enables men to have sex without emotional ties, and without placing domestic restrictions on their freedom.

Many of Bukowski's early speakers are on first-name terms with prostitutes, from 'A night of Mozart' and 'A 340 dollar horse and a hundred dollar whore'. Some of Bukowski's women are presented as whore and nymphomaniac, yet they are not nearly as 'diminished' as with Miller. This is the case in 'Fire station'. Its depiction of sluttishly unbridled female concupiscence is accompanied by a closing declaration of love, despite all that has gone before. Its Bilko-esque card-sharping narrator pursues casual pimping on the side, the extra irony being that the money taken is without her knowledge. She goes upstairs and several firemen go with her, in what is (an off-screen) serial gang-bang.

when the other guy came down
he gave me a

five.

"how was it, Marty?"
"not bad. she's got... some fine movements".[20]

The sexist comedy is in the last half phrase. Like Céline, Bukowski's work sees relations between the sexes as inextricably bound up with economics, sex bearing a commodity status. As 'Bardamu' observes in Celine's *Journey to the End of the Night*, "It's a sin...to be lecherous and poor".[21] In spite of this, the potential for love exists, even in the most deprived circumstances: this is what distinguishes Bukowski from both Miller and Céline. His women are more human, more rounded. He is nowhere near as bitter in his denunciations. After leaving the sexually-satisfied but fleeced firemen behind, the couple return to the bar, with his newly-won money. He explains that he "found some he didn't know he had". These ironies frame but do not invalidate the woman's declaration of love for him in the bar. The woman soon attracts attention:

"look at that sailor looking at me, he must think I'm a...a..."

"naw, he don't think that. relax, you've got class, real class. sometimes you remind me of an opera singer. you know,one of those prima d's. your class shows all over
you. drink
up".

Though the ironic tone tends to undermine it, the scene is epiphanic. The sentiments touch precisely because of the hard-edged world around it, and the all-too-human failings. The work plays with stereotypes - its male narrator is laconic, jokey, masterful, the woman is hysterical, gullible, nymphomaniac. But there is a degree of emotional depth between them. Here, sexual stereotyping does not deny or crush humanity - in fact it enhances it. There is tenderness at the heart. The dedication of 'Fire station' is, after all, "for Jane with love". Jane Cooney Baker appears in many guises, and was his Muse. Even late on, an uncollected poem, 'Pain like an old black and white snapshot', in a New York little (*Grinning Idiot*, 1982), further memorialises her, though she has then been dead for 26 years.[22]

Bukowski's women have quixotic physical attributes. They are generally well past their physical prime. In 'One of the hottest', a platinum blonde (a phrase associated with stars such as Jean Harlow) has "a huge painted mouth", a wrinkled neck but still "the ass of a young girl". This is also in 'I saw an old fashioned whore today': "I'm sure she drove off to someplace/ magic". Another says that "the dream" of a man is "a whore with a gold tooth"

and a garter belt,
perfumed
with false eyebrows..
salami breath

high heels
long stockings with a very slight
run on back of left stocking,

('A man's woman')[23]

    Clearly, Bukowski romanticises whoredom just as much as he does skid row. But this is far from the unreal perfection of *Playboy* centrefolds or soap opera starlets. She has the unreal imperfection of another kind of male fantasy figure: the slag, the vulgar, sexually voracious woman. These women show themselves to be tough cookies, ready with wisecracks. Their descriptions are written in a kind of shorthand, the reader knowing what they look like because they correspond to a pre-existing image. Once again, they can be tracked to the movies. These bar room belles are loud, sexy, like a drink: and they use lingo taken from Hollywood westerns with bar scenes. For example, in 'Shot of red eye', two unemployed daylabourers are sitting in a bar.

two big women came in and I mean BIG
and they sat next to
us.

shot of red-eye, one of them said to the bartender. likewise, said the other.

they pulled their dresses up around their hips and
swung their legs....

how old are you, daddy?

old enough to slice the melon, I said,
tapping my cigar ashes into my beer to give me strength.

can you buy a melon? she asked.[24]

    The phrase "shot of red-eye" (whiskey) is usually spoken by thirsty cowboys in need of a quick drink, but Bukowski uses it to bring all those Western associations to mind for the reader. This exchange depends upon the man's laconic machismo, and the woman's wit which undercuts it. The women's physical attributes, their witty, tough-talking, allied to their ability to manipulate men, enable the movie connection to be made with Mae West. She patented the steamy one-liner. West (1892-1980), only came to Hollywood at the age of 40, after a successful career on Broadway. In risqué film comedies *She Done Him Wrong* (1933), adapted from her own Broadway play *Diamond Lil; I'm No Angel* (1933),*Belle of the Nineties*

(1934) and *Every Day's a Holiday* (1935), she played essentially the same character, variously called 'Miss Lou', 'Diamond Lil' and 'Peaches O'Day '.

Nominally a saloon-bar singer, she was by implication a prostitute, announcing at the start of *She Done Him Wrong*, "I'm one of the finest women that ever walked the streets". Her scripts had a succession of innuendo-loaded wisecracks that deflated male sexual pretensions, and suggestive songs, 'I Wonder Where My Easy Rider's Gone' and 'I'm a Fast-Movin' Gal That Likes It Slow'. The character that she created shows a thinly concealed contempt for her male suckers, remarking "Diamonds are my career". West's characterisations exaggerated female sexuality; she was near to being a female impersonator, her swaggering walk oddly masculine. Her innuendoes implied that she was always available for a price.

Of course, Bukowski's steamy females are several rungs down the economic scale from this Mae West archetype. There are no diamonds for them, just more drinks. They have little economic independence ('Miriam' in 'Hot' had been 'wateing' all day). Many other strong, even domineering women feature in Bukowski's works, notably landladies ('The day Hugo Wolf went mad', 'The tragedy of the leaves'), and brothel madams. An early example takes the form of an exchange about the prospects for business, now that the war is over and soldiers, some wounded, are returning home. The madam says that "if they haven't shot off/ the other parts", these men will still want it:

men are men and
soldiers are soldiers and
they love to
fuck, don't
you?

amen, I said.
('A conversation on morality, eternity and copulation')[25]

Both agree that human nature is unchanging: men will pay for sex, and women will make themselves available at a price.

By contrast with this street-level perspective, another aspect of Bukowski's treatment of women is his occasional symbolic figures of womanhood. Bukowski is not the kind of writer to invoke 'The White Goddess' - he is no Robert Graves - which would involve a tone completely alien to his narrators. But he does find female archetypes and muse figures within the everyday. In '18 cars full of men thinking of what could have been', a physically spectacular woman transfixes a line of men stuck in traffic. She becomes a figure representing male desire - all the more powerful for being repressed - which 'causes' the poem. 'Eddie and Eve' works another angle on the woman as archetype theme. Its narrator visits an old friend after thirty years, only to find him aged and crippled by arthritis. His wife has also changed:

then his wife came out. the once slim Eve I used to flirt with.

210 pounds squinting at me.[26]

The comedy is in a single word, 'squinting'. This is further enhanced by her name, 'Eve', the archetypal temptress of mankind in *Genesis*. If ever so lightly, this invokes a deeply ingrained cultural myth, only to immediately deflate it. In fact, the poem cleverly plays off both male and female archetypes against the sorry fact of human ageing. It also makes a point about the 'dangers' to men of domesticity. Eddie has ended up in this state after 30 years in the same house with the same wife.

Bukowski is here echoing a U.S. tradition that regards women as the tyrant of the domestic realm, the enemy of male freedoms. The critic Leslie Fiedler long ago pointed out all those American male characters on the run from domestic responsibilities, who gravitate towards the unrestricted Frontier. Fiedler saw the American male writer as fearing 'maturity' above all things, "and marriage seems to him its essential sign....a compromise with society, an acceptance of responsibility and drudgery and dullness".[27] In this Literature of Masculine Protest, the original is Washington Irving's 'Rip Van Winkle', whose alcohol-induced sleep of two decades enables him to escape his shrewish wife, a representative of "a species of despotism under which he had long groaned, and that was - petticoat government".[28] She is especially hostile to his "insuperable aversion to all forms of profitable labor". Fictional descendants include 'Dean Moriarty', 'Walter Mitty', 'Randle P. McMurphy', and Bukowski's alter-ego in his fiction, 'Henry Chinaski'.

Bukowski's invective against domesticity is usually expressed in comic terms. To these literary characters can be added W.C. Fields (1879-1946), though he is oddly enough never mentioned by Bukowski. Yet his Fields-like stage delivery was remarked upon by many who attended his readings. Gerald Locklin commented in the early 1980s that Bukowski "has the sense of timing and construction (and the voice) of a W.C. Fields, which is one reason that his readings, no matter what his state of inebriation, continue to draw throngs".[29] Fields was famed for his hard-drinking curmudgeonly persona, both on and off screen. His rasping voice, bleary-eyed observations of the absurdities of life, his comedies of misanthropy, his deeply suspicious view of the world; all this relates to Bukowski. (Of course, certain other aspects don't: Fields' high falutin' tongue-twisting language and vaudeville 'routines'). Occasionally Bukowski's characters are mean to children and dogs. And think of all those 'hiding' in saloon bars, drinking and playing cards, concocting schemes with which to separate greenhorns from their money. 'Fire station' has a card-sharping narrator: one also appears in the early comic jail-drama 'Moyamensing prison'.

A number of poems make a disparaging connection between women and the workaday pressures that the male narrator wishes to avoid. 'The Sound of human lives' appeals to latent misogyny by contrasting its narrator's easy-going attitudes with the complaints of his 'strangely' ambitious girlfriend.

my dear, I say, there are men out there now
picking tomatoes, lettuce, even cotton,
there are men and women dying under the sun,...
you don't know how lucky we
are...[30]

When the woman leaves the bed and starts typing, he remarks that he "does not know" why people think "effort and energy" have anything to do with creation. He compounds this fatuous comment by remarking that in politics, medicine, history and religion "they are mistaken also". Here overt sexism has undermined his own best instincts as a writer. Women are said to lack the inspiration needed, their work compared to the futility of back-breaking labour in the fields. Such statements are not just as a macho put-down, but also a plea that art itself be a male preserve, a zone of freedom from female interference.

The rambling narrative of 'The days run away like wild horses over the hills' again makes negative links between a woman's writing and her sexuality. Its speaker calls upon a friend, and sees an attractive woman there; "the bitch had some poems she wrote and I read them/ and they were not bad considering she was built for/ other things". In 'A literary romance', the author of "very sexy poems about rape and lust" turns out to be a 35 year-old virgin. Following a failed attempt at seduction, she remains "a very bad poetess":

I think that when a woman has kept her legs closed
for 35 years
it's too late
either for love
or for
poetry.[31]

On one level, this fits in with Bukowski's authentic thesis that art must be informed by experience, that the artist who avoids involvement in human affairs is likely to produce mere word games. But C.B. often tries to have it both ways: a sexy woman cannot be a good writer, as in 'The Days Run...' and neither can an unsexy one. 'A literary romance' suggests that seduction could release her into art, giving her the masculine secret of creativity. This sexual interpretation of the artistic impulse is exactly the scenario of a similar but far more avuncular early poem, 'Experience'. It concerns "a lady down the hall" who paints butterflies and insects and "works with clay". Invited in for a drink, he remarks on a work-in-progress, a statue which is "messed up in the front, sort of". She invites him back in a week later to see the finished article, and the sex-magic has worked:

then I began to laugh and she laughed
and the work of art stood there,
a very beautiful thing.[32]

'John Dillinger and le chasseur maudit' again smears women's art. Its speaker finds "some sanctuary" in hearing about "desperate men"

Dillinger, Rimbaud, Villon, Babyface Nelson, Seneca, Van Gogh,
or desperate women: lady wrestlers, nurses, waitresses, whores,
poetesses[33]

These are loaded dice: the men are all highly differentiated within the reader's mind, and the "desperate women" (a rather different connotation) are merely types. Men are Saints of Opposition. Women, however, can only serve, or ape the masculine pursuits of wrestling...and poetry. Women artists who placed themselves away from the sexual control of men and still produced great work - from Jane Austen to Emily Dickinson and Marianne Moore - would hardly bear Bukowski's prejudices out. He aligns himself with a heavily masculine American cultural tradition.

But there are other types of ideal male figure than tough guys in his works. These are artists, and particularly the great Classical composers. Bukowski may have his feet set in American popular culture, but his eyes are on (usually European) high culture. The most striking references to 'high culture' are his frequent invocation of the lives, loves and sometimes works of classical composers. (Bukowski himself liked to refer to his typing as "playing the piano", as in the title of a collection published in 1979. There are photographs of him poised over a keyboard, but judging by his extended digits he was at best a two finger player). Frequent jokey juxtapositions of European high art with American low-life occur throughout his works. 'L.Beethoven, half-back' has Ludwig as a tough-tackling, tough-talking American football player; the madness of Hugo Wolf is viewed by his landlady. 'The Life of Borodin' is recounted. There are fantasies about fucking a Wagnerian soprano during a performance of *Siegfried* ('Climax'), or simply listening to a Wagner overture in the park ('Rain'), or an elegiac note, the exiled "Chopin with his bag of polish soil" ('One for the shoeshine man'). Especially late on, Bukowski registers his nightly regime of typing away while listening to music on a portable radio.

Music stands for an important element, pleasure - even spiritual uplift - ameliorating his often harsh world view. (Indeed, some of the most positive terms used in his work come from music of all kinds, for instance "the lilting high....anything that contains the original energy of/ joy").[34] The origins of Bukowski's taste for classical music may again owe something to his watching movies during the 1930s and 1940s. One clue came during a 1979 Vancouver reading: he read a poem, 'Schubert', about early memories of watching a bio-pic of the composer. Movies by major studios such as Warners and 20th Century Fox at this time very often had lush, lyrically romantic scores, by Max Steiner and Erich Korngold. They were European imports from the Germanic symphonic tradition, exponents of high art serving a popular audience: and as such an approximate model for Bukowski's own ambitions. Such composers enhanced the emotional impact of many movies that Bukowski saw. He refers to a whole range of composers: Russians (Tchaikovsky to Borodin) and Americans like Copland, but overwhelmingly to the Germanic romantics; Beethoven, Wagner, Brahms, and Mahler. As a further speculation, Bukowski's taste for Germanic music may relate to his boyhood experience of being taunted for his national origins ("Heinie"). Classical music was one area of German cultural superiority that he could identify with and attach himself to. But one way that C.B. brings high art down to the quotidian level is that his narrators almost invariably listen to the music alone, and on a cheap radio. Concerts are for the sociable, the cultural snobs and the middle classes.

A further necessary counterbalance to European high art can be seen in Bukowski's prolific depictions of a typically American, bluecollar environment - the racetrack. It might be thought that Bukowski went to the track to get away from his artistic life. But, as he informed the interviewer Robert Wennersten, it was closely connected to his writing, and he compared his attendance to that of Hemingway at the bullfights: "I go to the track, and try to get a rhythm going. Then I come back and drink and type. If I stayed in all day looking at the typewriter, it wouldn't work....There's a lot of death at the track, a lot of dead people. Maybe that's what I want to see".[35]

At the track, his characters, from vamps to hustlers, are again largely taken from Central Casting. Bukowski draws there as elsewhere, on a range of archetypes. Supreme among them is Humphrey Bogart, perhaps the most ubiquitous of all specimens of American rugged individualism. Bogart (1899-1957) has had a cultural sweep almost out of proportion to the actual films he appeared in, constructing an enduring icon of fictional masculinity. This is as the guy undeluded by the wiles of women and the corrupt practices of men, who nevertheless has a strong streak of hard-bitten romance within him, and sentimentality. Bogart played a succession of minor hoodlums before becoming the iconic private eyes 'Sam Spade', 'Philip Marlowe', and clubowner 'Rick ' in Casablanca during the 1940s. His characterisations are symbolic of inner integrity and masculine self-sufficiency, often against the authorities. His characters are domineering once-bitten romantics, liking liquor to dull the pain.

Steve Richmond once remarked upon Bukowski "playing Humphrey Bogart on the page and making it real".[36] His Bogart manner draws upon the latter's roles as an escaped convict, prospector, hobo, hoodlum, perhaps even the boozy tug-boat captain in *The African Queen*. There is for example a two page uncollected work, 'Bogart in the world of the dead', published in *The Willie* (San Francisco; Spring 1968). Another narrator recalls his youth, when he "looked like" Bogart and "rode boxcars through the bad-lands/ never missed a chance to duke it".

cigar in mouth lips wet with beer
Bogart's
got a beard now
but don't believe the gossip:
Bogie's not dead
yet.
('Maybe tomorrow')[37]

Hugh Fox also made the connection. He called Bukowski "the Man Against the Crowd. The Crowd is compromisers, sell-outs....I think that one of the big reasons for Buk's popularity is his straightforward morality. It's a Hemingway-Bogartish morality, the morality of the purity of the inner man, the losing tough guy".[38] Bukowski thereby latches onto not just movies, but onto specifically American cultural mythology. And eventually Bukowski 'himself' appears within his own work as a masculine archetype, inviting male readers to identify with him.

Celebrating these fictional images of masculinity, Bukowski role-plays, and sends up male attitudes. 'Iron Mike' refers at its outset to a famous cinematic image of domineering male behaviour, James Cagney pushing a grapefruit into Mae Clark's face in *The Public Enemy* (1931). The poem goes on to cut down Iron Mike's cocksman behaviour ("32 scalps dangling") and aggressive misogyny. (Written well before the nickname became Mike Tyson's, was Bukowski not only a poet but a prophet also?).

we talk about this film -
Cagney fed this broad
grapefruit
faster than she could
eat it and
then she
loved him.

"that won't always work", I told Iron Mike.[39]

Bukowski shows the breadth of his appreciation of Cagney - his range extended from the gangster genre to musicals and melodrama - in other poems. In 'Love and courage', he describes a particular movie in which the Cagney character earns money in the ring to enable his piano-playing brother to become a star at Carnegie Hall, ending up "punched-out and blind". In 'Silk', Bukowski recalls the effect of seeing women wearing silk stockings during the Depression:

silken legs for
Cagney and Gable and
all the boys in the neighbourhood.

The ironic perspectives of Bukowski's narrators question and subvert the attitudes and stereotypes that, on another level, they exploit. This fully extends to his more general treatment of symbolic figures in movie culture, cowboys and gangsters. This allows another layer to Bukowski's rendering of so-called 'realism' in mythic terms. Cowboys come in for frequent satirical stick. There are brief interpolations in works such as 'The difference between a bad poet and a good one is luck'. Set in a small town in Texas, the locals size up the stranger in their midst:

and they all came to her house -
all the cowboys, all the cowboys:
fat, dull and covered with dust.
and we all shook hands.
I had on a pair of old blue jeans, and they said
oh you' re a writer, eh?

and I said well, some think so. two weeks later they
ran me out

town.⁴⁰

This humour plays off against the heroic image in Hollywood Westerns. The collision between the urban writer and the fat, dull cowboys results in mutual incomprehension. By implication at least, the archetype is debunked. 'What a man I was' (seen by the critic Jack Byrne as a tribute to e.e. cummings' poem 'Buffalo Bill', though the stylistic kinship is hard to see) is spoken in a parodic drawl by a cartoon outlaw about to be lynched. His crime? He tells us that he shot "the Sheerf", and "everything that counts".⁴¹ The fabulatory 'Tough company', has poems "like gunslingers" who draw steel and threaten their creator, telling him to "get with it".

Bukowski brilliantly subverts Hollywood Western associations in 'Another academy'.⁴² Again, the poem depends on readers seizing on the divergence between reality and cinematic image, in this case John Wayne's. It starts by observing a group of down and outs, waiting outside a Mission Hall in Los Angeles, one of them still concerned about the late Oscar sentimentally awarded to Wayne for *True Grit* (1969). He was one of the best-known cowboys, associated particularly with John Ford movies. He was also a Republican champion of God, the Flag, family values, the Military, Free Enterprise. Bukowski's juxtaposition of the bums to Hollywood razzmataz undercuts all this. Theirs, after all, is the true grit, probably closer to the reality of the Old West than Wayne's impersonations of grizzled old soaks. The poem satirises the savage divergence between films and reality; the ultimate rich in American society versus the ultimate poor. (Hollywood being the purveyor, not just of illusions but of national cultural myths).

Bukowski even sends up the Frontier Myth in 'Yeah, man?', which enacts an ironically updated version of the pioneer experience. 'Larry' lives in a neighbourhood taken over by "little brown guys", probably Mexicans working in California. When his vehicle, that cherished machine of American freedom, is blocked in by their "smashed giant battleships of/ cars", a dispute arises. He forces them to move their cars at knifepoint and goes out to buy a celebratory six-pack. On his return, he finds that his furniture and belongings have been stolen, wrecked or covered in graffiti. His cat's tail lies bleeding in the toilet. Larry takes a swig of beer:

he decided
that it was about time
he moved
further west.⁴³

Gerald Locklin astutely commented that this is "not simply a nightmare tale of one man's misguided race relations; it is the demographic and demonological saga of white flight. [From the inner cities] Bukowski...is undeniably a chronicler of politically significant phenomena".[44] This invokes the historical westward migration in America. Attacks by marauding Indians (staples of Hollywood) have been replaced by white conflict with more recent immigrants. Larry has paid the price for his American desire to protect his freedom of movement and his own individual space. If he is an Angeleno, there is now nowhere for him to move to.

As with cowboys, what we know about gangsters has been provided by Hollywood, from *White Heat* to *The Godfather*. Again, Bukowski goes back to his youth. The exploits of gangsters were embellished in newspapers during the 1920s and 1930s, making folk heroes out of psychopathic characters robbing the Banks which had foreclosed on many tenant farmers during the Depression. This is indicated by their homely nicknames - 'Pretty Boy' Floyd, 'Baby Face' Nelson, 'Ma' Barker. As in movies, Bukowski's gangsters are far removed from reality - the cold-blooded killings, protection rackets, extortion, bootlegging, and sordid loan sharking. The early Hollywood suggested an enviable lifestyle in which sex, excitement and drink were prominent. George Raft is probably the least well-known 1930s Hollywwod gangster name now, but he was a particular favourite of Bukowski's. Like Bogart and Cagney, Raft had a surprising range: the young Hank may even have first seen Raft as a romantic lead, such as his role as a dancer in *Bolero* (1934), with Carol Lombard. He appears significantly in 'The night I saw George Raft in Vegas', in *What Matters Most*...(1999).[45] This recalls a similarly-titled work in the L.A. magazine *Canto* (Winter 1961). This latter poem is a fantasy about being in a Raft film, juxtaposing 'real life' with a dream of playing the casinos. The speaker smiles like "George Raft sizing up a French tart", then Raft himself walks in and speaks to him, "hello kid, back again?". The actor is further referred to in 'Finis'[46] as one of the celebrities often to be seen at California racetracks during the 1950s.

"The boxing matches and the racetracks are/ temples of learning", states 'Horse and fist'.[47] The racetrack is the movie set within Bukowski's work, the melodrama where one can see the masses having their dreams shattered, successful punters picked up by hookers and murdered. More mundanely, it is where many of his narrators avoid the 9-5 work routine, betting "against the crowd". It is the setting for a variety of moods, from sentiment, elegy, to broad comedy. For the latter, see 'Bad action', in *War All the Time* (1984). Disturbed several times by dubious characters, while trying to study the racing form paper, its narrator finally locates a secluded seat, and the public address system comes on:

"Ladies and Gentlemen, the Flag of

the United States of America".

we all stood up. the flag went up. we all sat down.

sometimes being at the racetrack is worse than being in the county jail.[48]

The track is so ubiquitous that Bukowski latterly anticipated readers' objections to "yet another horse poem": 'Cheer up' ("this might be the last one"). These appear in all phases of Bukowski's writing. *In War All the Time*, for instance, a lengthy story-essay-poem 'Horsemeat' presents vignettes of betting psychology, jockeys and horses. 'Valentine gift' is about the dubious pleasures of being recognized as a famous writer at the track. 'Space creatures' satirises blue-collar America. 'The day the epileptic spoke' is reminiscent of the much earlier 'The world's greatest loser'. The latter memorialises a newspaper seller at the track, a man with no legs who used a rotten board with roller skates to get around, and who only backed losing outsiders. It concludes by drawing a wider moral on why people are nevertheless drawn to the track:

...we're fools, of course -
bucking the inside plus a 15 percent take,
but how are you going to tell a dreamer
there's a 15 percent take on the
dream? he'll just laugh and say,
is that all?[49]

For Bukowski, the track is not just about betting. There is sex, in the pneumatic forms of racetrack hookers, and money to be made, systems to be tried. The narrator of 'A last shot on two good horses' good-humouredly lets his dog grab a ten-dollar bill from his winnings. The narrator of 'A night of Mozart', by contrast, is blackmailing a whore involved in the murder of a punter. The murdered man is a professional gambler, different in his motivations from the crowd:

he didn't come out to holler and get drunk
and get fucked -
he came out to make it, which is better
than punching another man's timeclock[50]

The best of these type of poems is 'A 340 dollar horse and a hundred dollar whore' (in its original publication a '350 dollar horse': perhaps Bukowski later realised 10 dollars' betting tax should be subtracted). This is a strangely moving poem, which goes to the heart of Bukowski's early writing identity. A roominghouse world counterpointed by poesy; with the hooker as an enabling Muse. The speaker admits to her that he is a poet, only to half-withdraw the claim at her laughter. He concludes with an image of the "ugly horse", who 'wrote' this poem. He had earlier told the reader:

don't ever get the idea I am a poet; you can see me
at the racetrack any day half drunk
betting quarters, sidewheelers and straight thoroughs[51]

Bukowski Man goes to the racetrack to be alone in the crowd (often unsuccessfully). And to beat the system, at its simplest betting against tipsters.

"who you like?" another guy asks me
and I say "the 3 horse", and he says
"the three is out", and walks off
and that is all I want to hear
and I put 20 to win on the 3
('The days run away like wild horses over the hills')[52]

Or, as one of the *Wormwood* Bukowski special issues titled it, 'Horses don't bet on people and neither do I'. This 1984 collection is the *locus classicus* of all Bukowski's racetrack poems, a sequence of narratives which range discursively over characters encountered and conversations overheard. 'The wavering line' sees the tragi-comedy of men at the track ("old, balding, macho but/ sexless") as a Broadway musical: "I am the critic and the/ audience and sometimes I'm on stage/ too". The title poem works another variation on the familiar incident of the narrator being interrupted:

"...say didn't I see you
in some movie? aren't you a movie star?"
"no".
"yes, it was a horror movie, you played a man
who fell out of a bell tower and crushed his
skull...."[53]

'Do you use a notebook?' again connects the track to writing, making the Hemingway self-comparison when talking to interviewers:

they don't understand - it's been a gamble to begin with
and nothing ever solidifies into surety....

I park between a Dodge van and a Volks rabbit
thinking, Ernie would have understood and surely,
Manolete, and all these people here ahead of me...[54]

    Locklin's comment on these track poems was that "It's a world Bukowski knows intimately, one he can treat as a microcosm, one where stories offer themselves - it is a world of inherent narrative tensions....He may prefer Hollywood Park to Hollywood premieres but he has been to the latter now as well".[55] David Glover's brief essay, 'A Day at the Races', points out that "the world of gambling breaks episodically into Charles Bukowski's narratives, usually as lucky breaks. In a sense, a concern with getting the breaks defines the Bukowski persona....Some of Bukowski's most trenchant remarks on the art of writing refer us back to the track".[56] These include mental discipline, intuitive insights; and the need to 'gamble' to win.
    What both the racetrack and the movies represent in differing ways within Bukowski's work are - as well as their sex and economic aspects - the human necessity for dreams and illusions. These are all the more alluring for being temporary or frequently shattered. As we can now see, many of Bukowski's speakers and characters are mythic in an identifiably cinematic way and derive from his experience of old Hollywood movies. The movie input into his poetry is one major way of making it accessible, instantly recognisable to readers. Not for Bukowski culturally esoteric allusions. And however much his speakers may sneer at the masses' bovine habits (cf. betting against the crowd) they are not linguistically divorced from them. Bukowski's playing with these sources, invoking and satirising them, tends to give the lie to interpretations of his work as being in any sense 'realism'. It also gives great flavour to his work, much of its enjoyment. And his pervasive recycling of U.S. cultural mythology suggests why his works were destined to be ultimately taken up by Hollywood itself.

Artwork by David Hernandez

Chapter 7

Bukowski and West Coast Poetry

"this land punched-in, cuffed-out, divided,
held like a crucifix in a deathhand,
...this is their land and
I walk on it, live on it a little while
near Hollywood...
('Crucifix in a Deathhand')

Bukowski's work is sometimes characterised, either as a compliment or a put-down, as "pure Los Angeles". He was himself sociologically a typical Angeleno, being born elsewhere, though he came there from Germany as a small child, his parents' 'goldschatz' (golden boy). Certainly he identified with it, and, though his oeuvre contains few if any 'Odes to L.A.', the city is an unstated presence in almost everything that he wrote. He found his subject matter in the conditions and characters that he encountered in its streets, roominghouses, lowdown bars and racetracks. It was the environment which gave him the permission to write. His poetry makes even more sense to a reader who has actually been to Los Angeles. You can literally see the street signs and place names, feel the heat, experience physical details that make his work vivid. A first-time visitor to Los Angeles is literally dazzled by bright sunlight; and then by the sharpness of sights unfolding on a drive through the city. There are corporate skyscrapers and futuristic architecture, slum neighbourhoods, streets where few walk except poor people or tourists. Car-jammed freeways, bordered by movie advertising billboards, eventually reach the literally cooler atmospheres of San Pedro and Long Beach. No wonder Bukowski moved to the coast as soon as he could; it's a great relief from urban pressures.

Anyone anywhere staring out of their windows at rain or cloudy skies can feel the fundamental appeal of Southern California. Its promise of a better life - or at least better weather - mixes in with Hollywood images, day-dreams of its youth culture, the sun-tanned young women often seen curving past on rollerblades. The underlying reality is somewhat different for most of its inhabitants most of the time. References in Bukowski's work to 'skid row', the fear of ending up there, represent no Steinbeckian sentimentality but the economic sword hanging over the lives of many working people fearful for their jobs. Perception of this state of affairs indeed informs the poetry of one of Bukowski's best contemporary successors, machinist-poet Fred Voss. Beneath the conspicuous consumption and advertising gloss, rhetoric about melting pots, American society is Darwinian competition. Economic victims and failures, often the old or black people, are highly visible, sitting on benches in broiling heat, or going through trash cans in alleys "where poor men poke for bottles" ('Layover').[1] It is the tension between Fantasy California and economic realities which gives urgency to Bukowski's perspectives. The American Dream, indeed the Californian Dream, cannot come true for most of his characters, who survive as best they can.

Los Angeles, according to C.B., "is where you hang it up and/ battle" ('A little sleep and peace of stillness').[2] It is one of the most extreme American cities, full of pitfalls and contradictions; exciting, vibrant, dangerous. It is a vehicular city of suburbs extending over a large area. Just as London has Covent Garden, Highgate, Golders Green, etc, all very different districts within the city, so L.A. has diverse areas like Silver Lake, Boyle Heights, Chinatown, Echo Park, and of course Hollywood. On a British scale, Greater Los Angeles, if superimposed on London, would stretch from Cambridge to Brighton. Conspicuous wealth and poverty are a world but often only a short drive away from each other. The cultural penetration of movies and television, their twin message of violence and 'family values', is almost total. Media coverage of celebrities is ubiquitous. Surgically-enhanced porn stars and expensively-suited tele-Evangelists appear on Cable TV channels, competing for viewers' dollars. Helicopters whirr overhead constantly. This is the modern urban, topographical backdrop. It is only partially reflected in Bukowski's fictional world. As we have seen, much of his work actually comes out of American cultural mythology, via books and movies imbibed during his youth. In his later books Bukowski harks back nostalgically to the pre-1939 California, its movie palaces and studio lots, orange groves, an era of 'simpler' values. But he was characteristically a writer of the urban setting, looking out to celebrate or elegize something happening around him in the city.

Though often regarded as a special zone of its own, L.A. is a Californian city, taking its place within a state of great variety, from desert to fertile valley to concrete jungle. In its geography, ethnicity and writing there are - to borrow Gerald Haslam's 1992 anthology title - not one but many Californias. Bukowski's verse and his career as a writer evolved within and out of a richly diverse West Coast literary tradition in which little magazines, small presses, and live performances were vital and perennial. The vitality associated with California during the past century and more has colourful literary characters such as the rhyming bard Joaquin Miller (a sensation when he marched into late Victorian drawing rooms in London) and the experience-soaked novelist Jack London. Post-1945, the San Francisco Bay Area was revitalized by the 'Berkeley Renaissance' poets, then the Beats either visited or resided in or near San Francisco. In the 1960s, West Coast underground papers were in the vanguard of the international movement, mouthpieces of the counterculture. Post-1970, the poetry scene in and around Los Angeles and Long Beach became 'where it was happening', a state of affairs for which Bukowski and his associates were catalysts. Indigenous talents and migrants to the State have made a positive virtue out of being far away from the New York/ East Coast 'establishment' of critics, mainstream magazines and publishers. Several anthologies over the past three decades, including one of Bukowski's own editing, have attempted to select, define and capture Californian or Angelenos' special niche in contemporary poetry. It remains a generally extrovert writing scene filled with grand energy, nurtured by workshops and 'slam' readings.

That Bukowski admired and learned from California residents Robinson Jeffers, William Saroyan, John Fante, and perhaps Henry Miller, has already been argued. The Californian context of Bukowski's work is important to it, and he in turn has been widely influential among succeeding generations of West Coast writers - male and female. That is, by 'freeing up' the poetic territory available, in style, attitude and subject matter. By de-mystifying the subject matter of poetry, bringing it down onto the street, simplifying its techniques. Bukowski was an immensely strong 'precedent' author; a mentor, a father figure. He was in touch with a whole range of authors of differing generations; some were California natives, but most had migrated there. He communicated with John Fante, and Henry Miller; with those born in the 1940s such as Gerald Locklin, Ron Koertge, A.D. Winans, Joan Jobe Smith *et al.* They all spread the word. His influence among the young was partly his own, in part through others' advocacy of his work.

His performances in public during the 1970s were an essential part of his career; and he read most often in Los Angeles and elsewhere in California. As he told Locklin, when turning one down, "No, no more readings. I never liked to read but I feel that when they got their money up I gave them something to remember" (uncollected letter, 13 August 1983). These events not only entertained and 'outraged', giving raucous audiences what they wanted, but affected his procedures as a poet. When he no longer needed the money and exposure, he stopped doing them. The bear-pit hostile atmospheres, the two weeks he said it took to recover, became too wearing. He had done it all and become bored with audiences' expectations of comedy and vulgarity. This is very apparent on one of his last recorded readings, at Redondo Beach in April, 1980.

In his comments, Bukowski usually snarls against Southern California's mass tastes, its celebrity culture, the crass commercialism of, say, Disneyland. Yet, as has been shown, his art has many of its roots in the old Hollywood. One can readily imagine the Bukowski family car trips down Sunset Boulevard during the late 1920s and early 1930s, celebrity-spotting. Or hanging around outside studio lots, seeing actors in costume dramas walking around or going to lunch. The often fantastic L.A. architecture, a mix of extravagant styles, and some of the streets, must have resembled a giant movie set. Current Hollywood he was rightly wary of, fearful for his artistic soul. He turned down screenwriting offers in the wake of *Barfly*. The $10,000 he received for it placed him nowhere near the earnings level of the top level screenwriter, but neither did he end up as a highly-paid lackey of the studio system, as had many novelistic greats - Scott Fitzgerald, William Faulkner, James Agee, Aldous Huxley - and John Fante. The film industry employed and was satirised most memorably by Nathanael West (incidentally the subject of Locklin's doctoral dissertation at Tucson during the 1960s). Bukowski was both author of the screenplay for a financially fairly successful movie, as well as the satirical novel *Hollywood* (1989). Further involvements might have been lucrative, but he hardly needed the money.

California, as a subject in itself, and as a residence for writers, has a rich and varied history. Supplementing indigenous talents are those who have been lured to the Golden State: an elite few by the wages of Hollywood, but many more for a variety of social, economic, and latterly sexual reasons. This history has been anthologised and wisely commented upon most recently by the critic and short story writer Gerald Haslam. Himself a fifth-generation Californian from a migrant 'Okie' background, his selections in *Many Californias: Literature from the Golden State* (1992), and his essays in *The Other California: The Great Central Valley in Life and Letters* (1990; 1994) combine literary criticism, autobiography, and sociological commentary. One of his general conclusions is that "this remains a seeker's state, so it invites redefinition of the spirit's quest for the possible".[3] He shows that California's literary as well as geographical landcape is inherently various: his subdivisions are either topographical ('The Greater Bay Area', 'Wilderness California') or implicitly psychological: "The Heartland", "Fantasy California". The area he designates as "The Southland" is of most relevance to Bukowski, his associates and followers, but all the other Californias clearly impinge.

This Southland, known as 'cow country' during the mid-19th Century, was very sparsely populated compared to today's urban sprawl, but had incredibly harsh conditions. The librarian Lawrence Clark Powell called Los Angeles at this time the toughest town in the west, "a cesspool of Frontier scum". Haslam refers to a hellish view of Los Angeles in the 1850s, *The Reminiscences of a Ranger* by Horace Bell - who was described by a contemporary as a "blackmailer, murderer, thief, house-burner, snake-hunter, and defamer of the dead".[4] Its literary history has had a genteel side as well. Helen Hunt Jackson's historical novel *Ramona* (1884), intended by its author as an exposé of the plight of Indians, famously sentimentalised the area's Spanish Mission past. Meanwhile, Jack London was busy romanticising his own unruly youth in San Francisco, his sea voyaging. A Southland literary group that included Hildegarde Flanner, 'poet laureate of Pasadena' also gave encouragement to the young Robinson Jeffers. Succeeding Californian names, all certainly read by the young Bukowski, were William Saroyan, sometimes alluded to, but criticised for sentimentality; and John Steinbeck - oddly, almost never mentioned. (He was perhaps too much of a vogue writer during the 1930s: Bukowski preferred the harsher tone of Fante and Hemingway). Haslam's books also recognise the variety of writers produced by the State's mixed ethnicity, a factor of increasing relevance in the post-1945 era and particularly in today's West Coast writing coteries.

'A History of Los Angeles in Poetry 1781-1981' formed the subject of a special issue of Helen Friedland's magazine *Poetry L.A.* Bukowski was conspicuously absent from its somewhat staid pages, but Locklin, Ron Koertge, and Michael C. Ford, often paying tribute to movie stars and landmarks, were set among an eclectic mix of current and historical local poets. The editor had clearly missed the title poem of Bukowski's 1965 collection *Crucifix in a Deathhand* which, unusually for him, included a mini-history of the area:

this land bought, resold, bought again and
sold again, the wars long over,
the Spaniards all the way back in Spain
down in the thimble again, and now
real estaters, subdividers, landlords, freeway
engineers arguing.[5]

Friedland pointed out in her editorial that "migration may be the most important constant", and that social introductions in Los Angeles are commonly followed by "Where are you from?"[6] This sanitised historical survey told a story of Indian decimation, Spanish and Mexican rule, and then waves of American immigration and development. In the period 1850-70, Los Angeles was known as Los Diablos or 'Hell Hole of the West'; its violent crime blamed (then as now) on drugs, alcohol, racial tensions, and the influx of undesirable migrants. In the late 19th and early 20th Century, the exploitation of gold, then oil, and water to irrigate the abundant land was fought over by the capitalist Robber Barons. Post-1945, she concluded wistfully, "suburbia grew, and grew, and grew".

Similar social, political and economic factors operated elsewhere in California, eventually attracting writers. Some were determined loners: Robinson Jeffers settled in Carmel on the coast during the 1920s. The more welcoming Henry Miller, in the Big Sur area during the 1940s, near his friend Anais Nin. The collectivity of values also played a part in the various groups emerging near San Francisco; before, during and after the Second World War. Kenneth Rexroth became a pivotal figure, despite his argumentative nature, linking the pre-war generation with the *arriviste* Beats. Rexroth, a former leftist organiser, had many links to Anarchists as well as to Eastern religious groups. His relationships and feuds, within the Communist Party and their ideological opposites, the Southern Fugitives, were legendary. He became a Hearst newspaper columnist, and a prolific radio broadcaster. Rexroth influenced a generation of writers living on the West Coast with his passionate advocacy of pacifism-anarchism, Oriental verse, and an ecological aesthetic. (His most obvious successor, one personally nurtured by Rexroth, is Gary Snyder). Rexroth's volatile literary soirées enabled contacts to be made, and he famously introduced the first reading of 'Howl' by Allen Ginsberg at the Six Gallery in San Francisco during October 1955. Rexroth's poetry-and-jazz performances suggested the genre to the likes of Kenneth Patchen and Lawrence Ferlinghetti. Bukowski's friend Jack Micheline followed, doing some of his best work in collaboration with jazz greats such as Charles Mingus.

Rexroth's own account of *American Poetry in the Twentieth Century* (1971) naturally emphasised West Coast writers at the expense of East Coast New Criticism-dominated poets.[7] Rexroth pointed out the Californian literary groups which emerged, not out of the seminar room but out of Depression work camps, the Civil Conservation Corps. They had wartime libertarian, pacifist elements. Key members of the San Francisco Anarchist Circle had been conscientious objectors, held in logging and labour camps within western States, among them being Robert Duncan, Jack Spicer, William Everson, Philip Lamantia and Rexroth himself. They formed the basis of the so-called 'Berkeley Renaissance'. The Anarchist

Circle itself had produced little magazines: *The Ark*, and George Leite's *Circle*. *City Lights* was a magazine edited by Peter Dean Martin - who later set up the City Lights bookstore in San Francisco with Lawrence Ferlinghetti in June 1953. Readings were an essential part of this artistic scene. As Ferlinghetti recalled in 1980, "The Poets' Follies, big public events, had happened several years in a row before the Beats came on the scene. There was an indigenous group of activists". Another factor in the vogue for live performances was the effect of the touring Welsh bard Dylan Thomas. Ferlinghetti remarked that "Thomas had an enormous influence on me and, I may say, on other San Francisco poets. He did two marvellous readings in San Francisco on his American tours".[8]

San Francisco was the artistic centre for many years, having long been associated with bohemian lifestyles, its authors looking back to Jack London and forward to Richard Brautigan. Indigent writers could spend a relaxed time there, finding it hospitable to immigrant cultures, relaxed about sexual orientations, and with a 'European' atmosphere. In Allen Ginsberg's recollection, the city had many advantages for artists and a great deal of cross-fertilisation. There was a free flow between artistic generations and genres:

> It had a tradition of philosophical anarchism with the anarchist club that Rexroth belonged to, a tradition receptive to person rather than officialdom....There had already been a sort of Berkeley Renaissance in 1948 with Jack Spicer poet, Robert Duncan poet, Robin Blaser poet, Timothy Leary psychologist, Harry Smith, great underground filmmaker.... They were there all around the same time, they didn't know each other well but they were passing in the street....And specifically there were little magazines like *Circle*...there was a tradition that didn't exist in the more money-success-*Time*-magazine-oriented New York scene.[9]

The anthologist Bill Mohr has also pointed to social and economic forces directing the post-1945 population influx to California. The massive expansion of the Defence Industry, populist cultural movements from the Beats to the Hippies, and the ever-expanding Entertainment sectors, movies and television. "The suburban cities in Los Angeles County which first expanded when World War II brought huge numbers of people to work in the defense industries saw another population surge during the longest war in the United States' history, Vietnam....Many young people were moving here simply to be 'where it was happening', which included peace marches and rallies as well as movies and the Sunset Boulevard music scene".[10]

This applied equally to Los Angeles and its environs. But L.A. has always had a very different cultural atmosphere to San Francisco: less relaxed, more self-centered. The nature and layout of the city itself tends to prevent like-minded writers coalescing together to form groups. Los Angeles has often been portrayed in fiction and movies as a haven for loners, and this is fully echoed by Bukowski. In his introduction to the 1972 *Anthology of L.A. Poets*, he commented that "a man or woman, writer or not, can find more isolation in Los Angeles than in Boise, Idaho".[11] The meaner and tougher atmosphere of L.A. was something he relished, and drew strength from.

Many of his first, last, and most raucous readings were at California venues, and he must have read most often in Los Angeles and its environs. At the start of his performing career in 1969-70, Bukowski appeared on local campuses, and in bookstores such as 'The Bridge' on Sunset Boulevard. He moved on to appear on the same stage as rock groups in nightclubs, dealing with hecklers and exchanging banter with audiences. Bukowski soon learned to vary his tactics; at colleges, he was not simply a sit-down comedy act. One of his earliest campus readings was at Pomona College Art Department. He was paid $100 - his minimum fee in the first year or so was $25. Guy Williams, a teacher who helped organise the reading, wrote to Lafayette Young (a San Diego bookseller), testifying to Bukowski's emotional powers:

> After three days, I must tell you this: I still can't erase that scene in Rembrandt Hall - Bukowski standing there behind the podium with all the poems in his fist, his blood and belly full of booze, staring us down. The genteel audience, his disdain and him hurting so hard behind that ruined face. A face from another time, place, planet. As I think of it now my stomach still turns over, aches....he made me use my feelings. Gave me a ride in the gut bucket.[12]

Bukowski was unable to face poetry audiences sober. He was hardly unique among poets in that, of course. But his drinking on stage was a hallmark gesture, living up to his image as an alcoholic bard. He certainly 'lost it' at times. Locklin recorded the horrors of a day of two Bukowski readings given at the Long Beach campus around 1972. The earlier reading at midday passed off "without incident", but an afternoon in the nearby 'Gold Rush' tavern had turned Bukowski into "his doppelganger: [an] unruly, rude, bullying, self-styled demented genius". His account continues:

> Bukowski could barely talk by then, let alone discern many of the words on the page. Between attempts at poetry, he flaunted his thermos, alternately encouraged and insulted questioners, performed the world premiere of a one-note 'Melancholy Baby', all the time rocking back and forth upon the podium....I sat in back, laughing in spite of myself, while

reeling off rosaries that he might not topple from the stage and break his neck....He had planned to read two hours. My prayers were answered - his thermos dry, he gave it up after one.[13]

Stephen Kessler also recalled the hazards of Bukowski at large, describing a Santa Cruz benefit reading in 1974, where "Bukowski enraged the feminists and delighted the subliterary slobs by being himself on stage, reading in that unshakably murderous monotone for his allotted time punctuated by slurps off his quart of screwdriver [vodka and orange], then heckling his colleagues from the audience. ('Read ten more!' he yelled at Snyder as the hour approached midnight and the crowd hushed reverently to receive some of Gary's Zen/ environmentalist wisdom)".[14] Bukowski often encountered hostilty himself at readings. Joan Jobe Smith's article, 'The Poet as Entertainment', a contemporary account later reprinted in the Bukowski Newsletter *Sure*, captures the adversarial atmosphere at the Moulton Theatre, Laguna Beach in August 1976. "The women were especially unkind to Charles Bukowski that night". This was after all 'enemy territory'; well-heeled, conservative Orange County.

> Bukowski seemed to feel the tension in the theater. His recitation lacked its usual flamboyance and playfulness of *sotto voce* and *falsetto* [used when imitating women's voices], becoming monotonal...Finally, for comic relief, he paused as he usually does at his readings, to chat with the audience, to break the ice with them, and to unleash the verbal flood of questions and appraisals. In this intimate theatre, seating no more than 100, there were conspicuous spatterings of coughs...The proverbial pregnant pause was aborted....'Is there any word you find offensive?" [one of] the women in the front row asked. 'Love', he said quickly, breathing the word into the microphone, making it sound like 'lurve'. Nervous laughter. Then someone [Linda King] hollered from the back row: "then why you always tellin' me you love me?" Honest laughter. They were beginning to warm up to him. "Who's your whore this week, Bukowski?" a young male hollered. At last they had the nerve to get really mean.[15]

Joan Jobe Smith recently commented on the importance to Bukowski of Linda King's attendance at his early 1970s readings: "there was much banter and call-and-response between them livening things up. Sometimes the audience would yell for her to get up there on stage and read too. After they broke up, Buk's readings took on a lonely, sombre tone. He'd lost his echo" (uncollected letter, 8 June 2000). Such antics were alcohol-fuelled, but they also served a purpose beyond self-advertisement. He was never fazed at interrupting a poem in mid-flow. This 'lowered the tone', and linked in with Bukowski's constant intention of getting away from the 'holiness' of poetry. He told Michael Andrews in 1980 that "the bullshit's all right, but it's not as good as the poetry. I like to mix them together. It takes away from the holiness, the so-called holiness of the poetry".[16] Bukowski was well aware of the strain of playing up to the image he had created in his poems and stories. The human cost of being Charles Bukowski in public became increasingly wearing as he neared 60. Any poet is reading words which only they fully know their emotional investment in, in a highly charged atmosphere - then having to do it all again the next day or next week. Bukowski observed in one *Notes* column that poetry audiences - or rather, the 'fringe benefits' of readings, drink and groupies - had "killed Dylan Thomas" and "sucked many other poets into a grand imbecility. The poetry audiences must be respected, and denied".[17]

Those recordings on tape and CD available now of Bukowski's last readings show how tired and cynical he became about fulfilling audiences' expectations of antagonism, comedy and vulgarity. He signalled his intention of giving up in a poem read as the finale of a reading in Hermosa Beach, California, during April 1980. It describes a horrible atmosphere, in "this place like a bar or nightclub./ sold out: poet and audience both/ drunk".

"GIVE US MORE BLOOD!"
screams a young boy
from the back.
it's the best poem
of the night.[18]

He "drinks his way/ to the finish", manhandles a woman reporter, finds that his $500 fee is reduced by $68 to pay for bouncers, and ends by failing to find a woman for the night. The last line, "the reading is over" meant exactly that for Bukowski. Aside from one occasion in a San Pedro bookstore late in life, that was the end of his public reading career. According to a recent letter from his publisher (10 March 2000), the last recordings made by Bukowski were "perhaps 15 years before his death" [i.e. 1979]. There were none I am aware of after he turned ca. 65". But he did give interviews, at least one of which included a poem, 'Do you use a notebook?', from *Dangling in the Tournefortia*, which must have been recorded around 1981-82. Bukowski also read selections from the Harper Collins anthology *Run With the Hunted*, a recording dated 1 December 1992.

Bukowski's often-expressed scepticism (veering on contempt) about the value of performing extended to other poets' readings, though he claimed to rarely attend any. His partners, from Frances Smith and Linda King to Linda Lee Beighle, were enthusiastic attenders of poetry readings, not just his own. Bukowski actually encouraged readings by those whose work he trusted and liked, notably Gerald Locklin and Ron Koertge, during the early 1970s. At least once he set up a reading for Locklin at 'The Bridge' bookstore, and was annoyed when the latter's crowded teaching schedule meant that he forgot to turn up. Bukowski continually satirised those he considered bad writers, or exhibitionists 'wanting love' from audiences. "Beauti-ful', from 1984, illustrates the point. It concerns a narcissistic poet who plants "a stringy-haired blonde" at his readings to audibly say "beautiful". After a change of girlfriends, his new one goes into the same routine, only to be trumped by the previous:

and then it came
from the rear
from one of the back
seats:
"no, it wasn't, it was a
piece of shit!"[19]

Over-emphasis on audience manipulation has its drawbacks! For Bukowski just as much as the unnamed narcissist and for many others during the 1970s and beyond. The widening gap between poetry intended for silent reading, the inner ear, and poetry for performance became ever more marked. Robert Lowell was pitifully heckled at St. Marks in New York in the mid-1970s, by an audience restless at being given classical allusions and difficult poetry. The poet of *Life Studies* - whose 'informality' was always more apparent than real - seemed sadly outmoded. Bukowski's work was changed by his bread-and-butter performances in public. It became ever more direct and conversational, ever less romantic and literary; it didn't 'matter' so much that he was constantly interrupted. Certainly there is a great difference from his surrealistic simile and metaphor-laden 1950s to early 1960s poetry, as he himself acknowledged: "The early poems are much more lyrical than where I am now....In my present poetry, I go at matters more directly, land on them and then get out. I don't believe that my early methods and my late methods are either superior or inferior to one another. They are different, that's all".[20]

Bukowski was participating in a wider vogue, for 'democratising' poetry, pushing it towards 'entertainment', performance and recordings, and away from silent contemplation. But not that far - after all, he has always sold many more books than tapes. Each phase of Bukowski's career had a relatively low success rate; perhaps one poem in ten really 'comes off'. (But even a dud Bukowski poem is inimitable). Reading for crowds' ever shorter attention spans certainly affected him; many of his 1970s poems go for cheap laughs, the frisson of dirty words in public places.

Listening now to the recordings, those done live and at home, on tapes and CDs, they are fascinating, if uncomfortable. Pleasure is at times compromised by his mood, his antics. The exchanges with the audience - the bits between the poems - generally work well, even when they become formulaic. Some of the best Bukowski poems of the 1970s, perfectly structured for performance, yet rich enough to repay many re-readings - some real winners such as 'The catch', 'Eddie and eve', and 'Waxjob' - were apparently never recorded by him.

'The catch' is an enigmatic, fabulatory narrative about a strange ugly creature caught on the end of one of three fishermen's lines.[21] It takes on a life of its own, entertains a gathered crowd, before thrashing around, and dying, then disappearing as quickly as it had arrived. It may be a reflection upon Bukowski's performing self. It can certainly be read as a comical fable about the artist not feeling 'at home' in the world. Or about the artist's relation to an uncomprehending public. The creature as described has some analogies to Buk-like behaviour at readings, which included farting and belching; it briefly rides on the merry-go-round (of life? of the poetry circuit?) and has beer poured over its head. But to push possible personal analogies would detract from what the poem enacts so deftly, with scarcely a surplus word. It has clear kinships to Carlos Williams' 'The Sea Elephant', and perhaps to the philosophical bleakness of Robert Frost's 'Neither Far Out Nor in Deep', and even to the comedy of Robert Graves' 'Welsh Incident': all works that Bukowski is likely to have known.

'The catch' also illustrates the way in which Bukowski's allegedly 'unliterary' poems set off connections, cultural echoes in their readers or hearers. As has been demonstrated, Bukowski's works actually address themselves to literate audiences capable of appreciating their slangy departures from other kinds of writing, more polite expression. They make their pleasurable impact precisely by being different - harder, barer, rougher in diction - than smoother poetry. Yet despite his democratising intentions, Bukowski actually appeals to a fraction of the population as a whole. The typical man or woman in the L.A. street or bar has never heard of Bukowski. (This may be different in, say, Germany). If his poems were drawn to their attention, would they think it was 'poetry' at all? They don't rhyme, or employ regular rhythms, or use capital letters to begin each line. His sales figures mean that he must be being bought by those who don't normally buy contemporary poetry or novels. But most of his readers will surely have some educational connection with literature. The typical buyer and reader of Bukowski's books is likely to be a student, a would-be writer, a hip poetry enthusiast. His appeal to mass tastes comes primarily through his Hollywood connections and filmic interpreters.

As his published correspondence shows - and there is a great deal unpublished - Bukowski was in constant contact with editors, publishers, fans, and writers all over the States and Europe. And particularly within California, where he could occasionally see and be seen by them. A generation resident in L.A. and Long Beach, poets born elsewhere during the 1940s - Gerald Locklin, Ron Koertge, Steve Richmond, Joan Jobe Smith and others - were important to his career and its subsequent influence. They were his allies, friends, critics, and sounding-boards. And to many younger writers, Bukowski has been inspirational; they will have been to his readings, or heard his recordings. Even Californian would-be writers to whom his work is not congenial are likely to have viewed his rise with interest, such is the American cult of celebrity. Bukowski's currently wide ambit is clear. His work is now entering the language, being picked up on in popular culture, used in headlines and songs. Young writers are writing in ways which would not have been possible if he had never existed.

Bukowski's influence can be tracked through a number of important poetry anthologies since 1972. They have showcased Californian and Los Angeles poets, either as a distinct entity or as part of a national picture. Five names have been recurrent: Bukowski himself, Locklin, Koertge, John Thomas and Robert Peters. Given these books' agenda-setting intentions, and their acknowledgement of Bukowski's wide appeal, it is paradoxical that he is often represented by some of his weaker or most attitudinizing works. And ironically, from the most largest and most recent anthology, *The Outlaw Bible of American Poetry* (1999), Bukowski is ostentatiously absent because of copyright problems. Nevertheless, his influence is all the more noticeable for it being implicit, refracted as it is through his contemporaries, imitators and authentic successors.

An Anthology of L.A. Poets (1972) was of modest size, brought out by Bukowski's own Laugh Literary imprint, in conjunction with Paul Vangelisti's Red Hill Press based in Fairfax. It was a mixed bunch, and enjoyed an elastic grasp of geography, with most of the contributors known personally to Bukowski and living outside Los Angeles proper. Bukowski's introduction depicted the works as populist and accessible, being written against the idea that poetry should be "an in-game, a snob game, a game of puzzles and incantations".[22] A group photograph taken in sunshine showed Jack Hirschman, Gerda Penfold, Holly Prado, Charles Stetler, Linda King, Steve Richmond, Neeli Cherkovski [Cherry], Paul Vangelisti, John Thomas, Robert Peters, Gerald Locklin, Ron Koertge, and Bukowski himself.

Bukowski's manner had by then already begun to be imitated, if not nearly as much as it would by the 1980s. But it would be an oversimplification to attribute all virtue and vice in contemporary Southern Californian poetry to him. Another seminal figure of a differing kind within this kind of West Coast writing has been the New York poet and anthologist Edward Field. His 'movie verse', his several widely appreciated anthologies, and not least his friendships with Locklin, Charles Stetler and others have been important. As a generalisation, that strain in West Coast poetry which facetiously plays with popular culture, especially movies, comes from Field - and from his friend Frank O'Hara. Bukowski never mentions Field. As Gerald Locklin, an advocate of both, has pointed out, Bukowski was never much interested in competing geniuses of the same generation (cf. Ginsberg and Kerouac). As a critic of wide sympathies, Field has been far more generous. Field's poetic background has been cosmopolitan, ranging from England during the War to the New York poetry scene. And especially to the expatriate gay American authors in Tangiers, notably Paul and Jane Bowles, the visiting Beats, and his friend the novelist-critic Alfred Chester. Field's influence on the West Coast scene, like Bukowski's, has been exercised through other people, with his early collections *Stand Up, Friend, With Me* (1962) and *Variety Photoplays* (1963) being cited as major influences by Locklin and by Charles Harper Webb.

Published in mass-market paperback, Field's *A Geography of Poets* (1979) was a large (more than 560 pages) agenda-setting book, reflecting an inclusive impulse. Its intention was to showcase the regional richness of American verse, "the grass roots direction of current poetry". Accordingly, Field's manifesto was generally though not dogmatically against academic poets; it was a project of the times recognising "cultural decentralization". It set itself against both Modernist/Postmodernist cultural elitism, and the perceived domination of New York/ East Coast editors and publishers. Organised on a regional approach, the subsections were accordingly geographical rather than stylistic or thematic. The Southern California section included Bukowski, Locklin, Koertge, Stetler, Thomas, the veteran Kenneth Rexroth, the Mexican-American Gary Soto, and the poet-critic Robert Peters. In a lengthy prefatory essay detailing his own discovery of modern poetry, and surveying national trends, Field paid tribute to the "loosening up" effect of the Beats. He also, at least by implication, pointed to the already noticeable effect of Bukowskian subject material and language.

Among the various poetry hot-houses in various areas of the U.S., Field singled out the "lively" scene around Long Beach. "Charles Stetler, Ron Koertge, and Gerald Locklin are writing poems that are direct, funny, and often filthy. Their vernacular style, sassy and jaded, is at the opposite pole from the issue-orientated, righteous poetry of the Bay area to the north". Field identified their works as being "typically rooted in the places, issues and language of their immediate lives".[23] These everyday settings were bars, supermarkets, racetracks, and movie theatres; the latter two being favoured locales of Ron Koertge's work. (Koertge probably saw Bukowski at the track often enough). The Northern California/ San

Francisco section also included plenty of Bukowski associates, former friends, and fans: Alta, David Barker, Harold Norse, Gerda Penfold, alongside Lawrence Ferlinghetti and Karl Shapiro. Linda King, who since her days with Bukowski had moved to Arizona, was represented in the South West section. One of her poems was a recognisable and unflattering portrait, "dedicated to C.B."

he lumbers from the bed like a
three hundred pound orangoutang...
the only ape in town who
uses yards and yards of
pink flowered toilet paper.
('The great poet')[24]

Field's democratic and inclusive impulse would have been applauded by Bukowski, if not all of his selections, and certainly not his emphasis on the usefulness of poetry workshops. Field modestly concluded that the book was "a New Yorker's attempt to pay a debt of recognition". The book's successor was *A New Geography of Poets*, published by Arkansas University Press in 1992. Significantly, it was co-edited with Gerald Locklin and Charles Stetler, long-time colleagues in the English Department at Long Beach State University. They commented that "in our geography are poets of a rainbow of backgrounds, of a post-melting pot consciousness....vernacular poetry growing out of populist sentiments has exploded with a compelling verve and energy".[25] They pointed out that the 'geography' of contemporary poets also meant the workplace (citing Fred Voss), the racetrack (Bukowski) and the inner mental landscape in which movie stars loom large (quoting from a Joan Jobe Smith poem). Their selection of Southern California poets included Koertge, Wanda Coleman, Chris Daly, Lisa Glatt, Pamala Karol ('La Loca'), Rafael Zepeda, and Charles Harper Webb. The latter two were also Long Beach departmental colleagues, and some of the others graduates of the Long Beach creative writing programme. The editors maintained that the "torch of innovation" has passed from the Bay Area to the Long Beach/ Los Angeles nexus:

> In a landscape the rest of the country fantasizes about, Southern California poets largely ignore the unreal lure of the Hollywood mirage, orange groves, the surfer beaches, and Disneyland, and find their material more often in the somewhat sleazy realities of life, commemorating the survival of humanity among the sleaze....The new poetry from the L.A./ Long Beach area is laid back, more related to talk than song, invoking stand-up comics, sassy comebacks, bartalk, and true confessions. As in the poetry of Charles Bukowski, the leading poet of the area...cynicism is pervasive - love is often portrayed as alleycats

fighting, and financial problems are never far away. The bar, the racetrack, and porno shop are common settings, as are ethnic neighbourhoods, or the banal atmosphere of a supermarket. The feminism that the women poets seem to be expressing is the independence to take and talk sex as forthrightly as men.[26]

Bill Mohr's first selection from the L.A. scene was *The Streets Inside*, published in 1978. Its follow up, the weighty *Poetry Loves Poetry: An Anthology of Los Angeles Poets* (1985), was brought out by his Momentum Press in Santa Monica. It was a worthwhile, implicitly Politically Correct attempt at connecting up the madly eclectic scene, featuring writers of many divergent social identities. The book's size and handsome appearance was made possible by grants from the National Endowment for the Arts and an oil company, the Atlantic Richfield Foundation. Mohr's introductory essay, 'Self-Portraits in Los Angeles', once again points to immigration as a fundamental factor, noting "the several hundred poets who have taken up permanent residence here in the past twenty years". He characterised them in general as loners, and as 'existential romantics', observing that the "huge majority" of these poets "write narrative poetry which emphasizes visual imagery".[27]

Appropriately for loners, he noted that "there isn't a social scene among the poets", unlike in San Francisco or New York. (The Long Beach poets in fact regularly used to meet each other in bars, a favourite venue being 'The Reno Room'). Mohr outlined those organisations and venues which have brought writers together in L.A., perhaps most importantly the Beyond Baroque Foundation which has run reading series and workshops since 1968. The Women's Building, as the name suggests, was a centre of feminist publishing activity. He acknowledged Bukowski's status as the best-known Los Angeles poet and "one of the most influential in the United States". Mohr saw his influence particularly in the "heterosexual warfare" at large in the work of many writers.

The anthology carried career details of 62 contributors of 390 poems; far too many for any real coherence to emerge. Mohr attempted to capture this vast range with the phrase "they have evolved an idiosyncratic blend of poetics which incorporates everything from O'Hara's 'Personism' to Olson's 'Projective Verse". In truth, the book's inclusiveness drew together poets diversified more by ethnicity and sexual orientation than by variety of styles. Most deployed an easy-talking free verse, writing about their lives and fantasies; and virtually none used any formal devices or regular metres. Many now seem workshop-produced poets of little distinctiveness. But there were some strong individual voices scattered throughout the book. Black women poets, such as Wanda Coleman who is published by Black Sparrow, and Michelle T. Clinton. Feminists were well represented by Aleida Rodriguez (editor of *Rara Avis*), Kate Braverman, Amy Gerstler, Holly Prado and Suzanne Lummis. Male gay poets were also conspicuous, easily the most accomplished being Dennis Cooper, editor of the magazine and publishing imprint *Little Caesar* from 1977 to 1983, Peter Cashorali, and Robert Peters.

Movers and shakers of the L.A. scene were well to the fore. Austin Straus, host for some years of 'The Poetry Connection' on KPAX Radio, which gave local and nationally-known poets welcome exposure for many years; Michael C. Ford, editor of *Sunset Palms Motel* and a Bukowski admirer since the *Open City* days; as was Bob Flanagan, connected with workshops at the Beyond Baroque Foundation. Also featured were Jack Grapes (who had been published way back in *The Outsider* and later became editor of *Onthebus*), P. Schneidre of publishers Illuminati, and Leland Hickman who edited the magazines *Bachy* and *Temblor*. Locklin, Koertge, Thomas, Webb, and Vangelisti were included; as were several younger writers with a Locklin connection, notably singer-songwriter Dave Alvin and Laurel Ann Bogen. A few true mavericks were to be found. The most original was the British tennis player-turned poet Nichola Manning, yet another Bukowski fan whose works were a Transatlantic species of humorous everyday surrealism. 'Come on, strangle me' - not included in the anthology but in a British magazine, *Ambit* - characterises her zany world. It describes what is essentially an S&M sex game, resulting both in a weird orgasm, and in grandchildren "popping out like bowling balls".[28] She gave a number of exuberantly funny performances during the 1980s, encouraged by her boyfriend the late Robert de Laura, before disappearing in true Dada fashion.

Charles Harper Webb has been for some years a Professor of English, alongside Stetler, Locklin, Rafael Zepeda, and Elliot Fried, at Long Beach, as well as a practising psychotherapist. His essay-anthology *Stand Up Poetry* (1990) continued the defining process, with an argument about the nature of the poetry of Los Angeles "and beyond". He included work by 22 writers, many of the usual suspects but also Billy Collins, Edward Field, Steve Kowit (editor of the 1989 collection *The Maverick Poets*, to which Bukowski contributed), Laurel Ann Bogen, James Krusoe, Wanda Coleman and Manazar Gamboa. Webb characterised L.A. Poets' difference from the 'insiders' of academic poetry partly in career and publishing terms. West Coasters: generally published by small, independent presses. Prize-winning poets and reputation traders: generally published by University presses and/or the East Coast publishing world. (There are exceptions. Certain collections by Ron Koertge; Billy Collins has since crossed over to East Coast publication. And Webb himself published a novel with Chatto & Windus, a major publishing house in London).

'Stand-up', like the word 'Beat', (Beats being acknowledged as predecessors) has for Webb at least a double meaning. A performing, comedy aspect; and the Edward Field-like 'standing up for your rights'. Though there are women poets included, perhaps there is an implicit third meaning to do with male sexual energy, a subject that Webb has also bravely tackled. The common characteristics he identified were as follows. Clarity (as opposed to the 'obscurity' of Modernism/Post Modernism); the use of ordinary, natural language; humour; performability; flights of fancy; direct address and asides to the reader; the breaking down of barriers between prose and poetry modes; and the use of popular culture such as movies and television.[29] Most, though not all, of these can be found in, perhaps even attributed to, Bukowski. But by no means all. Exceptions which spring to mind are that Bukowski almost never writes 'odes to' things, say, 'Beer' as Locklin does; or investigates the private life of comic strip Superheroes as Koertge does; or plays with kitsch movie characters as Field does in 'The Bride of Frankenstein'. Bukowski has his tributes to movies and movie stars. But an ode, however casually expressed, would be too self consciously literary, alien to his purposes.

West Coast poets are prominent in *The Outlaw Bible of American Poetry* (1999), edited by Alan Kaufman and S.A.Griffin, the latter a long-time Bukowski fan. This collection of dangerous characters actually achieved 'Book of the Month' status with a leading paperback club. At nearly 700 pages in length, it is a grand source of information on a host of neglected talents: d.a. levy, William Wantling, Kenneth Patchen, and the 'Meat Poets' (while leaving out prime mover Douglas Blazek). It spans a vast range, from the Dead Greats (Whitman, Carlos Williams, Ginsberg, Kerouac, Brautigan, even the actor James Dean) to anarchic street poets ('the Reverend Pedro') and singer-songwriters from Bob Dylan to Leonard Cohen. But mostly it is a compendious assembly of "Beats, Rappers, Slammers, Nuyoricans, Queers, Beatniks, Slackers, and Punks". It gives printed form to oral performers, the 'dub' poets, the shouters and extroverts, "from the clubs of Manhattan's East Village to the cafes of San Francisco to the rock stages of Venice West".[30] Women are prominent among the better-known performance poets, Wanda Coleman, Sapphire, Lisa Martinovich, and Karen Finlay.

Southern California poets feature in the book, though not as any 'school' or coterie. Their selection fills in 'gaps', but by no means all. Among those who surely merited inclusion were Robert de Laura, a surreal poet widely published in small magazines of the 1970s, and the aforementioned Nichola Manning. The late Bob Flanagan (1952-1996) was included: he conducted poetry workshops at Beyond Baroque for many years. His 'Bukowski Poem' treats the difficulty of a young writer trying to do what C.B. has already trademarked:

and she starts yelling and throwing
glasses and all of a sudden I realize
it sounds a lot like
a Bukowski poem....

What's wrong with you? she asks.
Oh, nothing, I say, it's just that
I'm starting to write like Bukowski....

And I go to the bathroom and feel
like vomiting but can't.
I fill the tub with hot water.
CHRIST! I yell.
I don't take baths; Bukowski takes
baths! I take showers![31]

Among the other West Coast poets featured, Fred Voss is the best-known and most highly regarded - at least in Britain. This is due to his being published by a leading press, Bloodaxe Books, his several reading tours, and to the widespread appreciation of his landmark collection *Goodstone* (1991). It was enthusiastically reviewed in the *TLS* and the national press, praised for its poetry of 'witness', and hailed as a contemporary classic. John Osborne, editor of *Bête Noire* which had previously published over a hundred Voss poems in successive issues between 1989-90, called his factory poems "without parallel in Anglo-American verse".[32] *Goodstone* is a fictional treatment of the machine shops in which Voss himself has worked for 20 years, after dropping out of a Ph.D in English. It consists of a multi-faceted series of portraits of masculinity under extreme pressure and factory conditions. Under the economic whip of short term Air Force contracts, the workers' siege psychology and survival tactics, management incompetence and implied corruption, are presented in telling vignettes. The human cost on individuals is added up without authorial sentimentality:

each morning when he came to work and put his hard hat on
there seemed to be a heavier weight on his head,
pushing him into the concrete floor
of the steel mill,
driving his neck and his head
down into his shoulders
as if he were a shaft being driven through concrete
by a jackhammer
('Termination')[33]

Voss's poems are powerful machines made of words. He has credited Bukowski with his beginnings as a writer; and he indubitably learned about a hammered-down style from him. Like Bukowski, Voss creates a narrowly-focussed, intense fictional world, with special attention to the socially and economically marginalised. There is a full range of emotions portrayed, from comedy, farce, anger to pathos; and a teeming cast of desperate or poignant characters. Yet Voss has also taken on the structurally simple language mode into areas other than the bohemian. Differences of tone and attitude immediately become apparent. Both may praise Beethoven, but Voss finds spiritual dimensions in the music that are almost completely absent from the resolutely materialist Bukowski. Voss is the foremost contemporary poet treating the essential subject of work, on either side of the Atlantic: readers often find that the stark but implicitly political analysis his poetry offers applies equally to offices as it does to the factory.

Characters in Bukowski's novels *Post Office* and *Factotum* comment adversely on the hellish and deadening nature of routinised work, but their view (*pace* the critic Russell Harrison) is more personal than political. In poems, of course, his characters are very often not working at all, though they may well be 'Looking for a job'. Bukowski himself regretted the 'wasted' time he had spent in factories; for Voss it is, in both senses, his work. He wrote to Voss that "Your poems about working at the machines, well, I liked them, understood them, sure. The way we fight to hold jobs that are killing us physically and spiritually but we are more afraid of no job at all so we swallow the shit and the abuse and pretend there's something left of us after we walk out of there. The bottle and the word saved part of me but there is a part I will never get back: the wasted hours, the wasted years given over to them". (uncollected letter, 1 May 1992)

Being from a much younger generation, Voss is far more attuned to a contemporary consciousness of sexual politics. As has been emphasized as of fundamental importance, Bukowski's personal ethos and literary values were formed in the 1930s-40s. Unsurprisingly, full appreciation of feminism, racism, and gay liberation escaped him. It doesn't escape Voss: he largely breaks with Bukowski's machismo. The San Pedro local paper *Random Lengths* reported on the growing reputation of "The Machinist Poet of Long Beach". Julia Stein noted that "Voss has absorbed Bukowski's influences yet expanded them". For Voss, it is the confines of work, "and the way they delineate and constrict the individuals who work with them", that are significant.[34]

Fred Voss's poetic career has gained lift-off during his marriage to the poet and magazine editor Joan Jobe Smith. She was a friend and correspondent of Bukowski's during the early to mid-1970s, and was often teased by him for her late-blooming academic studies, which resulted in an

MFA from the University of California at Irvine. Her collections *Jehovah Jukebox*, published by Event Horizon in 1993, and *The Pow Wow Cafe* (1998) are distillations of her life experiences. These include being a child taken to cosmopolitan Long Beach from a small town in Texas; romances as a 1950s High School Prom Queen; being a movie fan, mother, carer and divorcee; and working as a go-go dancer in clubs and bars for seven years. Her poems are necessarily personal but also constructed as a wider social witness, often to the sexual and economic exploitation of women:

...all the men drinking beer and laughing
and smoking cigars and cigarettes and watching
Robin whose name I didn't know yet dance some
dance I didn't know how to dance yet to the
Rolling Stones singing a song about a stupid girl
on the jukebox playing as loud as it would go...
first thing a drunken man in a beerbar ever asked me
my first day on the job, a go-go girl in the raw:
Is that chick up there on the rag or is she really
a fag with her balls tied up in a jock?
('Aboard the Bounty')[35]

Her publishing and editorial activities have been significant, helping to encourage new talent - not least her husband's - and 'connect up' the Long Beach/ L.A. poetry scene. In its initial incarnation, *Pearl* was a space for women's writing, its premise being "to present the feminine point of view of poetics in toto." But, stated its Winter 1974 issue, "having obliged this objective with two issues, and standing alone being the natural posture for statues [rather] than for woman...all subsequent issues will embrace the art and poetics of man". One of the all-female issues included poems by, among others, Ann Menebroker, Lyn Lifshin, Rochelle Holt, Smith herself; and Linda King, described as "sculptress, writer, bartender". A printed extract from a King letter, dated 9 October 1974, mentioned that she and Bukowski had "just got off a poetry trip to Salt Lake City....Bukowski claimed I stole the show, but I don't really think so. He did get too drunk to finish his reading".[36] The magazine was relaunched in the 1980s, co-edited with Marilyn Johnson and Barbara Hauk. Bukowskiana, poems and drawings, sometimes appeared. The magazine continues to have an international scope, while being based around a core of Long Beach writers.

Bukowski by no means appeals only to male sensibilities. Many women poets have learned from him, especially sassy Californians. The inevitable gender differences mean that they cannot imitate him as easily as young male poets can and do. Some have, in a general sense, been 'freed up' by their contacts and correspondence with him. This applies also to those whose relationship with Bukowski was solely with his work. Devreaux Baker comes to mind, based in Mendocino on the northern California coast, and a friend of Stephen Kessler who has been a regular commentator on C.B. Pamala Karol (a.k.a. 'La Loca'), a performance poet whose *Adventures on the Isle of Adolescence* was published in the City Lights Pocket Poets Series in 1989, has been a long-time admirer of Bukowski. Her uninhibited celebration of female sexual appetite and manners (e.g.'You should only give head to guys you really like'), working class content, and confessional 'openness' owes at least something to him:

...I filled the ears of the man of the house
full of his son's orgasm.
I was not what they wanted for him.
But it was the fire season
and their saber-toothed brawls with their boy
over leaving dirty creamers in the sink
were in weed,
dry,
waiting for a match.
('I received this woman's intimacies')[37]

The same general observation can be made about the poems of Lisa Glatt. One of the younger generation Long Beach poets, her work has been encouraged by Locklin and praised by Edward Field. Indeed, Locklin's endorsement on the back of her first collection *Monsters and Other Lovers* (1996) observes that she "writes about sex in as funny and convincing and touching a manner as any woman I have ever read. If there is to be such a thing as a female Bukowski, it will probably be Lisa...she is already influencing a generation of writers only slightly her junior". Her second and latest collection, *Shelter* (Pearl Editions, 2000) shows that she has already developed her range beyond this. Her highly 'driven' poems are obsessional, relatively explicit, though often humorously satirical about the sexual pretensions of 'boys'.

She re-works that perennial subject of female poets, the body, as well as the all-consuming mother-daughter relationship. But she also looks with a cold eye on the contemporary urban scene of Singles bars, pick-ups, and mornings-after; what Bill Mohr called "heterosexual warfare". Bukowski has been a kind of poetic (grand)father, almost a fantasy figure. He appears as a beneficent ghost in her 'Giving Charles Bukowski My Leg'. It is an intimate act of homage, incestuous and necrophiliac in its intensity, written with unblinking awareness of all those 1970s Bukowski poems about having sex with much younger women:

Like a dead father
he comes to me
in the night, sits
at the foot of my bed,
wanting things.
Like a dead father
he's ready to know me
now, only after the worms
have covered his rich face.

*It's so much easier
to want you from here*, he says.

I would bend over
if he even hinted
but it's not my ass
he wants; it's my leg....

I unscrew it at the knee,
offering him
my calf, ankle, and foot.
All my ugly things.

Ugly, he agrees.

And he is beautiful
then, opening his hand,
holding it, he is beautiful,
touching my few dark hairs,
lifting my weird leg
to the light, beautiful,
I tell you,
more beautiful
than any one
of my smooth skinned boys.[38]

    Glatt, like a number of the L.A./ Long Beach poets, is an excellent performer. And there have been many reading venues and opportunities for her and others. One favoured location for many years in Long Beach, where Fred Voss did some of his earliest readings, was 'Beneath Broadway', underneath an old downtown hotel. He also recalled, in a 1996 interview, 'The House of Chan', which was formerly the home of a Chinese herb doctor. At a nightclub called 'Bogart's' he once read with Timothy

Leary. The longest-running local reading series has been that under the auspices of *Pearl* magazine: it was "started in a deserted lot where the Pike Amusement Park and Cyclone Racer rollercoaster used to be, across the road from a tattoo parlour....and later held in a cafe where old Blues Greats like John Lee Hooker and Junior Wells play".[39]

These readings were and remain a vital proving ground for young writers. Back in Los Angeles during the 1970s, a series of readings was held (1976-77) at The Alley Cat, a restaurant in Hermosa Beach. These featured John Thomas, Michael C. Ford, Ben Pleasants, Steve Richmond et al., but also a variety of emergent voices including Michael Andrews, Deena Metzger, Kate Braverman, Eloise Klein Healy. Such informal venues abounded then, with readings in libraries, record stores, and bookstores such as Chelsea, Chatterton's, Papa Bach and George Sand; in the Poecentric Lounge, Gasoline Alley, The Sculpture Gardens, Bebop Records and Fine Arts, The Midnight Special bookstore, and the Los Angeles Theater Center. The Beyond Baroque Foundation has run regular reading series since 1973, notably under the direction of James Krusoe (editor of *Santa Monica Review*), Dennis Cooper, and Amy Gerstler.

In Southern California, poetry is crossed conspicuously with social factors, usually ethnicity and sexual orientation. (This extends to readers: there are numerous gay and lesbian bookstores. In San Pedro, Vinegar Hill Books was reportedly Bukowski's favourite). The diffuse and discontinuous scene of the 1970s-80s-90s produced a plethora of little magazines and small presses serving a variety of interests. Jack Grapes' *Onthebus*, from Bombshelter Press, announced itself committed to publishing writers "who deserve a wider audience". Grapes himself edited yet another anthology, *The New Los Angeles Poets* (1989), featuring young talents - the only recognisable name now being Lisa Glatt. There were postmodernist coteries also: Eliot Weinberger's *Montemora*, and *Sulphur*, edited by Clayton Eshleman, favoured Black Mountain poetics. Also prominently featuring Southern California writers have been magazines elsewhere in the States. Most notable current publication: the newspaper format *Chiron Review*, edited by Michael Hathaway from Great Bend, Kansas. This latter long-running magazine has been a rich source of commentary on Bukowski. *Pinchpenny*, edited by Tom Milner from Sacramento, California, and Jay Dougherty's Connecticut-based *Clock Radio*, regularly featured Bukowski and his associates during the 1980s.

Black Sparrow Press is the profitable summit of a mostly unprofitable but vital publishing pyramid. It has itself moved to several locations over the past two decades, from Los Angeles to Santa Barbara, then to Santa Rosa. Black Sparrow now has international clout and distribution, a wide roster of avant-garde American authors over the past 35 years. It is an exemplar for independent publishers, specialising in limited edition, signed or special copies. The colourful designs symbolise a rather different ethos from its only California rival, the mostly black and white City Lights editions. Bukowski remains far and away Black Sparrow's best seller. One of Bukowski's most admirable personal qualities was his loyalty to editors and publishers who believed in his work. By staying with Black Sparrow, he eventually reaped very high financial rewards. A statement in 1988 to interviewer Jay Dougherty reflected on this. It remains a substantially accurate view of his relations with his main publisher.

> Black Sparrow press has a limited circulation and this tends to hold down being known widely in the U.S. Yet they have published book after book of mine throughout the years, and most of the books are still in print and available. Black Sparrow and I almost began together and it is my hope that we will end together....If I had gone to a large New York publisher, I might have larger U.S. sales...but I doubt that I would continue writing in a workmanlike and joyful fashion. Also, I doubt that I would have the same uncensored acceptability that I have at Black Sparrow. As a writer I consider myself in the best of worlds: famous elsewhere and working here. The gods have spared me many of the pitfalls of the average American writer. Black Sparrow came to me when nobody else would....It would be ungrateful of me to seek a large New York publisher now. In fact, I don't have the slightest desire to do so.[40]

Back in the 1960s, Black Sparrow was a very small press. Small-scale publishing is and was the norm in California, and further afield. During the 1970s, John Kay's Mag Press, Bob Austin's True Gripp Press, and Paul Vangelisti's Red Hill Press were active. During the 1980s, Applezaba Press and Illuminati served local writers, as did Roy Shabla's Artaban Press (Downey, California), Kirk Robertson's Duck Down Press (Fallon, Nevada), the late Leo Mailman's Maelstrom Press (Cape Elizabeth, Maine), and Bill Mohr's Momentum Press (Santa Monica, California). More recently, a new and innovative publisher has emerged, Event Horizon Press located in Desert Springs, California. Editor-publisher Joseph Cowles has produced striking-looking books by Donna Hilbert, Joan Jobe Smith, Lyn Lifshin, Jennifer Olds, Locklin,Voss and others, fully using the new publishing technology.

The writing scene in California has therefore been formed and influenced by social and literary factors; by successive waves of immigrants, the local tradition of small press and little magazine activity, and an infrastructure of venues for readings. In addition, the National Endowment for the Arts has provided substantial funds; grants for example to the Beyond Baroque Foundation, many of the small presses and magazines, and numerous individual fellowships. But it would be simplistic to attribute the flowering of poetry in Southern California during recent decades to infrastructure, economics, or even the influence of leading authors like Bukowski and Edward Field. There is also the role of vital linking figures, often playing multi-roles as author, teacher, critic, impresario, and socialiser.

Such is Gerald Locklin, a friend and correspondent of both Bukowski and Field, and who is clearly the major inter-generational figure in L.A. and Long Beach during this period. He has been a small press titan and one-man renaissance for three decades. Locklin's influence has been exercised by his work, his personal example but also in his critical advocacy of Bukowski. More exactly, by his teaching of Creative Writing and personal effect on numerous young writers. Bukowski would never officially countenance academia, beyond accepting lucrative readings. Yet sympathetic academics were essential to Bukowski's reputation, and even, ironically, to the dissemination of his anti-academic approach to writing. The Bukowski-Locklin affinity was based firstly on their shared love of Hemingway, and progressed intermittently over two decades to become a mutually supportive literary kinship.

The archive of correspondence between the two men held at Long Beach shows their mutual regard, and that literary 'influence' was by no means all one way. (There is evidence for this. Bukowski's final novel, *Pulp*, a detective fiction moving uneasily between parody and symbolism, was clearly suggested to him by Locklin's much funnier and more sharply-written novella spoofing the genre, *The Case of the Missing Blue Volkswagen*. This was first published by Applezaba Press in 1984 - and their letters show that it was much appreciated by Bukowski). No flatterer in general, he constantly asked Locklin to send him publications as they appeared, telling him that they had 'saved his life'. Their correspondence also implies Bukowski's perhaps surprising deference to Locklin's academic status. Certainly he encouraged, confided in, gave advice about women, drink and writing to, and very rarely harangued, the younger man.

He also addressed several poems specifically to Locklin, who later returned the compliment in his own *Wormwood* sections. (The magazine at times became a channel of two-way communication between Bukowski and the younger generations of writers ushered in by Malone). Interesting among these poems, indicating their warm relationship, is 'A bit of light for the toad' - the toad being Locklin's early fictional persona. It sets him right about Linda King's liking for parties, her sculpting of Locklin's head ("making you look like a Greek god"), Neeli Cherkovski's Groucho Marx impressions and makes other personal observations.[41]

Bukowski's preface to one of Locklin's publications emphasises the Rabelaisian qualities which extend into his writing: "He swings from the heels, pukes from the bathroom. He's open and he calls the shots".[42] For his part, Locklin acknowledged that "there's no question that I learned a great deal from him, and that others have....Probably the most important thing I learned from Bukowski was that poetry could be about anything. Could be a story, joke, laundry list, letter-to-the-editor". (uncollected letter 9 February 1985). As with any writer strong in their own identity, there are ultimately major differences of tone and attitude between them. Locklin after all, learned equally from his fellow New Yorkers Nathanael West and Edward Field, and alongside his friend Ron Koertge at Tucson, Arizona. Locklin's work, moving as easily as Bukowski's between poetry and prose, uses popular culture facetiously. West Coast fads and fashions in the academic world, current orthodoxies of all kinds, are regularly sent up. Locklin is essentially a social satirist, with Long Beach as his *Main Street*. He has been a long-term critical observer of Bukowski's career, writing many articles and reviews, coming up with many insights. His view back in 1985 was that Bukowski was himself 'freed up' by refusing to act in any editorial capacity:

> He feels it is his job to write, and leaves the selection and evaluation to others. Thus, he is free to write a lot. The unevenness of his published work leaves Bukowski vulnerable to the critic with an axe to grind, who may select exclusively from the second-rate or from what he needs to prove his thesis. But such critics are easily refuted by anyone who has read along with Bukowski over the years.[43]

The Bukowski/Locklin imprint is visible in the works of a number of younger poets who chronicle their schooling in life-and-hard-knocks. Mark Weber, for instance, a native Angeleno musician-writer now resident in New Mexico who has published several joint chapbooks with Locklin, as has Rafael Zepeda. They have also marked the 'Taxi Poems' of Chris Daly, whose fictional world is that of mean streets Los Angeles, as seen by a detached but fascinated viewer. His poems report offhandedly to the reader about the urban poor, the nocturnal habits of prostitutes, pimps, drug dealers. They are stories spun to enliven a humdrum if dangerous occupation:

black girls are always
taking cabs from one house
to another in the middle of the night....

...and there's a bar at one
if not both ends of the trip. mex

ican girls i took

only once and they had
4 to 7 children between
three of them and they had me
stop on the way for a few minutes
of duking in the street with that bitch
bubbles who fucked
oscar. no pachucos were at
either end. orientals are
rare; once i sped an ageing
masseuse from one parlor to another...
('A little typewriting')[44]

Such glimpses, (of what is known in prose as Dirty Realism) are filled with characters abroad at a time when middle-class Americans are safely sleeping. Douglas Goodwin is another L.A. poet clearly of the urban angst and alienation mode. Bukowski showed his regard by writing forewords for Goodwin's collections *Half Memory of a Distant Life* (1987) and *Slamming It Down* (1993).

As Jeffrey Gomez, a fan in Ventura, California, rightly pointed out in a 1992 issue of *Sure*, "it's difficult to pick up a quarterly or mimeographed poetry magazine these days without feeling the omnipresent stamp of Charles Bukowski's style". His 'Tales of just plain ordinary' is a satirical vision:

last night the students of Charles Bukowski
came to my house
in a sleep walking state
mumbling something about pulling down the shades in small
rented rooms...

I ran to the post office for safety and a sign said
NO MORE STAMPS
because the fans of Charles Bukowski
had bought them all
in order to submit their poems to small magazines...[45]

Certainly anyone editing a literary magazine in the Western world now will regularly receive would-be contributions in a sub-Buk mode: slangy-titled slim poems full of words such as guts, beer and agony. As well as inspiring young writers to find their authentic own voices, Bukowski has also inevitably spawned a thousand-and-one duds - mainly because his work makes poetry look 'easy'. "They're all little BUKOWSKIS!" was his own reported comment. Locklin wryly pointed out that these imitators were more into a lifestyle interest than an artistic one: "they'll do the drinking but won't listen to Beethoven".[46] Bukowski, and those taking his legacy forward, knew that so far as mastering the art of poetry is concerned, there is no substitute for a lifetime.

Bukowski's death in March 1994 had an emotional effect on many writers. On those who had known him personally, and those who didn't but to whom his work has meant so much. In an interview published in *Chiron Review* shortly afterwards, John Bennett, long-time editor of *Vagabond*, was asked about a story he had written about his 'adventures' with Bukowski, 'The Party to End All Parties', and whether he was "the wild man we read about in his poetry and fiction". Bennett responded: "Bukowski? The man had his fears and foibles and petty side, but he also had compassion and awareness and sanity". In the same issue, Dan Nielsen, editor of *Black Gun Silencer*, remarked that after the death of his favourite author "it feels like we're all tied for last".[47]

Among the small press tributes which then emerged, the one which stands out was *Das Ist Alles*, a beautifully produced anthology by numerous hands, including Frances Smith a.k.a. 'Franceye', (mother of Bukowski's daughter Marina) and edited by Joan Jobe Smith for Pearl Editions. Another heartfelt contribution was *Last Call: A Legacy of Madness* (1995), put out by Lummox Press and Vinegar Hills Books in San Pedro. Editor Raindog gathered together poems and prose by himself, Locklin, Jay Alamares, Tracey Young-Cleantis, and - a young 'son of Bukowski' - T. Thrasher. Raindog's preface states that "Bukowski spoke to me. Even though the experiences of our lives were very different, he spoke to me....The essence of his tale was that of survival, one man's attempt to beat the odds. A man against the elements; except in this case, the elements aren't the capricious whims of the indifferent natural forces, but the indifferent and self-serving human race".[48] Bukowski's self-mythologising had clearly worked brilliantly. T. Thrasher, yet another Creative Writing student of Locklin's at CSULB, is widely published in the area's magazines and shows signs of making a breakthrough to a high energy poetry that partakes of 'slams' but is more satirically subtle. He rewrites the bohemian life of drink and difficulties with women with postmodern ironies, and almost embodies Bukowski's plea at the end of the 1966 'Rambling Essay on Poetics and the Bleeding Life...' for "some surly [young] hardhead to come on through".[49]

Bukowski's impact in California and beyond has been both individual and collective, to do with freeing language and even sexual politics. It is available to be worked with or rejected by succeeding generations. The man who had such anxiety over his actual father, and in giving credit to his artistic fathers, eventually became a paternal figure himself. He can be seen as an exemplary West Coast author, both typical and extraordinary in his artistic struggle. It was more than horse-racing that Jack Micheline invoked when he called Bukowski "The longest shot that ever came in!".[50] Such a career showed that a poet published exclusively by small presses could come to prominence given the right conditions. (Allen Ginsberg was a comparable figure, but he gained international repute far earlier in his career). Many young writers in Southern California will want to escape Bukowski's huge shadow, while others will not be able to. His manner now seems part of the established landscape of modern poetry. He is, say current Black Sparrow blurbs, "arguably" America's "most influential and imitated poet". Locklin has pointed out that with the death of Bukowski, and Marvin Malone of *Wormwood Review*, an era in L.A./ Long Beach writing has come to a close.[51] Things will have to change and move on. In retrospect it was the larger historical context of Californian literature, and the specific conditions under which West Coast authors operate, that made Bukowski's work possible. He in turn is still very much a living presence in its contemporary writing, which is highly conscious of all ironies implicit in the term 'The Golden State'.

Chapter 8

Das Ist Alles : Charles Bukowski Reconsidered

"regard me, even as dead, more alive than
many of the living"
- 'Regard me'[1]

If one of the essentials of an important poet is quotability, then this so-called 'Poet Laureate of Los Angeles low-life' will surely survive. The ability to live beyond the grave and enter the culture, the general language of everyday, is, at its most basic, about providing bite-sized chunks for readers to carry around in their heads. For novelists to cannibalise as titles, and for newspaper sub-editors to use as headlines. Bukowski has many candidates for inclusion in future hip anthologies of quotations. His book titles alone might provide a rich source. *The Days Run Away Like Wild Horses Over the Hills* and *Tales of Ordinary Madness* have both already been used several times in British and U.S. newspapers. Other probabilities are *Burning in Water, Drowning in Flame*; *Love is a Dog From Hell*. (Titles of posthumous books seem to have tailed off somewhat). He has a host of memorable lines and passages, richly elegiac words which resonate within lives once read and - with more difficulty - understood by experience. In essence, his subjects were actually the age-old business of poetry: *lacrimae rerum* (the sadness of things) and *carpe diem* (seize the day). He simply gave them human form, the shadow of American myth, and set them walking the streets of L.A. A further aspect of his quotability lies outside the scope of this book: his *Notes* columns, seething as they are with jokey aphorisms such as a park bench Oscar Wilde might have been proud of: "The difference between art and life is that art is more bearable".[2]

The poet and critic Richard Howard, writing six years after T.S. Eliot's decease, loftily discoursed on that phase in the life of a poet's work which "generally begins only after his death and after a certain nimbus - sulfurous or celestial - has ceased to aureole his figure among us. It is the phase in which, at last, we may read what a poet says without the extensions of scandal or scripture".[3] That period where his poetry must stand or fall without its creator has been reached. Bukowski stands at the very end of the long line of Romanticism, begun back in the late 18th and early 19th Centuries, the individual life of the mind magnified. Further Romantic comparisons suggest themselves. He must create, Wordsworth wrote, speaking of the 'authentic poet', the taste by which he is to be enjoyed. Sales of Bukowski artefacts - books, tapes, fanzines, artwork, t-shirts, postcards, and memorabilia - indicate that this has happened. Keats urged that that which is creative must create itself. As we have seen, it was a lengthy process by which the derivative, omnivorously-reading, somewhat father-fixated Henry Charles Bukowski, Jr. became the authoritative Charles Bukowski we recognise. He remains a great example not just of dedication but of how to create yourself, how to find the courage to become one's own authentic artistic self. For Bukowski, this transformation from anxiety into self-assurance was well underway during the 1960s, and achieved by 1970 and his decisive escape into freelance authorship.

Bukowski's relatively unselfconscious writing practices are a great corrective to overly careful poets, and academics forever problematising, and theorising the act of poetry. By contrast, his pragmatic approach viewed poetry as a part of his everyday life, and it involved the handmaids of quasi-sexual pleasure - music and drink. His message to young writers was that 'doing it' was more important than talking about doing it. Such attitudes allowed him to be prolific, concerned solely with creation. They were often accompanied by ill-informed sideswipes at the Creative Writing industry, which is still one of the fastest-growing areas in American higher education. The arch-individualist professed to despise any aspect of the pseudo-collaborative, particularly the poetry workshop. Even in the early 1970s he was sending them up:

"...Leroi Jones, Ray Bradbury, lots of big
boys...they said this stuff was
good..."

"it's bad poetry, man. they are powdering your ass".
('The black poets')[4]

Bukowski's spartan view was that the only place to write was alone at a typewriter (later at a PC). His prejudices put down not just workshops, but the whole idea that creativity can be taught. And as a corollary, he badmouthed 'schools' of poets, even when such a label was simply academic shorthand for a wide variety of individual poets - 'The Black Mountain School', 'The New York School'. As Joe Wolberg pointed out, Bukowski's image as a writer was never an untutored one but self-tutored: poetry as a dialogue with the self. He learned by decades of self-directed reading, by formative contacts with others, by experience and practice. In this kind of development he followed some of America's greats, notably Samuel Langhorne Clemens a.k.a. Mark Twain, Henry Miller, and even Ernest Hemingway. His autodidacticism comes out in intuitive, usually negative statements about writers and writing judged 'too careful' or 'too intellectual'. Bukowski's literary intelligence was enabled, if also restricted, by a defensive refusal to discuss writing, ideas or issues in any other than life-related terms.

Bukowski's inspirational appeal is to would-be artists, but also to readers, offering a fount of hard-bitten worldly wisdom. Why did Bukowski's work become popular, even hip, especially among the young? At its most obvious, it was a matter of psychological identification. A seeming rebellion against straight society has its appeal. And one didn't have to be an aspiring 'tough guy from L.A.', to find all this highly attractive. The playwright Patrick Marber once recalled his own younger self in 1982, living in "a festering north London bed-sit" and doing his "inaugural Bukowski Ramble". As he amusingly explained in *The Observer Magazine*, "being a white, middle-class English boy, Charles Bukowski's tales of L.A. bums, hoodlums, winos and dead-beats were right up my crescent. I took to the night, muttering truths, observing the world through slanted eyes".[5] To those suffering from a painful case of tradition-bound English Lit., Bukowski's work is the perfect antidote. To people disaffected from polite writing, from their jobs and/or lives, Bukowski appeals as an exemplar of rejection - even while being something of a monster. His persona is a monster of rampant ego and appetite, gratifyingly able to tell the world to go fuck itself. He is a kind of humorous man-destroying Grendel in our literature. And people love monsters! After all, fiction and the movies are full of them, from Dracula and Frankenstein to Hannibal Lector. Bukowski became ever more 'himself' as he grew older, traded upon his persona, and exploited his notoriety. Even his appearance eventually attracted women and readers, and was responsible for selling a lot of books. The journalist Bernard Levin once described the author's picture on a British edition of *Post Office* as "surely that of Boris Karloff in the throes of becoming Mr Hyde".[6]

Having achieved self-creation, artists must then find a paying audience for their wares. What makes a particular author 'speak' to a reader is clearly a matter of individual selection psychology. For myself, the colourful Black Sparrow and chromatic City Lights volumes stood out on the shelves of 'Compendium', still the best U.K. bookshop for avant-garde American poetry, located in Camden Town, North London, about twenty years ago. The first purchases were a mixed bag of poems, stories and a novel: *Burning in Water...Women* and *Erections...*, and, reader, I was hooked. By what, exactly? No doubt there was a quasi-sexual attraction to his content. And perception of Bukowski's sheer difference from almost everything else there, his slangy departures from what Al Alvarez famously termed 'the gentility principle' in English poetry. By contrast, this was hilarity and extremity in writing, a stimulating lack of restraint. Sexual explicitness and 'bad language', to an extent rare in poetry, then as now. His very prophane wit and 'knock-off the bullshit' manner. Offensive laughter, often at odds with one's own best liberal instincts. The vicarious pleasures of reading about lives lived on the economic, social, and moral edge; a 'Lower Depths' plunged several degrees lower than, say, the stories of Raymond Carver. Glorious impertinence, at the same time making poetry exciting, vital, and relevant to life. Bukowski does indeed speak particularly to young males dissatisfied with their lot. The poet Bob Flanagan recalled his own discovery of Bukowski, and why a particular book saved his life:

> I was living in a basement apartment of a Masonic Temple. There were no windows. I spent my days making the most of my job at a local auto parts manufacturer....My job was slowly killing me....The book was *Post Office* and the timing of its arrival was perfect. I read everything of his I could get my hands on....It took a few years but all the richness of the available works were mine. Reading and re-reading Buk evened out the rough spots over the years. Virtually memorizing 'If you let them kill you, they will' helped save my faith in myself at a very critical time. Stand-up material by a stand-up guy.[7]

In identifying more general reasons for the commercial success of Bukowski's poetry, its most basic qualities are easy readability, 'autobiographical' gestures, and an anti-depressant humour. Compared to his Post-Modernist contemporaries, Bukowski's works are not ironised out of existence, flat and uninflected. Anything but; they are always very readable, and moreover can be read by anyone. Bukowski packs so much human interest into his poems, which are often life-enhancingly funny or poignant to read, that he makes most others seem dull by comparison. This was the basis of Jon Edgar Webb's complaint to Bukowski, that he'd 'ruined' other poets for him.

With Bukowski, readers are invited to relax and enjoy themselves, crack open a beer or a bottle of wine, read about extreme experiences in safety. Notwithstanding Bukowski's many women readers, there is an element of masculine wish-fulfilment within his works. A downmarket but enticing world of male interests and fantasies - sexually available women, gambling, drink - is conjured up on his pages. An escape from everyday routines, respectable morality and the work ethic is suggested, a satirical critique of social norms. The reader is invited to imagine what things might be like if they were to live by their wits, like a bum (or an artist), and light out for the territory ahead of the rest. The majority of Bukowski's readers are male, and therefore highly susceptible to his street-wise, engaging narrators. Certainly feminist criticism has barely begun to engage with Bukowski's works; the majority of commentary on Bukowski has been written by men. But he should not be regarded simply as a writer of male escapist fantasy. Rather, Bukowki's is a promotional plea for that American Ideal, the life of freedom, a continuity of concerns with the most characteristic U.S. literature. This freedom, as has been argued, aligns itself with Bukowski's practices as a writer, his subject matters, his reworking of American popular culture and myth - and with the avant-gardist's anti-bourgeois rhetoric.

His books have thus far been translated into at least twenty languages. *Interview* magazine surmised that during the last years of his life he was the most widely read contemporary American author in translation. His works are especially popular in continental Europe: Germany, France, Italy, Spain, and Greece. He is also well known in Latin America. He enjoys widespread name-recognition in Britain, though as a cult rather than a mainstream figure, despite many enthusiastic reviews and articles in newspapers and leading periodicals. In the States, his verse collections have had dozens of printings. There is a ready market for the virtually annual Black Sparrow publication, the most recent being *Open All Night: New Poems* (2000). Death has hardly slowed him down - there are more volumes of poems, letters and perhaps stories to come for the forseeable future. Black Sparrow's financial success has had less to do with absolute numbers of sales - hardback first editions of his books were usually between 500 and 1,000 copies, with typically 5,000 in paperback - than with the expensive signed and special editions which collectors and bibliophiles have been more than willing to pay for. (And of course royalties from foreign language editions).

Bukowski's European vogue can be attributed in large measure to the acuity of his translator Carl Weissner, and to having access to mass-market paperback publishers in Germany and France. His popularity in France perhaps has more to do with cultural traits, their famously high regard for American popular culture. That much-quoted endorsement of Bukowski by Jean-Paul Sartre and Jean Genet ("the best poet in America") was made up by Weissner for a German edition blurb. In fact, Genet was an admirer, having seen Bukowski's poems in *The Outsider*. Bukowski himself later turned down the chance to meet Sartre when in Paris. He had the good grace to admit that "I curse myself about Sartre...then I think 'what the hell we'd probably just've ended up boring each other'".[8] This was also a symbolic gesture: turning down theorised, ethical, and politicised approaches to literature.

Publications relating to Bukowski by European admirers have started regularly appearing in English translation. Most recently, the Italian Nanda Pivano's *Laughing With the Gods*, which consists of two interviews recorded at Bukowski's house in San Pedro during 1980 and 1984. There is also material relating to Marco Ferreri's film 'Tales of Ordinary Madness', and photographs by Joe Wolberg. Pivano, a leading Beat collector and critic in Italy, had acted as Jack Kerouac's interpreter during a visit there during the 1960s. Despite some moments of unintentional comedy, due to language difficulties, it is an enyoyable and sympathetic exchange, if not especially illuminating. By this stage in his life, Bukowski was playing, for the benefit of interviewers, twin roles as sage and cynical book huckster. Pivano's introduction records that at first he "had the unmistakable look of someone who would rather be somewhere else". Bukowski comments good-naturedly on his antagonistic public image ("a little over-exaggerated"), the reactions of feminists to his work, and concludes that "[it] all helps to sell books, because people who tend to hate you are good readers too....This false image all helps sales". As ever, he disingenuously maintains that there are few things easier than writing: "when people tell me how painful it is to write, I don't understand it, because it's just like rolling down a mountain, you know. It's freeing. It's enjoyable, it's a gift, and you get paid for what you want to do".[9] The Swiss Jean Francois Duval's *Buk Et Les Beats* (1998) is scheduled for forthcoming publication in English by the same publishers.

The first half of his career attracted a small press audience only, eccentric or dismissive critical attention, and no prospect of earning a living with his typewriter. While this was a frustrating, often financially difficult situation, it did mean that he was able to develop at his own pace. He became 'Charles Bukowski' without conforming pressures from mainstream publishers, agents, and the mass media, or simply the burden of expectations caused by reputations made too early. By the fifth and sixth decades of his life, when Bukowski had achieved a measure of fame, and the film industry had begun to cannibalise his writings, he continued to show the same mistrust of celebrity, the dangers of over-exposure to the public. He refused invitations to hype his work on network television programmes '60 Minutes' and 'The Johnny Carson Show'. He was no determined self-publicist, no Norman Mailer, Gore Vidal or Truman Capote. He was also no Jack Kerouac, whose embrace of long-delayed fame drove him into ultimately fatal drinking. (Though he had a 'beer image', Bukowski of course latterly drank wine, and grew ever more moderate in consumption under the care of his wife Linda). By the time he came to prominence, he was mature enough to handle the situation. When *Barfly* was being promoted, he restricted his mass-market interviews to *People*, a supermarket tabloid beloved of the masses.

Bukowski's primary objectives constantly remained the job of writing, and the freedom to write on his own terms. As Gerald Locklin noted back in 1985, Bukowski had "no illusions about invitations to the White House. His books do not even appear among the finalists for the *Los Angeles Times* Book Prizes. Thus, with plenty of money and permanently alienated from the literary establishment, Bukowski has no reason to compromise what may be the greatest freedom enjoyed by any published writer in American literary history".[10]

Indeed, freedom is what Bukowski's work was all about. Bukowski insisted on independence and free speech. This also meant freedom to pepper his texts with words and phrases deliberately insulting to decent, civilised, liberal values. For instance, 'Independence day' sends up America's national holiday, at least by implication, and with brutal humour also debunks a national shibboleth: respect for maternal feelings (cf. 'Mom and Apple Pie'). Its narrator is living with "an Alvarado Street whore". During a drunken argument, the woman starts crying over her absent children:

"I miss my children", said the
whore, "I wonder if I'll ever
see Ronnie and Lila again?"

"don't mourn, Lilly", I said,
"you give a great blowjob
and that counts for something".[11]

Though Bukowski always exercised the freedom to write whatever and as much as he liked, the fact that there was by the 1980s a market for all his wares encouraged his prolificness. Any glance at the C.B. collector's shelf will indicate how his volumes fattened up during these years. The last published in his lifetime, *War All the Time* (1984), *You Get So Alone at Times That it Just Makes Sense* (1986), and *The Last Night of the Earth*

Poems (1992), are enormous by the usual standard size of poetry volumes, each being well over 400 pages. The critic Gay Brewer estimated that Black Sparrow Press had published only about 50% of the total poetry output. Bukowski himself informed Kurt Nimmo, editor of *Planet Detroit*, that John Martin "has thousands and thousands of my poems...a build-up of 20 years of sending him work. He could run off 5 or 6 or 7 more books of my poetry". (uncollected letter, 3 March 1986)

Bukowski was no languid aesthete, nor did he show the fastidious reluctance to publish of a Philip Larkin, whose publishers were prepared to wait a decade between rigorously-selected collections *The Whitsun Weddings* (1964) and *High Windows* (1974). (It is a pity that Bukowski probably never read any Larkin - or vice versa. Thematically they have common ground, though formally at different ends of the poetic spectrum). Bukowski's critical standing was probably adversely affected by his sheer productivity. One of his first published stories has the unusually Latinate title 'Cacoethes Scribendi', meaning "an irresistable urge to write". He clearly regarded writing as a quasi-sexual act, as an offhand comment in a letter to Weissner makes clear: "still the force of the word springs from the individual and if there is enough individual force the language comes alive like a sperm-mad cock, no matter what its failures are". (no date, 1966)

Another liberty taken is a cavalier attitude to category restrictions. To take just one example: an eccentric rich man's desire to write an opera 'The Emperor of San Francisco' recurs in a poem ' Did I ever tell you?' (1957), a 1966 essay, and in the novel *Factotum*. Certainly repetitiousness detracts from his greatness as a writer. That there are two different poems in *Love Is a Dog From Hell* with the same title, 'Trapped', is a mere curiosity. But by his last volumes, Bukowski was not only recycling stories and phrases but titles, re-using quite a number such as 'Hot' or 'Peace'. Even more redundantly, in certain collections, (mostly though not all posthumous), a poem re-appears a volume later. And much earlier works are reprinted, placed within volumes of mostly new poems, somewhat out of context. For instance, 'Poem to a man in jail' (originally, *Second Coming*, 1974) appears in a substantially variant version in *What Matters Most*...(1999) under a slightly different title. But all this doesn't seem to matter. When Randall Jarrell praised Whitman and W.C. Williams' "wonderful largeness" which was "more important than any faultlessness", he was surely also anticipating the right approach to Bukowski's oeuvre.[12]

Bukowski's created impression of devil-may-care spontaneity made his work easy meat for parodists and snide jokers. Ron Padgett, teaching at the Naropa Institute in Colorado during August 1975, came up with a funny put-down when lecturing to students on the subject of freeing-up approaches to language:

It's very interesting to pretend you're from a foreign country and writing in very bad English, as bad as possible. You get to throw the words away and not worry about it. Anyway....The next one: "Six puppies ran urine down pipes encrusted with night-time invalids alive with lust".
Q: That's obviously a New York poet.
R.P.: Oh no, it's more like Charles Bukowski as a veterinarian.[13]

For all his offhandedness about it, Bukowski, in a very real sense, lived for writing. During a rare period of Writer's Block during the 1960s, Bukowski wrote to a friend that "sometimes I just climb in bed and...listen to sounds ...this way I can work it out pretty good, in a kind of black cave of my mind, making little quiet adjustments like a tailor".(To Weissner, no date, 1966) This image of Bukowski as a tailor, sewing words together patiently and relentlessly, gives a fairer if less theatrical image than the machinegunning typist he liked to be known as. He had a therapeutic sense about writing, calling it a process of "easing the monsters in the brain by moving them to paper". Just as his work evolved in style, so it did in subject matter. Skid row dramas gave way to track and freeway dramas. A 1989 interview made this clear:

Poems about whores showing their panties and spilling beer on my fly no longer seem quite apt. I don't mind nearing Death; in fact, it almost feels good. But different paints are needed for the damned canvas....As I go on, I write as I please and as I must. I don't worry about critics or style or fame or lack of fame. All I want is the next line as it truly comes to me.[14]

That phenomenon associated with famous, recently-deceased authors, analysis by academic critics, has begun in earnest. There have been to date two Ph.D dissertations, several Master's studies, and articles in scholarly publications such as *The Journal of American Studies*. Back in 1985 *The Review of Contemporary Fiction* focussed the first extended critical attention on his prose works. Seamus Cooney, editor of the three volumes of Bukowski correspondence so far published, teaches English at Western Michigan University at Kalamazoo. Gay Brewer, author of the study *Charles Bukowski* (1997) in the Twayne U.S. Authors series, teaches at Middle Tennessee State University. Russell Harrison, author of *Against the American Dream: Essays on Charles Bukowski*, published in 1994, has been a Fulbright lecturer and a teacher at Hofstra University.

The latter study is a treatment of the themes of work and class in Bukowski's stories and novels, mostly with reference to *Post Office* and *Factotum*. Certain poems are singled out, but it's clear that Harrison's main interest is not in them, or aesthetics, but in their larger social view. Such an emphasis on class content and critique of American society is at least a welcome corrective to the pervasively autobiographical and subjective interpretations that Bukowski's work has been usually subjected to. Harrison sees Bukowski as offering a criticism of U.S. late capitalist society, "from a working class point of view", and regards this as the major factor in the 'rejection' of his work by mainstream critics. (In terms of his poetry, hostility in certain quarters has been more than compensated for by an incredible amount of acceptance in others - not least by his army of readers).

Harrison claims a still embattled status for Bukowski's writing in the U.S. But he tends to exaggerate the extent of Bukowski's critical undervaluation, insisting that "the working-class content...rather than any so-called 'banality'...is the sticking point for academic critics and others".[15] In general, despite many perceptive political insights, Harrison's own reading of Bukowski's work is a distinctly selective one. Prose works which do not fit Harrison's thesis, notably the late novels *Hollywood* and *Pulp*, are ignored. Central to his contention is that politics, "broadly defined", has played an important if surreptitious role in Bukowski's work, and that the "most successful" of them (i.e. the ones that most fit his interpretation) depict "as class experience what might otherwise be viewed as confessional material". Again, the evidence in Bukowski's poetry, is that Bukowski is not interested in the working class as a group, only as individuals. As we have seen, his narrators consistently bad-mouth collective solutions to individual problems.

The poems Harrison singles out as the "finest", such as 'Sparks', its narrator showing solidarity with fellow workers, might easily be contradicted by the very many more with narrators who are alienated, mistrustful or contemptuous. Many of his narrators do not even have work colleagues to despise. Bukowski celebrates this estrangement rather than lamenting it. While valuable in some ways, Harrison's book is marred by academic jargon, obfuscating Germanic terms, of a kind that Bukowski himself loathed, and badly serving an author who demanded accessible idioms.

I would also maintain that the evidence is against Harrison's other main contention, that Bukowski writes "against" and questions the American Dream, and indeed that he is the only major post-1945 U.S. author to do so. There are habitual assaults on routinised work, anti-bourgeois and anti-consumerist rhetoric throughout Bukowski's oeuvre - except that it does evolve, does 'accept' the benefits of consumer capitalism. By the 1980s there are poems relishing the fact that the author is able to buy a black BMW or two for cash. The whole trajectory of Bukowski's career surely indicates that he fulfilled the American Dream of riches through hard work. From poverty and obscurity to wealth and the beginnings of an academic industry on his work - this sounds like an exemplification, both of success and the Dream itself. It might be more persuasive to observe that Bukowski denies the efficacy of the Californian Dream - there are no *Baywatch* beaches in his fictional landscape.

Two full-length biographies, published by major publishing houses Random House and Canongate Books, have now appeared. While neither is definitive, they do at least give a great deal of evidence for Bukowski's personal struggle, and that he was far more artist than mere autobiographer. *Hank* (Random House, 1991) by his associate Neeli Cherkovski is a restricted portrait, as C.B. was still very much alive. One of its best aspects is the intriguing material found out about Bukowski's solidly middle class ancestors in Germany. But much material appeared to have come from Bukowski himself, either as anecdotes or, more dubiously, as quotations from the works themselves. As a biographer, Cherkovski was too close to the material and, perhaps understandably, far too uncritical. He embellishes rather than interrogates the Bukowski legend. Admiration sinks to bathos when he calls Bukowski "the philosopher of L.A.", "old Mister Cool" and "a sex genius".

Hank is not entirely a hagiography. Cherkovski does not omit Bukowski's drunken thrashing around in public, and he mentions incidents such as the infamous appearance on the long-running popular French television show 'Apostrophes' in 1978. Bukowski appeared drunk on live television, allegedly pulled a knife on a security guard, then was pulled off the set. As Carl Weissner remarked, he "got a great press next day".[16] Bukowski's sometimes shabby treatment of former lovers and associates is recorded, but criticism is again muted. Cherkovski's approach to the stories and poems treats them as autobiography. A refusal to read fiction as fiction leads to reductive summaries of Bukowski's best work. 'Something for the touts...' becomes "an anthem for the working man", while the comic riches of 'Fire station' are reduced to "a series of funny incidents...in Los Angeles".[17] By doing so, Cherkovski tends to diminish Bukowski both as an artist and as a person - definitely not what was intended. However, Cherkovski's portrait of Bukowski as one of *Whitman's Wild Children* (1988, revised 1999) is far more convincing. It places him within a definite context, a group of inter-related writers loosely in the Whitman tradition, and told some fine anecdotes. Bukowski himself praised this latter book, and it is essential reading for anyone interested in the human side of post-war Californian poets.

What the best biographers do is to set an artist's works within the context of their times, tracing the direct and indirect ways in which they emerge out of life events. A truly informed literary appreciation was at times missing from Howard Sounes' *Locked in the Arms of a Crazy Life* (1998). But his book certainly succeeds in lively narrative and in diligent journalistic research. There are many aspects of Bukowski's life and writing contacts finally revealed, and especially his women. Sounes tracked down photographs of and interviews with the many females in Bukowski's life, particularly triumphing with the first-known picture of Jane Cooney Baker, and in speaking to Pamela Miller a.k.a. the legendary 'Cupcakes'.

One of the quasi-political aspects of Bukowski's writing career - strangely passed over for comment by Russell Harrison - has been the way in which the inexorable workings of Consumer Capitalism have caught up with it. Collecting Bukowski can require a bank loan now. A relatively recent way in which prices have risen has been the international competition bidding for Bukowski artefacts on website auctions, notably on eBay. As with the major Beats whose prices are roughly comparable, Bukowskiana varies in value enormously. Signed or special edition books, rare magazines, and individual drawings or paintings can involve thousands of dollars. Tapes and CDs, photographs, even books of matches with his visage on them are somewhat more affordable. In total the trade must add up to a substantial business. Several rare bookdealers have specialised in Bukowski, the most distinguished being the late 'Red' Stodolsky of the 'Beyond Baroque' bookstore on Sunset Boulevard, a friend of the man himself and memorialised in several poems. (Stodolsky's gruff manner was designed to put off all but the most ardent Bukowskiphile, and those with substantial money to spend. A perennial sign on his door said 'NOT A BROWSING BOOKSHOP').

All of Bukowski's novels have been optioned for movie production. These include *Post Office* (sold several times), and *Women* bought for $300,000 by Paul Verhoeven, a prominent Hollywood operator, the Dutch-born director of *Robocop*, *Basic Instinct* and *Showgirls*. At the time that the latter was released, Verhoeven was quoted in *The Guardian* as saying that he planned to make a low-budget version of the novel: "It's all about fucking, isn't it. Forty women. We might reduce it to 10. It would be the ultimate 18 cert hard porno art flick".[18] It has yet to be made. Sean Penn (who dedicated his movie *The Crossing Guard* to Bukowski's memory) has expressed the wish to do a Bukowski project someday. He repeatedly offered to act in *Barfly*, for a dollar, with Dennis Hopper directing.

The music industry has cottoned on to Bukowski's 'Street Cred': punk bands have long worn Bukowski t-shirts, invoked his name in songs. This international appeal includes Ireland's U2 and Hull's own supergroup The Beautiful South. A recent feature in the *Los Angeles Times* (12 August 2000) has detailed his influence on rock stars and bands, "few, if any, writers have reached as many modern musicians as Bukowski...the list of Bukowski acolytes goes on and on". Among the performers cited are Kurt Cobain, Bono, Gavin Rossdale of Bush, Richard Ashcroft of The Verve, and singer-songwriters Tom Waits, Jewel, Johnette Napolitano and Lucinda

Williams. Bands tipping their hats to C.B. have been the Red Hot Chilli Peppers, The Boo Radleys, and San Francisco's Buddhakowski. The irony is, of course, that Bukowski himself disliked rock and pop music! (But then he also loathed much contemporary poetry).

Bukowski, like Hemingway before him, eventually gathered the esteem of film stars, the company of the rich and famous. His affiliations with experimental, tough-guy and existential authors have been commented upon. Most of these began in poverty and obscurity, but ended up with money, fame, high status with literary critics, and name-recognition amongst a popular audience. This is the career pattern in western liberal democracies, under Consumer Capitalism's inevitable conversion of the once radical into desirable commodities. It is a process ruthlessly accelerated in the United States. Artists within groupings such as the Surrealists, the Abstract Expressionists, to Andy Warhol and beyond, have been hurried by the art market, critics and academia into safe enclaves. What was originally a critique of art and society became the province of the art-buying super rich. The same pattern has occurred in the American post-war literary avant-garde, though the money involved is clearly far less. Nevertheless, this neutralisation of critique has applied to the Beats, the New Yorkers and the Black Mountaineers, all colonised by academia and rewarded with big prizes. Bukowski's work too, though less intellectual or 'acceptable', is well on its way to the Museum of 20th Century Culture.

If Henry Miller and Allen Ginsberg can be thus incorporated, afforded guru status, then Bukowski certainly can. C.B's works, after all, were never prosecuted. But once again, Bukowski is closer to the Hemingway career model, if one takes out the latter's Action Man component. He began as a journalist, then became an experimentalist within expatriate American circles of the Parisian avant-garde. His prose was first championed in little magazines and small presses. He gathered the equivocal support of other artists, then of critics; his books became bestsellers, earning still larger amounts from film and television deals in the latter years of his life. Despite his suspicion of the studios, Hemingway had plenty of film contacts. There is one satisfying movie connection between C.B. and E.H. Photos in the published screenplay of *Barfly* show the author on the set of the movie. One shows Bukowski talking to Isabella Rosselini, the daughter of Ingrid Bergman - who had been one of the glamorous movie friends in Hemingway's social circle. Hemingway was a stylist, influencing young writers for decades, but whose work has latterly become unfashionable, 'politically incorrect'. Something of this sort of fashion change may happen to Bukowski.

Like Hemingway, again and again one finds Bukowski echoing American cultural mythology. He drew upon the essential figments of this;

namely, that beneath his conformist exterior, every American is trying to get along in a corrupt world, patrolling the mean streets, doing what a man's got to do and 'telling it like it is'. This of course is exactly what Hollywood trades upon. The Americanness of Bukowski's work is in its recourse to national myths, as well as the American speech he made so brilliantly into poetry.

Bukowski lived out the romantic image of the poet, one whose ramshackle life is redeemed by his work. He knew that life is a continuing process of loss, and that as he told Doug Blazek, "the horns of grief need no honing" (4 November 1964). His work is informed by this, reflecting on the losing human struggle with time, ageing and death. He had real genius for narrative, whether in poetry or prose. But what made Bukowski as a writer was not his parents, his acne-ridden adolescent looks, nor even his near-death experience in the charity ward, his years in dead-end jobs, cheap roominghouses or at racetracks. All these experiences were important, and became deeply-rooted in his psyche. But it was the period of his self-directed voracious reading during the war years, when he devoured whole sections of the Los Angeles Public Library, and other libraries, which formed him. It constituted his higher education. The discoveries he made, the decisions he took then, the attitudes imbibed, informed all his subsequent writing. 'Hey, Ezra, listen to this', a poem in *War All the Time*, even states as much, finally accepting that influence.

The young Bukowski reacted against the tameness of his forebears, but eventually he had the grace to praise them. He had, for instance, always valued independent men of letters, particularly H.L. Mencken - with the John Fante connection - and Mencken's now-largely forgotten contemporaries Christopher Morley and Lewis Mumford. (During the 1975 'Bukowski Symposium' at the *L.A. Free Press* he even managed to praise a poem by John Crowe Ransom). Revisionism proceeds apace in his last volumes. He is more generous to his parents, even his father, and to the previously despised masses. Libraries provided his youthful refuge from the world, an escape into the private world of reading, the necessary precondition for his life as an artist. 'The burning of the dream' records the destruction by fire of the Los Angeles Public Library: "and with it went/ a large part of my youth....I was a bibliophile, albeit a/ disenchanted/ one/ and this/ and the world/ shaped me". 'Kenyon Review, after the sandstorm' reflects maturely on his debts to the 'professors' of literature:

I knew I would never be able to write
in that manner, yet I almost wanted to be
one of them or any of them: being guarded,
fierce and witty....

I also sensed that there might be something else.[19]

It was this early inculcation of the ideology of the avant-garde - the artist in advance of public taste or antagonistic to it, who eventually finds acceptance, wealth, and recognition, which sustained him for decades. Given the willingness that U.S. postal authorities show in putting fairly recently-dead cultural figures on stamps, it is a fair bet the former postal worker's face will adorn letters within a decade or so. Further movies will surely be made from his works. Innovative theatre groups such as 29th Street Rep in New York have adapted his fictions. Recently the play 'South of No North; Stories of the Buried Life', directed by Leo Farley and Jonathan Powers, ran from 24 February to 26 March 2000.

Like any important writer, Bukowski recorded movements in the society around him. His heyday was no era of bland consensus in art or politics. Encouraged by his two publishers and excited by having a popular, rapid-fire platform for his writing in the underground press, he perfectly captured the free wheeling late 1960s, early 1970s American society. Later on, as he became world famous and the society around him changed, got uglier, more materialistic and less idealistic, one can see this in the later works. In the interviews he gave in the last five years or so of his life, the mask had become stuck, as he adopted a sage-like stance. Even Bukowski suffered to some extent from the coarsening effects of celebrity.

Bukowski was also sustained in his career by friends, lovers, editors, and by readers. Eventually, his life and art did connect up. The alienation he had experienced was transmuted into art, and, over several decades, he managed a full acceptance of humankind. Gerald Locklin made this point in a 1996 interview in *Pearl* magazine: "He had his poses...and would slant things against humanity and for himself. And while that could be iconoclastic and great in many ways, I really believe that there is a perennial and enduring quality in his late poems. I think he takes a step up amongst the great poets and philosophers. He realized his union with humanity, that he was not different from the rest essentially".[20] Despite Jeffers-like diatribes, many of his poems actually show a positive affirmation. The Welsh poet Douglas Houston once enthused about 'Waxjob', whose subject is a Korean veteran's deliberate drinking himself to death. (Published in 1974, it may possibly be an oblique narrative 'about' the poet William Wantling, with drink standing in for the latter's fatal addiction to heroin). Houston wrote that in it Bukowski "has such an attractively unadulterated view of the shabbiness of human behaviour which yet permits something that might or must be called LOVE to suffuse his lines".

He was fundamentally serious, however often comedy, or anarchic narrative interruptions intrude. He was a great in at least this sense: he was one of the handful of modern poets to have created a new style, albeit a mongrel style, thereby permanently enlarging the possibilities of poetry. His admirers and imitators have propagated this, perhaps to excess. And if the greatest art conceals art, Bukowski was formidable. He was part of a movement towards greater accessibility inspired by the Beats, but also the Robert Lowell of *Life Studies* during the late 1950s. It grew to affect a great deal of Anglo-American poetry, and stimulated the vogue for performance and subjective manner which is still dominant today.

His eventual status is still open to debate, clearly, but certain critics already rate him alongside, say, Henry Miller. Indeed, as Gerald Locklin points out, he shares with Miller and e.e. cummings the characteristic that their works are "read out of a sense of pleasure rather than a sense of duty".[21] Bukowski certainly ranks alongside his near contemporaries Ginsberg, Kerouac, O'Hara, Creeley, Bishop, Plath, Ashbery, as different as they all are. He was part of a distinguished post-1945 American generation, now largely passed away. In contrast to their more intellectual delights, his is a 'physical' species of writing that seems to appeal directly to the senses, like a whiff of invigoratingly pungent air while passing a bar. His poems do have great resonance, speaking directly to readers. And for many he was the funniest, most entertaining poet of our times, a reluctant but decided showman.

Listen to his live recordings - despite his professed dislike of them, he worked best with an audience. From the mid-1970s onwards, he had a great, truly authoritative voice. He was able to traverse that fine boundary between reassurance (the feeling that as a reader 'one is in good hands') and dangerousness. When Bukowski succeeds, there is something ultimately indefinable about how he does it, some magical momentum and energy not entirely accountable. His was an instinctive talent but far more deliberated than he is given credit for. How many Bukowski poems deserve to become classics remains with posterity, and depends upon the future workings of critics and anthologists. The standard line of many fellow poets is that one could make a truly great 200 page Bukowski volume by selecting only the very best. His future *Selected Poems* - which is likely to be somewhat more bulky - will showcase work that is wonderfully alive, spanning the whole range from comedy to elegy.

Ezra Pound, writing in *Poetry* during 1915, maintained that "The essential thing in a poet is that he builds us his world".[22] Bukowski indubitably does this. We can take leave of Charles Bukowski most appropriately at his own world-in-itself, the racetrack. It remained the richest single subject for his life and writing, and within which he felt quite at home. 'The condition book' appeared in his favourite little magazine, *Wormwood Review*, in the year of his death. A moving and accepting work, it reads in its entirety as a Whitmanesque farewell.

the long days at the track have idented themselves
into me:
I am the horses, the jocks, I am six furlongs, seven
furlongs, I am a mile and one sixteenth, I am a
handicap, I am all the colors of all the silks, I am all
the photo finishes, the accidents, the deaths, the
last place finishes, the breakdowns, the failure of
the toteboard, the dropped whip and the numb pain
of the dream not come true in thousands and thousands
and thousands of faces. I am the long drive home in the
dark, in the rain, I am decades and decades and decades
of races run and won and lost and run again and I am
myself sitting with a program and a Racing Form.
I am the racetrack, my ribs are the wooden rails, my
eyes are the flashes of the toteboard, my feet are
hooves and there is something riding on my back. I am
the last curve, I am the home stretch, I am the longshot
and the favorite, I am the exacta, the daily double and
the pick 6.
I am humanely destroyed, I am the horseplayer who
became the
racetrack.[23]

Artwork by David Hernandez

NOTES

Footnotes have been kept to a minimum; therefore, the quotations from Bukowski's correspondence are not footnoted. They are, however, identified by recipient and date, and can be found in the three volumes published by Black Sparrow Press listed in the bibliography. It is assumed that most readers will have, or have access to, copies of at least some of Bukowski's collections, especially those discussed in Chapter Five. Extracts from the poems are identified; titles have been standardised by capitalising only the initial word. All other quotations, paraphrases, and opinions are noted as follows.

Introduction
1. 'He beats his women', *Second Coming* vol.2, #3, (San Francisco, 1974).n.p.
2. Ed. Helen Vendler, *The Faber Book of Contemporary American Poetry* (London, 1986), 7.
3. J. Bennett interview with Oberc, *Chiron Review* Vol. XIII #3 (Autumn, 1994), 22-23.
4. H. Sounes, *Locked in the Arms of a Crazy Life* (Edinburgh, 1998), 228.
5. *Mockingbird Wish Me Luck* (1972), 156.

Chapter 1
1. Preface, *Poems...8 Story Window* (Salt Lake City, 1968; 1975), n.p.
2. Letter in *Laugh Literary and Man the Humping Guns* #2 (L.A., 1969) n.p.
3. Ed. Malcolm Cowley, *Walt Whitman's Leaves of Grass* (1959; Harmondsworth, 1977), 18. Edward Field, *A Frieze For a Temple of Love* (Black Sparrow Press, 1998), 53-56.
4. 'Translating Bukowski and the Beats': Weissner interview with Jay Dougherty, *Gargoyle* #35 (1988), 68-86.
5. Ed. Cowley, *Leaves of Grass*, 13.
6. Andrew Linick, *A History of the American Literary Avant-Garde Since World War Two*, unpublished Ph.D dissertation (Univ. of California, Los Angeles, 1965), 247. Len Fulton comment in Morris Edelson, *Six Little Magazines*, unpublished Ph.D

dissertation (Univ. of Michigan, 1973). C.B. interview with Jay Dougherty, *Gargoyle* (1988)
7. Morris Edelson, 'St. Bukowski' in *A Bukowski Sampler* (2nd edition, 1975); Ken Tucker, review of LP Bukowski Reads his Poetry, Rolling Stone, c.1980.
8. M. Seymour-Smith, *Who's Who of 20th Century Literature* (London, 1976); N. Cherkovski, *Whitman's Wild Children* (1999), 306
9. C.B. preface to *Ask the Dust* (1939; Black Sparrow Press, 1979), 6.
10. Piers Brendon, *The Dark Valley: A Panorama of the 1930s* (London, 2000), 87. *Olé* #3 (November 1965), n.p. *Dangling in the Tournefortia* (1981), 13.
11. K. Shapiro interview with Michael Anania and Ralph J. Mills Jr., *Triquarterly* #43 (Fall, 1978), 210.
12. R. Creeley interview, in ed. Donald Allen, *Contexts of Poetry: Interviews 1961-1971* (Bolinas, California, 1973).
13. Ed. Malcolm Cowley, *Leaves of Grass*, The First (1855) Edition (1959; Harmondsworth, 1977).
14. Ibid.
15. *Burning in Water, Drowning in Flame* (Black Sparrow, 1974), 89-92.
16. 'A Rambling Essay Written While Drinking a Six Pack (Tall)', reprinted in *A Bukowski Sampler*, (Madison, Wisconsin, 1969), 9-15. Russell Harrison, *Against the American Dream: Essays on Charles Bukowski* (Black Sparrow Press, 1994), 30.
17. *Burning in Water...*, 64-66.
18. *Shakespeare Never Did This*, Section 21 (City Lights Books, 1979), n.p.
19. C. Lynn Munro, 'Charles Bukowski', in ed. Frank N. Magill, *Critical Survey of Poetry* (New Jersey, 1982), 354-365.
20. *Burning in Water...*, 38.
21. *Burning in Water...*, 145-6.
22. *Roominghouse Madrigals*, 15-16
23. F. Stephanile, *The Outsider* #3 (1963)
24. C. Bukowski, ibid
25. L. Fiedler, *The Return of the Vanishing American* (London, 1968), 23.
26. Whitman, in ed. Louis D. Rubin Jr., *America's Humor* (New Jersey, 1973), 254.
27. This paragraph is indebted to John Osborne, 'American Male Mythology and Ken Kesey's *One Flew Over the Cuckoo's Nest*', *Bête Noire* #1 (Autumn, 1984), 50-65.
28. L. Fiedler, *Love and Death in the American Novel* (New York, 1960), 77.
29. A. Kazin, 'The Self as History: Reflections on Autobiography', in ed. Albert E. Stone, *The American Autobiography* (Englewood Cliffs, New Jersey, 1982), 31-43.

Chapter 2

1. Epigraph: uncollected *Notes* column, reprinted in Jory Sherman, Friendship, Fame... (Augusta, Georgia; 1981), 35-38. Al Fogel, *A Comprehensive Price Guide & Checklist 1944-1999* (Surfside, Florida, 2000).
2. David Montrose, 'Third Coming', *New Edinburgh Review* #52, (1980), 30-31.
3. C.B. 'A Rambling Essay...' in *A Bukowski Sampler*.
4. *The Kenyon Review*; 1940, 4 issues, and vol. 6, (1944).
5. C.B. 'A Rambling Essay...' in *A Bukowski Sampler*.
6. *Story* magazine; details in *Triquarterly* #43 (1978).
7. *Portfolio* magazine, details ibid.

8. *The Roominghouse Madrigals*, 82.
9. Ibid, 114.
10. *The Outsider* #3 (1963)
11. Ed. Seamus Cooney, *The Bukowski/ Purdy Letters 1964-1974* (Sutton West & Santa Barbara, 1983).
12. *A Bukowski Sampler*, 50.
13. Fogel, *Price Guide...*, 59.
14. *The Outsider* #3.
15. *A Bukowski Sampler*, 38-39.
16. L. Fulton, Small Press Review, in J. Sherman, *Friendship, Fame...* 13
17. Jim Burns, *Poetry Information*, 20-21 (Winter 1979-80), 131-137.
18. Jon Edgar Webb Memorial Issue, *Wormwood Review* #45 (1972).
19. *The Outsider* #3,
20. Author's Introduction, *Burning in Water...*(1974), 5-8.
21. *Bukowski/ Purdy Letters*, 55.
22. Ormonde Plater, 'Tough Poems', *Vieux Carré Courier* vol.2, #14 (28 May 1965), 6.
23. Introduction by G. Woodcock, Al Purdy, *Selected Poems* (Toronto, 1972), 8.
24. *Bukowski/ Purdy Letters*, 12.
25. Purdy, *Selected Poems*, 106-107.
26. Joe Wolberg, 'The People's Poet: Bukowski', *Oui*, (n.d., 1980), 44-49, 118-120.
27. Ed. Alan Kaufman, *The Outlaw Bible of American Poetry* (New York, 1999).
28. *Olé* #1.
29. Ibid,
30. *Olé* #4,
31. Harold Chapman, *The Beat Hotel* (Montpelier, 1984), 6.
32. C.B. to Weissner.
33. *Open Skull* #1 (San Francisco, 1967).
34. Eric Mottram, 'Sixties American Poetry, Poetics and Poetic Movements', in *History of Literature in the English Language*, Vol.9, American Literature Since 1900 (London, 1975), 271-311.
35. Ed. T.L. Kryss, *A Tribute to Jim Lowell* (Cleveland, Ohio,1968), n.p.
36. *Wormwood Review* # 24(1966), n.p. (fold-out list of magazines).
37. Ibid.
38. Flyer kindly supplied by poet & bookseller Alan Halsey of Hay-On-Wye.
39. Mottram, 'Sixties American Poetry...', 302.
40. Interview with Mark Weber, *Wormwood Review* #145-146 (1999), 16-18.
41. M. Edelson, *Six Little Magazines*.
42. Hugh Fox, *Charles Bukowski: A Critical and Bibliographical Study* (Somerville, Massachussetts, 1969)
43. Ed. John Bryan, *Open City* #83 (20 December 1968).
44. In Jory Sherman, *Bukowski: Friendship, Fame & Bestial Myth* (Augusta, Georgia, 1981), 28.
45. In *Poems Written Before Jumping Out of an Eight Story Window* (2nd edition, Salt Lake City, 1975), n.p.
46. T. Quagliano, 'The Ground in Los Angeles', *Schist* #4/5 (1976), 37-42.
47. R. Offen, *Chicago Literary Times* (September 1965), 4-5.
48. *The New York Times Book Review*, 5 July 1964, 5.
49. Dabney Stuart, '7 Poets and a Playwright', *Poetry Chicago*, Vol. 104, #4 (July

1964), 263-264.
50. J.W. Corrington, introduction, *It Catches My Heart In Its Hands* (New Orleans, 1963).
51. J.W. Corrington, 'Charles Bukowski and the Savage Surfaces', *Northwest Review*, Vol. VI, #4 (Fall,1963), 123-129.
52. Fox, *A Critical and Bibliographical Study*.
53. Wolberg, *Oui* article, 119.
54. Ibid.
55. Dedication, *At Terror Street and Agony Way* (Black Sparrow Press, 1968).
56. C.B. to Weissner.
57. Trans. Carl Weissner, *Gedichte die einer schrieb* (1974), 102.

Chapter 3

1. *Triquarterly* #43.
2. Stephen Moore, 'Sheri Martinelli: A Modernist Muse', *Gargoyle* #41 (1998), 28-54.
3. A. Ginsberg, 'Encounters with Ezra Pound', *Composed on the Tongue* (Bolinas, California, 1980), 1-17.
4. John Bennett interview, *Chiron Review* (Autumn 1994), 22. *Intrepid* # 21-22 (1971),
5. C.B. preface, in Al Masarik, *Invitation to a Dying* (Washington, 1971).
6. John Tripp, *2nd Aeon* #19/21, (1974), 237.
7. P. Finch, *2nd Aeon*, ibid.
8. Interview with Weissner, *Gargoyle* #35 (1988).
9. LP sleeve notes, 'A Cold Turkey Press Special', Rotterdam Poetry Festival 20-24 1972.
10. C.B. interview with Arnold L. Kaye, *Chicago Literary Times* Vol 2, #3 (1963).
11. C.B. interview with Don Strachan, *L.A. Free Press*, Vol. 8, #30 (23 July 1971), 4.
12. C.B. interview with Robert Wennersten, *London Magazine* Vol. 14, #5 (December,1974), 35-54.
13. Paul Ciotti, 'Bukowski', *Los Angeles Times Magazine*, (22 March1987), 12-19, 23.
14. Ed. Linda King, *Me and Your Sometimes Love Poems* (2nd edition; Phoenix, Arizona, 1994), n.p.
15. Ibid.
16. *Second Coming*, vol.2, #3 (1974), n.p.
17. A.D. Winans, *The Charles Bukowski/ Second Coming Years* (Coventry, 1996),
18. Joe Wolberg, sleeve notes, *Poems and Insults* (LP 1975; CD with extra poems, Grey Matter,1995). .
19. *L.A. Free Press* 'Bukowski Symposium', extract reprinted in Steve Richmond, *Spinning Off Bukowski* (Northville, Michigan, 1996), 83.
20. Hayden Carruth, *Harper's*, (March, 1975).
21. G. Esterley, 'The Pock-Marked Poetry of Charles Bukowski', *Rolling Stone* #215 (17 June, 1976), 10-17.
22. *Mockingbird Wish Me Luck*, 31.
23. *Love Is a Dog From Hell*, 79-80.
24. P. Mickelson, in *Triquarterly* #43.
25. K. Shapiro interview, ibid.
26. Weissner interview, *Gargoyle* #35 (1988).

27. *Shakespeare Never Did This*, Section 16 (San Francisco, 1979), n.p.
28. Audio cassette, 'Bukowski: The Viking Inn, Vancouver', (October 1979).
29. Review of *Post Office, The Times*, (n.d., 1980).
30. *Septuagenarian Stew* (1990), 26-30.
31. Ciotti, *Los Angeles Times Magazine* (22 March 1987).
32. 'The Whole World Mourns the Death of a Poet', *Random Lengths* (San Pedro, 17-31 March 1994), 3.
33. L. Rolfe, *L.A. Village View* (March, 1994).
34. S. Kessler, *Mendocino Outlook* (1994).
35. Interview with Jay Dougherty, *Gargoyle* #35 (1988).

Chapter 4

1. *War All the Time*, 15-17.
2. 'Horse on Fire'.
3. *Mockingbird...*, 102-103.
4. *The Days Run Away...*, 115-120.
5. *Penguin Modern Poets 13* (1969), 22-23.
6. Ed. Linda Wagner, *Interviews with William Carlos Williams*, (New York, 1976).
7. S. Fredman, 'The New American Poetry', *PN Review* #28 (1982), 42-44.
8. *Second Coming* vol.2 #3 (1974), n.p.
9. Jimmie Cain Jr, 'Bukowski's Imagist Roots', *West Georgia College Review* #19 (1987), 10-17. *The Days Run Away...*, 31.
10. W.C. Williams, 'The American Idiom', in *Interviews...*, 101-102.
11. *Mockingbird...*, 156.
12. E. Hemingway, *The First Forty-Nine Stories* (1944; London, 1968).
13. C. Bukowski, 'He Beats His Women', *Second Coming* (1974), n.p.
14. *Burning in Water...*, 37.
15. E. Hemingway, *A Moveable Feast* (1964; St. Albans, 1977), 21.
16. G. Stein, *Three Lives* (1909; London, 1970), 9.
17. E. Hemingway, *Fiesta/ The Sun Also Rises* (1927; London, 1976), 128.
18. E. Hemingway, 'Up in Michigan', *The First Forty-Nine Stories*, 79-83.
19. D. Lodge, *The Modes of Modern Writing* (London, 1977), 156.
20. *Burning in Water...*, 67-70.
21. E. Hemingway, *Death In The Afternoon* (New York, 1932), 122
22. *Play the Piano...*, 18-19.
23. *Mockingbird...*, 71.
24. See Ted Olson, 'Two Poets Listening to Life', *Sure* #4, 2-8.
25. R. Jeffers, *The Double Axe* (New York, 1948).
26. *You Get So Alone At Times That It Just Makes Sense* (1986), 288-289.
27. *Penguin Modern Poets 13* (1969), 28-29.
28. R. Jeffers, *manifesto* (1928).
29. Ferlinghetti interview with Gavin Selerie, *The Riverside Interviews* #2 (London, 1980).
30. D. Thomas, *Collected Poems 1934-1952* (1952), 8.
31. A. Breton, 'First Manifesto', in ed. Edward R. Germain, *English and American Surrealist Poetry* (1978), 29-30.
32. Ibid., 35.

33. *Penguin Modern Poets 13*, 85-86.
34. *Burning in Water...*, 33-34.
35. *Penguin Modern Poets 13*, 47-48.
36. *Dangling in the Tournefortia* (1981), 241-245.
37. J. Osborne, Arts Faculty lecture series, Hull University, 1978, 'The Form of Modernism'.
38. A. Ginsberg, 'Howl', *Howl and Other Poems* (1956), 9-22.
39. *Penguin Modern Poets 13*, 26-27.
40. *Chicago Review* (1970).
41. John Clellon Holmes, *Nothing More to Declare* (London, 1968), 117.
42. *Bukowski/ Purdy Letters*, 43-44.
43. N. Podhoretz, 'The Know-Nothing Bohemians', in ed. Park Honan, *The Beats* (1987), 216-229.
44. J.E. Webb, reprinted in *Bukowski/ Purdy Letters*, 58.
45. S. Cooney, ed, *Screams from the Balcony*, 357
46. Foreword, *The Roominghouse Madrigals*, 5-6.
47. *Burning in Water...*, 223-225.
48. *Wormwood Review* # 53 (1974), 22-23.
49. Interview with Gary Snyder, in ed. Arthur and Kit Knight, *The Beat Vision* (New York, 1987), 1-27.
50. J. Campbell, 'Beat, Beaten and Blue: Charles Bukowski and the Beats', *Bananas*, (1981), 48-50.

Chapter 5
(Poems generally not footnoted; see respective books)
1. *A Bukowski Sampler*, 49; 41.
2. Ed. Edward Mendelson, *The English Auden* (Faber, 1977), 163.
3. Ed. Louis D. Rubin, Jr., *America's Humor*.
4. 'I met Hank in 1968', *The Kerouac Connection* #27 (Winter 1995), 49-50.
5. *Beat Scene* #22 'Hank and Georgia', 25-26
6. 'Bukowski Live in Hamburg May 1978', audio cassette.
7. Ed. Seamus Cooney, *Reach for the Sun* (1999), 181.
8. 'Run With the Hunted', audio cassette (Caedmon/ Harper Collins, 1993).

Chapter 6
1. Poem in Bukowski/ Locklin correspondence, California State University, Special Collections. *Mockingbird...*, 26-27; 100-101. "Wait on the word...", C.B. quoted in *The Orange County Register* (11 March 1997), 6.
2. *You Get So Alone...*, 280.
3. The details in this paragraph are partly indebted to 'America in Isolation', in Piers Brendon, *The Dark Valley: A Panorama of the 1930s* (London, 2000), 422-444.
4. *The Days Run...*, 29.
5. *Betting On the Muse*, 46-49.
6. Ibid., 366-370.
7. *Burning in Water...*, 18.

8. Audio cassette, 'King of the Hard Mouthed Poets', *Nola Express* 1968. *The Memoirs of Roger Vadim*, (London, 1986), 158.
9. *Intransit*: The Andy Warhol - Gerard Malanga Monster Issue (1968), 192.
10. *Septuagenarian Stew*, 26-30.
11. C.B. interview with Michael Andrews, *Easy Reader* vol. X #31 (April, 1980), 8-12.
12. *Play the Piano...*, 51.
13. *A Bukowski Sampler*, 39-40.
14. *Burning in Water...*, 161-162.
15. Ibid., 113-114. *The Days Run...*, 17-18.
16. E. Hemingway, 'God Rest You Merry, Gentlemen', *The First Forty-Nine Stories*, 322-326.
17. *War All the Time*, 243-245.
18. Both *Tropic of Cancer* and *Tropic of Capricorn* were banned in the U.S. until 1960.
19. K. Millett, *Sexual Politics* (London,1977), 312.
20. *Play the Piano...*, 38-44.
21. L-F. Céline, *Journey to the End of the Night* (1932), 312.
22. *Grinning Idiot* (New York, 1982), 14.
23. See also 'I saw an old fashioned whore today', *Mockingbird...*,122;138.
24. *Burning in Water...*, 123-126.
25. *The Roominghouse Madrigals*, 132-133.
26. *Burning in Water...*, 179-180.
27. L. Fiedler, *Love and Death in the American Novel* (New York, 1960)
28. Washington Irving, 'Rip Van Winkle', *Selected Prose* (1961), 92.
29. G. Locklin, *Charles Bukowski: A Sure Bet* (Sudbury, MA, 1995), 30.
30. *Burning in Water...*, 214-215.
31. Ibid., 21-22.
32. *A Bukowski Sampler*, 48-49.
33. *Burning in Water...*, 132-133.
34. *Love Is a Dog...*, 305-307.
35. Interview with Robert Wennersten, *London Magazine* (1974).
36. S. Richmond, *Second Coming* vol.2 #3 (1974), n.p. *The Willie* (1968).
37. *Play the Piano...*, 101.
38. H. Fox, *Second Coming*, n.p.
39. *Love Is a Dog*, 83-84. Dangling..., 51-52; 17-18.
40. *Burning in Water...*, 147-148.
41. *The Days Run...*, 13-15. Jack Byrne, 'Bukowski's Chinaski: Playing Post Office', *Review of Contemporary Fiction*, 46.
42. *Mockingbird...*, 21-22.
43. *Dangling...*, 59-65.
44. G. Locklin, *A Sure Bet*, 31.
45. *What Matters Most Is How Well You Walk Through the Fire* (1999), 63-64.
46. *Betting On the Muse*, 339-341.
47. *Play the Piano...*, 108-109.
48. *War All the Time*, 220-221.
49. *Mockingbird...*, 14-15.
50. *The Days Run...*, 70-71.
51. *Burning in Water...*, 47-48.

52. *The Days Run...*, 115-120.
53. *Wormwood Review* # 95 (1984), 119.
54. Ibid, 120-121.
55. G. Locklin, *The Review of Contemporary Fiction* vol.5 #3 (1985), 34-36.
56. D. Glover, 'A Day at the Races: Gambling and Luck in Bukowski's Fiction', ibid., 32-33.

Chapter 7
1. Epigraph: *Burning in Water...*52-53. *A Bukowski Sampler*, 50.
2. *Burning in Water...*, 137-138.
3. Ed. G. Haslam, *Many Californias: Literature from the Golden State* (Reno, Nevada, 1992). G. Haslam, *The Other California: The Great Central Valley in Life and Letters* (Reno, Nevada, 1994).
4. Ibid., 64.
5. *Burning in Water...*, 52-53.
6. Ed. Helen Friedland, 'A History of Los Angeles in Poetry 1781-1981', *Poetry LA* #3 (Fall/Winter 1981-82), iv; 51.
7. K. Rexroth, *American Poetry in the Twentieth Century* (1971).
8. Ferlinghetti interview with G. Selerie, 1980, *The Riverside Interview*, 2, 7-8.
9. Ginsberg interview with Yves Le Pellec, in *Composed on the Tongue*, (Bolinas, California, 1980), 86.
10. 'Self Portraits in Los Angeles', ed. Bill Mohr, *Poetry Loves Poetry: An Anthology of Los Angeles Poets*, (Santa Monica, 1985), i-xv.
11. C.B., Introduction to ed. Bukowski, Cherry, Vangelisti, *An Anthology of L.A. Poets* (Fairfax, Los Angeles, 1972).
12. G. Williams letter, 18 November 1970, in *Second Coming*, vol.2 #3 (1974), n.p.
13. G. Locklin, 'Two Poets', ibid.
14. S. Kessler, 'Notes On a Dirty Old Man', *The Review of Contemporary Fiction* (Fall 1985), 60-63.
15. J. Jobe Smith, 'The Poet as Entertainment', *Sure* #4 (1992), 35-41.
16. C.B. interview with Michaėl Andrews, *Easy Reader*.
17. C.B. Notes, in J. Sherman, Friendship, Fame...(Augusta, Georgia, 1982), 37.
18. *Dangling...*, 171-175.
19. *War All the Time*, 173-176.
20. C.B. foreword, *The Roominghouse Madrigals*, 5-6.
21. *Burning in Water...*, 185-186.
22. C.B. introduction, *An Anthology of L.A. Poets*.
23. Ed. E. Field, *A Geography of Poets* (New York, 1979), xxix-xlvi.
24. Ibid., 175-176.
25. Introduction in ed. Edward Field, Gerald Locklin, Charles Stetler, *A New Geography of Poets* (Fayetville, Arkansas, 1992), xvii-xxix.
26. Ibid.
27. *Poetry Loves Poetry*, iii.
28. *Ambit* #108 (1987), 48.
29. Ed. Charles Harper Webb, *Stand Up Poetry: The Poetry of Los Angeles and Beyond* (Los Angeles, 1990).
30. Ed. Alan Kaufman, *The Outlaw Bible of American Poetry* (New York, 1999).

31. Ibid, 614-615.
32. "Fred Voss [has]...constructed a discontinuous long poem whose directness of address to factory experience is without parallel in contemporary Anglo-American verse", John Osborne, *Bête Noire* #8/9 (1989-90), 354.
33. *Outlaw Bible...*, 411-412.
34. J. Stein, 'The Machinist Poet of Long Beach', *Random Lengths* (2-15 May, 1997), 1,8.
35. *Outlaw Bible...*, 413-414.
36. Linda King letter 9 October 1974, and poems, *Pearl* (Winter 1974), 56-59.
37. La Loca, *Adventures on the Isle of Adolescence* (City Lights Books, 1989), 9-12.
38. Lisa Glatt, *Monsters and Other Lovers* (Long Beach, 1996), 42-43.
39. F. Voss interview with Jules Smith, *The Reater* #1 (Winter 1997), 90-100.
40. C.B. interview with Jay Dougherty, *Gargoyle* #35 (1988).
41. *Wormwood Review* # 53 (1974), 26-28.
42. C.B. statement on various Locklin books, including *The Case of the Missing Blue Volkswagen* (Long Beach, 1984; North Cave, England, 1999).
43. G. Locklin, 'Setting Free the Buk', *Review of Contemporary Fiction*, 27-31.
44. C. Daly, *The Last Peepshow and Other Poems* (Sacramento, 1986).
45. Jeffrey Gomez, 'Tales of Just Plain Ordinary', *Sure* #4 (1992), 33-34.
46. Locklin interview with Jules Smith, *Pearl* #27 (Fall/ Winter 1998), 26-34.
47. John Bennett and Dan Nielsen interviews with Oberc, *Chiron Review* (Fall, 1994), 22-23; 14.
48. Ed. Joan Jobe Smith, *Das Ist Alles: Charles Bukowski Recollected* (Long Beach, 1995). Other posthumous tributes included: ed. Gregory Smith, *Atom Mind* (Summer 1994); ed. Ana and Dave Christy, *Charles Bukowski and Alpha Beat Press 1988-1994* (New Hope, Pennsylvania, 1994); ed. Mitchell Smith, *The Kerouac Connection* #27 (Winter 1995), 45-62. Introduction, in ed. Raindog, *Last Call: A Legacy of Madness* (San Pedro, 1995).
49. See Thrasher's hilarious 'Allen Ginsberg had taken Art hostage' in the 'Men of Long Beach' issue of *Pearl* #22 (Fall/ Winter 1995), 63-64. C.B. 'A Rambling Essay...', *Sampler*, 14.
50. J. Micheline, 'Long After Midnight', *Second Coming* (1974), n.p.

Chapter 8
1. *The Roominghouse Madrigals*, 176.
2. *Notes of a Dirty Old Man* (City Lights, 1972)
3. Richard Howard, sleeve notes, 'The Waste Land and Other Poems' read by T.S. Eliot (Caedmon, 1971).
4. *Mockingbird Wish Me Luck*, 52-3.
5. Patrick Marber, *The Observer Magazine*, 13 March 1994.
6. Review of *Post Office*, in *The Times* (n.d., 1980).
7. B. Flanagan, 'On Bukowski & his Paintings', *Sure* #4 (1992), 9-11.
8. 'Pen and Drink', *Weekend Guardian*, 14 October 1981.
9. N. Pivano, *Laughing With the Gods* (Sun Dog Press; Northville, Michigan, 2000),
10. G. Locklin,'Setting Free the Buk', *Review of Contemporary Fiction*, Vol.V, #3, 28.
11. *Dangling...*, 26-30.
12. Randall Jarrell, *Poetry and the Age* (1955; Faber, 1973), 218
13. R. Padgett, 'Stoically Bedazzled', *Talking Poetics From Naropa Institute*, Vol. 1

(Boulder and London, 1978), 117.
14. Bukowski interview, *Gargoyle* #35 (1988).
15. R. Harrison, *Essays on C.B...* (1994).
16. Weissner interview, *Gargoyle* #35 (1988).
17. N. Cherkovski, *Hank*, (New York, 1991).
18. *The Guardian*, (8 January 1996).
19. *Wormwood Review* #95 (1984), 121.
20. Locklin interview with Jules Smith, *Pearl* #27 (Fall/ Winter1998), 26-34.
21. *Burning in Water...*, 187-189. Douglas Houston, letter to Jules Smith, 27 October 1988. Locklin comment quoted in *The Orange County Register* (11 March 1987), 6.
22. *Poetry*, (June 1915).
23. *Wormwood Review* #132 (1994).

BIBLIOGRAPHY

PRINCIPAL POETRY WORKS

Flower, Fist and Bestial Wail (Eureka, California; Hearse Press, 1960)
Poems and Drawings (Crescent City, Florida; Epos, 1962)
Longshot Pomes For Broke Players (New York; 7 Poets Press, 1962)
Run Withced the Hunted (Chicago, Illinois; Midwest Poetry Chapbooks, 1962)
It Catches My Heart In Its Hands (New Orleans; Loujon Press, 1963)
Crucifix In A Deathhand (New Orleans/ New York; Loujon Press/ Lyle Stuart Inc., 1965)
Cold Dogs In The Courtyard (Chicago Literary Times-Cyfoeth, 1965)
The Genius Of The Crowd (Cleveland, Ohio; 7 Flowers Press, 1966)
At Terror Street and Agony Way (Los Angeles; Black Sparrow Press, 1968)
Poems Written Before Jumping Out of an 8 Story Window
(Ravendale, California; Poetry Xchange, 1968);
reprinted with correspondence, (Salt Lake City, Utah; Litmus Press,1975)
A Bukowski Sampler (Madison.,Wisconsin; Quixote Press, 1969);
reprinted with essay by Morris Edelson (Houston, Texas; Quixote Press, 1979)
The Days Run Away Like Wild Horses Over The Hills (Los Angeles; Black Sparrow Press, 1969)
Penguin Modern Poets 13 [with Philip Lamantia and Harold Norse] (Harmondsworth, Middlesex; Penguin Books, 1969)

Fire Station (Santa Barbara; Capra Press, 1970)
Mockingbird Wish Me Luck (Los Angeles; Black Sparrow Press, 1972)
Burning in Water, Drowning in Flame: Selected Poems 1955-73
(Los Angeles; Black Sparrow Press, 1974)
Love is a Dog From Hell (Santa Barbara; Black Sparrow Press, 1977)
Play the Piano Drunk Like a Percussion Instrument Until the Fingers Begin to Bleed a Bit (Black Sparrow Press, 1978)
Dangling in the Tournefortia (Black Sparrow Press, 1981)
War All the Time (Black Sparrow Press, 1984)
You Get So Alone at Times That It Just Makes Sense
(Santa Rosa, California; Black Sparrow Press, 1987)
The Roominghouse Madrigals: Early Selected Poems 1946-1966
(Black Sparrow Press, 1988)
In the Shadow of the Rose (Black Sparrow Press, 1990)
Septuagenarian Stew [includes stories] (Black Sparrow Press, 1990)
The Last Night of the Earth Poems (Black Sparrow Press, 1992)
Betting On the Muse [includes stories] (Black Sparrow Press, 1996)
Bone Palace Ballet (Black Sparrow Press, 1997)
What Matters Most Is How Well You Walk Through the Fire
(Black Sparrow Press, 1999)
Open All Night: New Poems (Black Sparrow Press, 2000)

PROSE WORKS

Confessions of a Man Insane Enough To Live With Beasts (Bensenville, Illinois; Mimeo Press, 1965)
All the Assholes in the World and Mine (Bensenville, Illinois; Mimeo Press, 1966)
Notes of a Dirty Old Man (North Hollywood, California; Essex House, 1969; reprinted City Lights Books, 1973)
Post Office (Los Angeles; Black Sparrow Press, 1971); reprinted (London; Melbourne House, 1980)
Erections, Ejaculations, Exhibitions and General Tales of Ordinary Madness (San Francisco; City Lights Books, 1972)
South of No North (Los Angeles; Black Sparrow Press, 1973)
Life and Death in the Charity Ward (London; London Magazine Editions, 1974)
Factotum (Santa Barbara; Black Sparrow Press, 1975); reprinted (London; W.H.Allen and Co., 1981)
Women (Santa Barbara; Black Sparrow Press, 1978)
Shakespeare Never Did This (San Francisco; City Lights Books, 1980)
Ham on Rye (Santa Barbara; Black Sparrow Press, 1982)
Hot Water Music (Santa Barbara; Black Sparrow Press, 1982)
The Most Beautiful Woman in Town and Other Stories (San Francisco; City Lights Books, 1983)
There's No Business (Santa Barbara, Black Sparrow Press, 1984)
Bring Me Your Love (Santa Barbara; Black Sparrow Press, 1983)
Hollywood (Black Sparrow Press,1989)

Septuagenarian Stew [with poetry] (Black Sparrow Press, 1990)
Pulp (Black Sparrow Press, 1994)
The Captain is Out To Lunch and the Sailors Have Taken Over the Ship [with illustrations by Robert Crumb] (Black Sparrow Press, 1998)

PUBLISHED CORRESPONDENCE (all edited by Seamus Cooney)

The Bukowski/ Purdy Letters 1964-1974 (The Paget Press, Sutton West and Santa Barbara, 1983)
Screams From the Balcony: Selected Letters 1960-1970 (Black Sparrow Press, 1993)
Living on Luck: Selected letters 1960s-1970s (Black Sparrow Press, 1995)
Reach for the Sun: Selected Letters 1978-1994 (Black Sparrow Press, 1999)

ARCHIVES WITH BUKOWSKI CORRESPONDENCE

University of Arizona, Special Collections
Brown University, John Hay Library
California State University, Long Beach, Special Collections [Gerald Locklin Archive]
University of California, Los Angeles, Special Collections
University of California, Santa Barbara, Special Collections
Centenary College, Samuel Peters Research Library, Shreveport, Louisiana
The State University of New York at Buffalo, Poetry Rare Book Collection
The University of Southern California, Rare Books Collection
Temple University, Special Collections

MISCELLANEOUS BUKOWSKI CORRESPONDENCE

Consulted: uncollected letters to Professor Geoffrey Moore, Joan Jobe Smith, Fred Voss, Kurt Nimmo.

Letters concerning Charles Bukowski received by Jules Smith from: Carl Weissner, John Martin, Jim Burns, Chris Challis, Howard Sounes, Joan Jobe Smith, Fred Voss, Douglas Houston, Joe Wolberg, Nichola Manning, Pamala Karol, Devreaux Baker, Jack Madigan, Chris Daly, Marvin Malone, Kevin Ring.

CURRENT MAGAZINES WITH BUKOWSKIANA

Beat Scene, ed. Kevin Ring:
27 Court Leet, Binley Woods, near Coventry, CV3 2JQ, England.
Chiron Review, ed. Michael Hathaway:
702 North Prairie, St.John, Kansas 67576-1516, USA.
Pearl, ed. Joan Jobe Smith, Barbara Hauk and Marilyn Johnson:
3030 E. Second Street, Long Beach, California 90803, USA.

Sure: *the Bukowski Newsletter* [1992-1996], ed. Edward Smith: PO Box 1183, Ojai, California 93024, USA.

CRITICAL SOURCES ON BUKOWSKI'S WORK

Anderson, Elliot, ed. 'The Little Magazine in America: A Modern Documentary History', *Triquarterly*, 43, (Evanston, Illinois, Fall 1978)
Andrews, Michael, 'No Holds Barred Interview', *Easy Reader*, Volume X, no.32, (Los Angeles, April 1980) 8-12
Barker, David, *Charles Bukowski: A Bibliographic Price Guide* (Salem, Oregon, 1984)
Barker, David, *Bukowski, The King of San Pedro* (Del Mar, California, 1985)
Bennett, John, ed., [poetry anthology, with drawings by Bukowski] *Six Poets* (Ellensburg, Washington, 1979)
Blazek, Douglas, ed., *Olé*, nos 1-8 (Bensenville, Illinois, 1964-66)
Blazek, Douglas, ed., (letters) *Life in a Common Gun* (Madison, Wisconsin, 1968)
Blazek, Douglas, ed., (letters) *Open Skull* (San Francisco, 1967)
Blazek, Douglas, ed., *A Bukowski Sampler* (Madison, Wisconsin, 1969); reprinted with essay, Houston, Texas, 1979). Contents:
Morris Edelson, ' St. Bukowski'
Douglas Blazek, ' A Few Notes... '
William Wantling, ' A Letter from Bukowski... '
Walter Lowenfels, 'Buk is the Houdini... '
Charles Bukowski, 'A Rambling Essay on Poetics and the Bleeding Life Written While Drinking a Six-Pack (Tall)'
Brewer, Gay, *Charles Bukowski* (Twayne's U.S. Authors Series #684; New York, 1997)
Bryan, John, ed., (underground newspaper) *Open City*, 83 (Los Angeles, 20 December 1968)
Bukowski, Charles, and Neeli Cherry, eds., *Laugh Literary and Man the Humping Guns*, nos 1-3 (Los Angeles, 1969-71)
Bukowski, Charles, Neeli Cherry and Paul Vangelisti, eds., *An Anthology of L.A. Poets* (Fairfax, California, 1972)
Burns, Jim, 'Bukowski's Book ', *Poetry Information*, 12/13, (London, Spring 1975) 25-30
Burns, Jim, 'The Outsider', *Poetry Information*, 20/21, (Newcastle, Winter 1979) 131-137
Cain, Jimmie, 'Bukowski's Imagist Roots', *West Georgia College Review*, 19 (1987), 10-17.
Campbell, James, 'Beat, Beaten and Blue: Charles Bukowski and the Beats', *Bananas*, (London, 1980) 48-50
Challis, Chris, 'Drain a Last Tired Beer', *Houdini*, 1, (Bristol, 1980) 5-7
Cherkovski, Neeli, *Whitman's Wild Children* (1988; Vermont, 1999), 5-39
Cherkovski, Neeli, (biography) *Hank* (Random House, New York, 1991)
Christy, Jim, and Claude Powell, *The Buk Book: Musings on Charles Bukowski* (Toronto, 1997)
Ciotto, Paul, 'Bukowski', *Los Angeles Times Magazine*, (22 March 1987), 12

Cooney, Seamus, ed., *The Bukowski/ Purdy Letters 1964-1974*, (Sutton West and Santa Barbara, l983)
Corrington, J.W., foreword, *It Catches My Heart In Its Hands* (New Orleans, 1963), 5-10.
Corrington., J.W., 'Charles Bukowski and the Savage Surfaces', *Northwest Review*, Volume VI, no. 4, (Eugene, Oregon, Fall 1963) 123-129
Creeley, Robert, 'Think What's Got Away', *Poetry Chicago*, Volume 102, no.1, (April 1963) 48
Cunningham, Valentine, review of *Post Office*, *TLS*, 4030, 20 June 1980
Dorbin, Sanford, *A Bibliography of Charles Bukowski*, (Los Angeles, Black Sparrow Press, 1969)
Dougherty, Jay, 'Charles Bukowski and the Outlaw Spirit', *Gargoyle*, 35 (1988) 92-103
Dougherty, Jay, 'Translating Charles Bukowski and the Beats: An Interview with Carl Weissner', *Gargoyle* 35 (1988) 68-86
Duval, Jean Francois, *Buk Et Les Beats* (Switzerland, 1998)
Edelson, Morris, 'Six Little magazines' [Doctoral dissertation], (University of Michigan, 1973)
Esterly, Glenn, 'The Pock-Marked Poetry of Charles Bukowski', *Rolling Stone*, 215, (New York, 17 June 1976) 10-17
Fante, John, *Ask the Dust* (1939); introduction by Charles Bukowski (Black Sparrow, Santa Barbara, 1979)
Finch, Peter, review of 'Erections..'. , *2nd Aeon*, 16/17 (Cardiff, 1973) 234-235
Fogel, Al, *Charles Bukowski: A Comprehensive Checklist 1946-1982* (Miami, Florida, 1982)
Fogel, Al, *Charles Bukowski: A Comprehensive Price Guide & Checklist* 1944-1999 (Surfside, Florida, 1999)
Fox, Hugh, *Charles Bukowski: A Critical and Bibliographical Study* (Somerville, Massachussetts, 1968)
Fox, Hugh, 'The Living Underground: Charles Bukowski', *North American Review* (Fall 1969), 57-58
Fulton, Len, 'See Bukowski Run', *Small Press Review*, 16 (May 1973)
Gannij, Joan Levine, 'Hank and Georgia', *Beat Scene* 22, 25-26
Glazier, Loss, ed., *All's Normal Here: A Charles Bukowski Primer*, (Fremont, California, 1985)
Gloor, Dan, and Brock Yancey, 'Ode to Long Beach Writers' [article], *University Magazine*, (1983) 4-9, 33-35
Graalman, Bob, 'Charles Bukowski', *Dictionary of Literary Biography vol. 5: American Poets since World War II* (Detroit, 1980)
Grapes, Jack, 'This Thing Upon Me', *Poetry East* 34 (Fall 1992), 7-23
Grimes, William, [obituary] *The New York Times* (11 March 1994)
Hand, Alex, and Alan Turner, eds., *Iconolatre* 18/19 (West Hartlepool, 1966)
Harrison, Russell, *Against the American Dream: Essays on Charles Bukowski* (Santa Rosa, Black Sparrow Press, 1994)
Hoare, Philip, 'Tales from Skid Row', *The Guardian* (31 January 1987)
Hoare, Philip, [obituary] *The Independent* (14 March 1994)
Hollywood, Rikki, ed., *The Bukowski Scrapbook* [fanzine tribute] (London, 1994)
Hollywood, Rikki, ed., *Bukowski Unleashed: Essays On a Dirty Old Man* (London, 2000)

Howard, Mel, and Thomas King Forcade, eds., *The Underground Reader* (New York, 1972)

Hughes, John, [article] *The Orange County Register*, (11 March 1997)

Kaye, Arnold L., 'Charles Bukowski Speaks Out', *Chicago Literary Times*, Volume 2, no. 4, (March 1963) 1-2

King, Linda, [with Charles Bukowski], *Me and Your Sometimes Love Poems* (2nd edition; Phoenix, Arizona, 1994)

Krumshansl, Aaron, *A Descriptive Bibliography of the Primary Publications of Charles Bukowski* (Black Sparrow Press,1999)

Kryss, T.L., ed., *A Tribute to Jim Lowell* (Cleveland, Ohio, 1966)

Langton, Roger W., ed., *Surviving Bukowski: The Relationship Between Ann Menebroker and Charles Bukowski* (Boulder, Colorado, 1998)

Levin, Bernard, review of *Post Office*: *The Sunday Times* (n.d., c.1980)

Lewis, David N., [obituary article] *Random Lengths* (San Pedro, 17-31 March 1994)

Linick, Anthony, 'A History of the American Literary Avant-Garde Since World War Two' [Doctoral dissertation], (University of California, Los Angeles, 1965)

Locklin, Gerald, review of *Dangling in the Tournefortia*, *American Book Review*, Volume 4, no. 5, (July 1982) 6

Locklin, Gerald, review of *The Roominghouse Madrigals*, *The Kindred Spirit*,Volume VII, no.3, (St.John, Kansas, 1988) 15

Locklin, Gerald, [essays] *Charles Bukowski: A Sure Bet* (Sudbury, Massachussetts, 1996)

Long, Philomene, ed.,[with John Thomas] [memoir] *Bukowski in the Bathtub* (Venice, California, 1997)

Lowe, Erica, [interview with Bukowski] *Arete* (July-August 1989)

Lowenfels, Walter, ed. [anthology] *Poets of Today* (New York, 1964)

Lowenfels, Walter, ed. [anthology] *Where Is Vietnam?* (New York, 1967)

Lykiard, Alexis, 'Wine, Women and Work; The World of Charles Bukowski', *Palantir*, 19, (Preston, 1984) 33-39

Malone, Marvin, ed., *The Wormwood Review*, 45, [John Edgar Webb Memorial Issue] (Stockton, California, 1972)

Mohr, Bill, ed., *Poetry Loves Poetry: An Anthology of Los Angeles Poets* (Santa Monica, California, 1986)

Montrose, David, 'Third Coming ', *New Edinburgh Review*, 52, (Edinburgh, November 1980) 30-31

Moore, Geoffrey, [anthology] *The Penguin Book of American Verse* (1977; revised, Harmondsworth, Middlesex, 1983)

Morrow, Bradford, and Seamus Cooney, eds., *A Bibliography of the Black Sparrow Press* (Santa Barbara, California, 1981)

Moser, Norman, 'Charles Bukowski', [entry] *Contemporary Poets* (London, 1980)

Munro, C. Lynn, ' Charles Bukowski ', [entry] *Critical Survey of Poetry*, ed. Frank N. Magill, (Englewood Cliffs, New Jersey, 1982) 354-365

Norse, Harold, 'To Know You Has Been Grace', *Small Press Review*, (May 1973), 7-8

O'Brien, John, ed., Bukowski/ Butor Number, *The Review of Contemporary Fiction*, Volume V (Elmwood Park, Illinois, Fall 1985). Contents:

Ernest Fontana, 'Bukowski 's Ham on Rye and the Los Angeles Novel '
Jimmie E. Cain, Jr, 'Women: the Siren Calls of Boredom'
Jack Saunders, 'Writing the Great American Novel on the PC'

Keith Abbott, 'Some Tough Acts to Follow'
Gerald Locklin, ' Setting Free the Buk'
David Glover, 'A Day at the Races: Gambling and Luck in Bukowski's Fiction'
Gerald Locklin, 'Bukowski's War All the Time and Horses Don't Bet on People and Neither Do I'
Thomas McGonigle, 'A Bottle Stain'
Loss Glazier, 'Mirrors of Ourselves: Notes on Bukowski's Post Office'
Jack Byrne, 'Bukowski's Chinaski: playing Post Office'
Norman Weinstein, ' South of No North: Bukowski in Deadly Ernest '
Julian Smith, 'Charles Bukowski and the Avant-Garde'
Stephen Kessler, 'Notes on a Dirty Old Man'
Offen, Ron, 'Apocrypha for the Marriage of Heaven and Hell', [review of Crucifix...] *Chicago Literary Times*, (September, 1965) 4-5
Oliver, Myrna, [obituary] *The Los Angeles Times* (10 March, 1994)
Osborne, John, and Peter Easy, 'Wanted: A Good 'Beat' Critic', *Over Here*, Vol.4, no.2 (Autumn, 1984) 16-24
Packard, William, ed., 'Charles Bukowski', The Poet's Craft: Interviews from *The New York Quarterly* (New York, 1987), 318-323
Penn, Sean, 'Tough Guys Write Poetry', *Interview* (September 1987), 94-100
Perret, Christopher, 'Open Letter', *Wormwood Review*, No.21, (Stockton, California, 1966), 16-17
Pivano, Fernanda, [interviews] *Charles Bukowski: Laughing with the Gods* (Northville, Michigan, 2000)
Plater, Ormonde, 'Tough Poems', *Vieux Carré Courier*, Volume 2, no.14, (New Orleans, 28 May 1965) 6
Quagliano, Tony, 'The Ground in Los Angeles', *Schist* 4/5, (San Francisco, 1976-78) 37-42
Raindog, ed., [tribute anthology], *Last Call: A Legacy of Madness* (San Pedro, 1995)
Reed, Christopher, [obituary] *The Guardian* (11 March 1994)
Richmond, Steve, [memoir] *Spinning Off Bukowski* (Los Angeles, 1996)
Ring, Kevin, ed. 'The Bukowski Letters', *Beat Scene* 20 (1994), 14-18
Robbins, Doren, 'Drinking Wine in the Slaughterhouse with Septuagenarian Stew: For Bukowski at 71', *Onthebus* (1992), 282-285
Shapiro, Karl, [interview] *Triquarterly* 43 (Evanston, Illinois, Fall 1978) 210
Sherman, Jory, *Bukowski: Friendship, Fame and Bestial Myth*, (Augusta, Georgia, 1981)
Smith, Joan Jobe, ed., *Charles Bukowski: Essays, Epistles and Poems 1975-1996* (private photocopy, Long Beach, California, 1996)
Smith, Joan Jobe, 'The Poet as Entertainment', *Sure: The Charles Bukowski Newsletter*, (no.4, 1992), 35-41
Smith, Joan Jobe, ed., *Das Ist Alles: Charles Bukowski Recollected* (Pearl Editions, Long Beach, 1995)
Smith, Jules, 'Introducing Six Poets From L.A. and Long Beach', *Bête Noire* (Winter 1987) 122-125
Smith, Jules, review of *Septuagenarian Stew*, *TLS* (7-13 September 1990)
Smith, Jules, review of *Hank*, *TLS* (29 November 1991)
Smith, Jules, review of *The Last Night of the Earth Poems*, *TLS* (18 December 1992)

Smith, Jules, review of Russell Harrison, *Essays on Charles Bukowski*, *TLS* (24 March 1995)

Sounes, Howard, [biography], *Charles Bukowski: Locked In The Arms of a Crazy Life* (Canongate Books; Edinburgh, 1998)

Strachan, Don, ' An Evening with Chuck Buk ', *Los Angeles Free Press*, Volume 8., no. 30 (23 July 1971) 4

Strawson, Galen, review of *Factotum*, *TLS*, (4 September 1981) 1000

Stuart, Dabney, '7 Poets and a Playwright ', *Poetry Chicago*, Volume 104, no. 4, (July 1964) 263-264

Tripp, John, review of *Mockingbird Wish Me Luck*, *2nd Aeon*, 19/21, (Cardiff, 1972)

Tucker, Ken, review of L.P. ' Charles Bukowski Reads His Poetry', *Rolling Stone*, (New York, c.1980)

Webb, Jon Edgar, ed., *The Outsider*, 3, (New Orleans, 1963). Contents:
Letters from Bukowski to the Webbs
'Editors Congratulate Bukowski'
R.R.Cuscaden, 'Charles Bukowski: Poet in a Ruined Landscape'
J.W.Corrington, 'Charles Bukowski:. Three Poems'

Wennersten, Robert, 'Paying for Horses: An Interview with Charles Bukowski', *London Magazine*, Volume 14, no.5, (London, December 1974) 35-54

Weissner, Carl, translator, *Gedichte Die Einer Schrieb...* (Augsburg, Germany, 1974)

Winans, A.D., ed., *Charles Bukowski Special Issue, Second Coming, Volume 2*, no.3, (San Francisco, 1974). Contents:
Steve Richmond, 'Gagaku'
Jerry Kamstra, 'Buk'
Jack Micheline, 'Long After Midnight'
Harold Norse, 'The Worst Thing You Can Say To Him Is I Love You'
Gerald Locklin, 'Two Poets'
G.J.Melling, 'Notes to a Dirty Old Man'
Linda King, 'To Think I Fell In Love With a Male Chauvinist'
Hugh Fox, 'What Bukowski Has Really Done/ Is Doing to U.S. Poetry'
Charles Bukowski, 'He Beats His Women'

Winans, A.D., *The Charles Bukowski/ Second Coming Years* (Beat Scene Press, Coventry, 1996)

Wolberg, Joe, 'Bukowski: The People's Poet', *Oui*, (c.1981) 44-49, 118-120

Wordsworth, Christopher, review of *Factotum*, *The Guardian*, (2 September 1981)

Young, Elizabeth, 'Bum Steered', *New Statesman and Society* (17 June 1994), 37-38

Jules Smith was born in Gosport, Hampshire, and awarded a Ph.D. in American Studies by the University of Hull in 1990. A reviewer for the TLS, he has also contributed to *The Oxford Companion to Twentieth-Century Literature in English* (1996) and *The New Dictionary of National Biography* (OUP, forthcoming 2004).